W9-CZU-375

THE NON-PROLIFERATION OF NUCLEAR WEAPONS

THE NON-PROLIFERATION
OF NUCLEAR WEAPONS

GEORGES FISCHER

Research Director, Centre National de la Recherche Scientifique

translated by
DAVID WILLEY

ST. MARTIN'S PRESS
NEW YORK

CARL A. RUDISILL LIBRARY
LENOIR RHYNE COLLEGE

First published in France, under the title *La Non-Prolifération des Armes Nucléaires*, by Librairie Générale de Droit et de Jurisprudence in 1969. Revised by the author for this English edition, 1970.

© Georges Fischer 1971

Library of Congress Catalog Card No. 72-189811

All rights reserved

For information, write: St. Martin's Press, Inc., 175 Fifth Avenue, New York, N.Y. 10010

Printed in Great Britain

First published in the United States of America in 1972

341.73
F52N
82137
Feb 1973

AFFILIATED PUBLISHORS: Macmillan & Company, Limited, London – also at Bombay, Calcutta, Madras and Mebourne – The Macmillan Company of Canada, Limited, Toronto.

Contents

CONTENTS

CONTENTS

vii

Abbreviations

ABM	Anti-Ballistic Missile
ANF	Atlantic Nuclear Force
COPREDAL	Preparatory Commission on the Denuclearisation of Latin America
IAEA	International Atomic Energy Agency
ICJ	International Court of Justice
MIRV	Multiple Independently-targeted Re-entry Vehicle
MLF	Multilateral NATO Force
NATO	North Atlantic Treaty Organisation
NPT	Non-Proliferation Treaty
OAS	Organisation of American States
OPANAL	Agency for the Prohibition of Nuclear Weapons in Latin America
SHAPE-SACEUR	Supreme Headquarters Allied Powers in Europe – Supreme Allied Commander Europe
SIPRI	Stockholm International Peace Research Institute
UNCTAD	United Nations Commission for Trade and Development
UNIDO	United Nations Industrial Development Organisation
WEU	Western European Union

INTRODUCTION

SINCE the end of World War Two, the endless, difficult debate over disarmament has been going on inside and out of the United Nations in a
hurly-burly of propaganda, national prejudice and self-interest, misunderstanding, idealism, and a sense of compromise. Cynics, who are fond
of historical precedent, might care to recall the Russian note of 2 April
1816, proposing a general simultaneous reduction in weapons aimed at
weakening the British Navy.[1]

But in a field where the future of the human race is at stake, cynicism is
not appropriate. Our duty as citizens, of our country and of the world, is
to oppose the waste of resources, oppose man's folly,[2] oppose the annihilation of our civilisation.

Of course, negotiations about disarmament appear endless and sometimes futile. But lawyers, even more than other people, ought to remember
that "negotiations are the ordinary method by which governments exercise
their mutual relations, discuss, compromise over, and settle their disputes".[3] Given the complexity of present-day international society, and
the very nature of its organisation, these negotiations can only be long and
difficult. They demand, on the part of both statesmen and citizens, exceptional calm and patience. *Détente* and disarmament condition and influence
one another, according to the circular causation theory of Gunnar Myrdal,
who postulates the interdependent relationship of social factors, each of
which becomes alternately cause and effect.

The Nuclear Non-Proliferation Treaty, approved by the United Nations
General Assembly[4] on 12 June 1968 was opened to signature on 1 July
1968. It entered into force on 5 March 1970. On that date it had been, in
accordance with Article 9 of the Treaty, ratified by the three States whose
governments were appointed depositaries (USA, United Kingdom and the
Soviet Union), and by more than forty other signatories. The Treaty is not
exactly a step towards disarmament, but it does underline the exceptional
overwhelming character of nuclear weapons in comparison with con-

---

[1] Cf. M. Bourquin, *Histoire de la Sainte-Alliance* (Geneva, Georg, 1954), p. 186.
[2] Title of a book written by Jules Moch (Paris, R. Laffont, 1954).
[3] French Government Memorandum, PCIJ Series C, No. 84, p. 205.
[4] Resolution 2373 (XXII) which does not include the word "approval", but in
which the Assembly "welcomes the Treaty".

ventional ones. It expresses the hope of a more rational, safer world and, at the same time, opens up new disarmament possibilities. It represents a measure of arms control which, although only partial, forces the international community to regulate and restrict these weapons which now exist independently in so many countries, if it cannot actually ban them. For this reason, and also because it is an effect and a factor of *détente*, the new Treaty must be welcomed by all those who care about peace.

This work aims at giving a rapid review of the origin, drawing up, and provisions of the new Treaty, and introduces and comments upon the relevant texts. The legal problems involved are few in number but the author considers these, and also touches upon questions of politics and international relations.

The subjects to be dealt with, in order, are: the origins, the problem of non-proliferation, the drawing-up of the Treaty, the ban on the transfer, receipt and manufacture of nuclear weapons, control machinery, international co-operation in the field of peaceful uses, final clauses, the security of non-nuclear States, and collateral measures.

1. ORIGINS

It is not the aim here, nor is it even possible, to describe the development of theory and negotiation in the field of disarmament. It will suffice to give some account of those agreements which led directly to the conclusion of the Non-Proliferation Treaty.

I. TRENDS

It does seem possible to detect a tendency to proceed from the general to the particular, from the complete to the fragmentary. The Baruch-Lilienthal Plan aimed at the strict control of all atomic activities through an international body. Both the Western Powers and the Soviet Union during a preliminary period made proposals for general and complete disarmament.

Slowly, however, much more limited aims were put forward. The cause of this new trend was atomic weapons testing, and in particular the thermo-nuclear weapons tests carried out by the United States in the Pacific in March 1954. The radioactive fall-out caused by these experiments contaminated Japanese fishermen, their boats and their hauls, and consequently had an emotional impact all over the world.[1] The Japanese Diet, Mr Nehru, and the Bandung Conference in particular, protested, and in the 1955 United Nations General Assembly, the Soviet Union demanded as a first step the conclusion of an agreement on the stopping of all kinds of nuclear weapons tests. This proposition was rejected. On 23 July 1956, Sir Anthony Eden, in the House of Commons, said he was ready to examine the limitation of tests, separately from general disarmament and arms control. In the United States, Senator (later Vice-President) Humphrey asked, in agreement with Governor Stassen, for the separation of a test ban from the rest of the disarmament question which was subject to over-strict control measures.[2] So it was by turning away from a "global" approach towards

---

[1] Cf. G. Fischer, *L'Energie atomique et les Etats-Unis* (Paris, Librairie générale de Droit et de Jurisprudence, 1957), pp. 366 *ff*; M.-F. Furet, *Expérimentation des armes nucléaires et Droit international public* (Paris, Pedone, 1966), *passim*.

[2] E. H. Voss, *Nuclear Ambush, The Test Ban Trap* (Chicago, Regenry, 1963), p. 125. Even during the 1956 Presidential campaign, Stevenson had demanded the stopping of tests, which earned him extremely violent attacks from his opponents. Cf. R. E. Lapp, *The New Priesthood* (New York, Harper and Row, 1965), pp. 120–30.

partial measures that a solution was sought. And the whole subject was characterised by a lethargy that can and indeed must be deplored, but that shows up the political and psychological difficulties that hold up agreement in the field of disarmament and arms control.

II. SOME CONVENTIONAL PROVISIONS

The Peace Treaties of 10 February 1947, it will be recalled, forbade Italy,[3] Bulgaria,[4] Finland,[5] Hungary,[6] and Romania[7] to possess, manufacture, or test atomic weapons. The same ban is contained in the Austrian State Treaty of 15 May 1955—and this ban is extended to cover chemical and biological weapons.[8] On 1 December 1959 an important instrument, the Antarctic Treaty, was signed. Although it may be of interest to only a limited number of States, it is none the less of considerable importance as it reserves Antarctica for purely peaceful activities and envisages the neutralisation and a kind of internationalisation of this region, matched by controls exercised by both parties.

According to Article 5 of the Treaty, "Any nuclear explosions in Antarctica and the disposal there of radioactive waste material shall be prohibited." This text covers not only nuclear weapons tests but also peaceful experiments to which the area was particularly adapted. But we are back in 1959—these tests appeared to be useless, and above all world public opinion was so hypnotised by nuclear tests that it was only interested in a total ban. It looks as if the provisions of Article 5 are a technological sacrifice (which at the time appeared unimportant) aimed at soothing the anxiety of Latin American countries in particular.[9]

A new step forward was made on 20 June 1963 when the United States and the Soviet Union signed the agreement for the establishment of a "hot" line between their two Heads of State.[10] Another advance was made by the United Nations General Assembly Resolution unanimously adopted on 13 December 1963 and entitled "Declaration of legal principles governing the activities of States in the exploration and use of outer space".[11] Most of the provisions of the Declaration were adopted in the Treaty of 27

[3] Art. 51.   [4] Art. 13.   [5] Art. 17.
[6] Art. 15.   [7] Art. 14.   [8] Art. 13.
[9] Cf. R. J. Dupuy, *Annuaire français de droit international*, 1960, pp. 111–132; H. J. Taubenfeld, *Disarmament and Arms Control*, Spring 1964, pp. 136-149.
[10] *Department of State Bulletin*, 8 July 1963, pp. 50–51. The line passes through London, Copenhagen, Stockholm and Helsinki for messages between heads of State. Service messages (concerning upkeep of the line) are transmitted via Tangiers. The agreement contains provisions about equipment, coding, and sharing of expenses.
[11] Rseolution 1962 (XVIII). See also Resolution 1884 (XVIII) of 17 October 1963.

January 1967 on the Principles Governing the Activities of States in the Exploration and Use of Outer Space. This instrument demilitarises the moon and other celestial bodies and denuclearises outer space under exploration at that time. Under Article 4, "States Parties to the Treaty undertake not to place in orbit around the earth any objects carrying nuclear weapons, or any other kinds of weapons of mass destruction, install such weapons on celestial bodies, or station such weapons in outer space in any other manner". Another provision of the same article bans weapons tests of all kinds on celestial bodies.

There has been criticism of the imperfections, ambiguities, obscurities, and gaps in this Treaty in which so many concepts, as for example that of weapons of mass destruction, remain undefined. But it must be understood that this is a text that reflects the worries of the two Super-Powers, and is a compromise between their respective interests. Even if neither of the two had any intention of putting nuclear weapons into outer space and on celestial bodies, each one could be in permanent fear of the other doing just this.[12] So the Treaty was a sort of mutual guarantee, a coincidence of hidden fears between the United States and the Soviet Union, the expression of the technological balance that exists between them. They gave up developing projects whose cost and difficulty made them superfluous. At the same time, conscious of their advance over other nations and of the scope of their gentleman's agreement within the framework of a multilateral instrument, the United States and the Soviet Union were in a hurry, as soon as consensus seemed possible, to put it down in black and white, without worrying about legal niceties or imperfections or ambiguities in the text of the Treaty, which was the visible result of their agreement. It is important to emphasise this aspect of the problem which characterises all the Treaties examined here: although they purport to be multilateral instruments, they are only clear for most of the time to the two Super-Powers. They alone have the power to interpret the conventional language, whose lack of clarity does not seem to bother them.

III. THE MOSCOW TREATY

Now let us return to the Moscow Treaty of 5 August 1963, which banned nuclear tests in the atmosphere, in outer space and under water. Underground nuclear tests are banned only if they "cause radioactive debris to be present outside the territorial limits of the State under whose jurisdiction or control such explosion is conducted". The legal problems raised by this

[12] W. C. Clemens, Jr., "Strategy and Arms Control", *Bulletin of Atomic Scientists*, November 1967, pp. 24–28.

Treaty have already been widely studied.[77] Here an attempt will be made to bring out some of the characteristics of the Treaty in so far as they help to shed light on its provisions.

1. The partial test ban

First of all, the Moscow Treaty partially bans nuclear tests. We have seen that in 1955 the Soviet Union was the first to put forward the idea of separating the problem of a test ban from that of general disarmament. It was not until 19 January 1959 that Britain and the United States for their part officially agreed to no longer make a test ban dependent upon progress over disarmament negotiations. As soon as the possibility of agreement emerged, the two problems tended to be linked once more, as Mr Krushchev did on 9 September 1961. In the end, agreement was reached only over the banning of tests, and only of certain kinds of tests at that. Yet during the negotiations, well before the conclusion of the Treaty, Britain and the United States adopted a maximalist position which is remarkably like that taken now by certain countries over the Non-Proliferation Treaty. These two States recalled the fact, at first sight elementary, that peace is endangered by the manufacture of the nuclear bomb rather than by tests.[14]

The Soviet Union, in a note to Peking on 3 August 1963, stated that if under present conditions it was not possible to solve at one and the same time and in its entirety the problem of general and complete disarmament, the only reasonable solution was to refuse to recognise the dilemma of "all or nothing at all", and to go forward step by step. Moscow foreshadowed a method of gradual approach, a sort of evolution by easy stages. This point of view seems to be more and more common.

2. The multilateral Treaty: the work of the Big Three

It is interesting to note that the Moscow Treaty bans nuclear weapons experiments in time of peace. In the past, prohibitions in the armaments field used to apply as a general rule to use in time of war. Again, many provisions of the Treaty—which is a short one—are imprecise and vague. There is no authentic interpretation to shed light on the meaning of certain terms used. In my work quoted above, I have shown that the

---

[13] See for example G. Fischer, "The Partial Banning of Nuclear Tests", *Annuaire français de droit international*, 1963, pp. 1–34; Schwelb, *American Journal of International Law*, July 1964; M.-F. Furet, *Explosion des armes nucléaires et droit international public* (Paris, Pedone), 1966.

[14] H. K. Jacobson and G. Stein, *Diplomats, Scientists and Politicians, the U.S. and the Nuclear Test Ban Negotiations*, (Ann Arbor, Univ. of Michigan Press, 1966), pp. 18–20, 42–45.

interpretation of the American State Department does not conform to the ordinarily accepted meaning of the expression "territorial waters". To give another example, it is not clear exactly what the term "underground tests" covers. The most important stipulations of the Moscow Treaty were negotiated in secret among the Big Three. They alone know exactly what they meant, for they thought it was neither necessary nor perhaps useful to give details to other parties of the exact contents of and precise reasons for their agreement.[15] This is again an idea that has already been expressed here—viz. that the delicate character of negotiations between the Super-Powers and of the problems on which they do reach agreement, leads the two States to withdraw into a sort of half-light from which they feel it is better not to emerge.

Some commentators deplore this situation and contrast it with a sort of legal Utopia which this author at least finds quite unrealistic.

3. Arms control reflects the supremacy of the Big Two

The Super-Powers were unable to agree on the banning of underground tests, as the detection and banning of these tests gave rise to complex problems to which we shall return later. Since the United States made the banning of these tests conditional upon the acceptance of on-site inspection, refused by the Soviet Union,[16] the partial, limited solution was the one which prevailed in 1963. So the Moscow Treaty is covered by no international control mechanism, and this has been the subject of regret in some quarters. Here again, allowance must be made for the political and diplomatic difficulties which led the Super-Powers to choose the solution adopted by the Moscow Treaty. Of course, legal formulae cannot as if by magic solve such problems, which will be dealt with later on. It is sufficient to indicate here that the Big Two and perhaps some other States have at their disposal sufficient technical means to detect possible violations of the Treaty. But on this level there is an obvious lack of equality between these States on the one hand and the rest of the Treaty signatories on the other. The Swiss Federal Council has deplored it by declaring that "for most

[15] This has been clearly stated by W. C. Foster, Head of the United States Agency for Arms Control and Disarmament, *Nuclear Test Ban Treaty, Hearings, Committee on Foreign Relations*; U.S. Senate, on Executive M., August 1963, p. 445 (referred to hereafter as *Hearings 1963*).

[16] In 1960, the Soviet Union accepted the idea of two to three annual inspections. This was considered insufficient by the United States, which led Moscow to withdraw its offer in 1963. In fact, as an eminent scientist has pointed out, the number of inspections is not a technical problem, but a political one, which must be resolved as such. Sir John Cockroft, *Disarmament and Arms Control*, Winter 1963–4, pp. 16–21. See also this volume, Chapter 9. I. 2. for a discussion of the possible banning of underground tests.

Parties to the Treaty, including Switzerland, there is no possibility of scientific verification of respect for the nuclear test ban".[17]

So there does exist a lack of equality between the Contracting Parties, three alone of whom have after all, because of the Treaty, given up research that they had been effectively pursuing until then.

This sort of private arrangement within a more elaborate Treaty framework is illustrated by an incident that happened in January 1965. Following a Soviet test that was presumed to have taken place underground, radioactive fall-out was detected by the Americans in the atmosphere outside the frontiers of the Soviet Union. What was going to be the attitude of the United States to what seemed to be at first sight a violation of the Moscow Treaty? Discreet contacts took place in Washington between the State Department and the Soviet Ambassador. On 9 March the State Department announced that the Soviet test might constitute a technical violation of the Moscow Treaty, but that in any case it presented no danger to the national security of the United States.[18] So respect for the letter of the Treaty was examined in the secrecy of Chancelleries, by discreet consultation between the two governments who knew exactly what to expect from each other and, at least in the technological field, spoke a common language. In any case, one of the negotiators of the Treaty felt that among the reasons why the Treaty was concluded was the acceptance by the United States of a purely national verification system.[19]

Having said this it is useful to note that all underground tests set free radioactive waste in the atmosphere and that the contaminated air must, in the course of its natural movement, pass the territorial limits of the State which has carried out the test. It seems that this fact was not known or taken into consideration at the time the Moscow Treaty was drawn up. Since then the United States have carried out numerous underground tests of which at least sixteen have set free radioactive waste and, in certain cases, this radioactivity has been sufficient to be detected over other countries. The Soviet Union, for its part, has carried out three tests with the same characteristics. Of course, we have much more information about American tests than about Russian ones,[20] yet there does seem to exist a tacit agreement between Russia and America over these tests. Neither of the

[17] Message from the Swiss Federal Council to the Federal Assembly, 13 September, No. 8831.
[18] J. H. McBride, *The Test Ban Treaty: Military, Technological and Political Implications*, (Chicago, Regnery, 1967), pp. 58–60.
[19] A. Dean, *Test Ban and Disarmament: The Path of Negotiation* (New York, Harper and Row), 1966, p. 58.
[20] See *SIPRI Yearbook of World Armaments and Disarmament*, 1968–69 (London, Gerald Duckworth, 1969), pp. 249–251.

two Super-Powers protests against violation of the Treaty by the other, for both now know that by going ahead with such tests, they risk a violation.

4. Legality of tests

The overwhelming majority of members of the international community have signed the Moscow Treaty. Those refusing to sign, apart from China and France, are: Albania, Cambodia, Congo (Brazzaville), Cuba, Guinea, North Korea, North Viet-Nam and Saudi Arabia.[21] So, in general, international society recognizes that nuclear tests and the radioactive fall-out resulting therefrom constitute a danger for the human race. President Kennedy, in a declaration of 26 July 1963, recalled that the increase in artificial radioactivity, although insignificant, was an act of man. And he added: "The loss of even one human life or the malformation of even one baby who may be born long after we are gone should be of concern to us all". Radioactive fall-out does have a genetic and somatic effect on human, animal and plant life, without it being possible to define exactly the nature and extent of this effect. But a recent observation does give some indication. On the island of Rongelap, contaminated by consecutive doses of fall-out in the American tests of 1954, it has been observed that of nineteen children who were under ten years of age in 1954, all but two now suffer from a disease of the thyroid gland.[22]

Yet it is still true that the Moscow Treaty does eliminate nuclear pollution of the atmosphere and water as completely as possible. By allowing underground tests only in so far as they do not cause radioactive fall-out to be present outside the territorial limits of the State making the test, it does try to be objective. The rule it makes seems to go further than that given in the judgement in the *Fonderie du Trail* case. In that case, the trial judge held that a State could not use its territory to the prejudice of another State, but that the international responsibility of the State concerned was involved only when the incriminating act had serious consequences.[23] The International Court of Justice was less restrictive in the *Corfu Channel* case, stating the above principle more categorically and more absolutely.[24]

[21] The following countries have also not signed: Barbados, Guyana, Lesotho, Monaco, South Yemen. In addition, certain countries which have signed the Treaty have not ratified it up to the present time. They are: Algeria, Argentina, Burundi, Cameroon, Colombia, Ethiopia, Haiti, Mali and Swaziland.
[22] *The Times*, 4 July 1968. An American expert, E. J. Sternglass, whose view has been challenged, maintains that tests have had regrettable effects on infantile mortality. See the discussion in *Bulletin of Atomic Scientists*, April 1970, pp. 18–20, October 1970, pp. 26–32, December 1970, pp. 23–34.
[23] United Nations, *Reports of international arbitral awards*, Vol. III, p. 1965.
[24] ICJ, *Reports*, 1949, pp. 22, 45.

But the Moscow Treaty does not protect nationals and foreigners under the same heading. Consequently it takes a more traditional position than the doctrine according to which modern international law must protect human rights in general.[25]

The problem of the legality of nuclear tests can only be sketched here.[26] First of all reference must be made to a new concept, of uncertain definition, recognised by Articles 53 and 64 of the Vienna Convention on Treaty Law of 23 May 1969. This is the *jus cogens*, that is to say imperative norms of international law, from which States cannot depart, even by Treaty, and which are recognised as such by the international community as a whole. Some believe these imperative norms are established as a result of multilateral general Treaties signed by a large number of States. According to this way of thinking, the ban imposed by the Moscow Treaty has become an imperative norm originating from the *jus cogens*. This is what seems to explain France's solitary hostile vote at Vienna.[27] France also quotes, in opposition to the view expressed above, the fact that the Moscow Treaty allows each signatory to withdraw from its Treaty obligations, if, in the exercise of its national sovereignty, it "decides that extraordinary events related to the subject matter of the Treaty have jeopardised the country's supreme interests". This could be answered by showing that the provision only repeats another norm arising from the *jus cogens*, the right of legitimate self-defence. But a study of the preparatory work, or at least of the statements made and explanations given to the United States during the ratification procedure, does not lend much weight to this theory. In fact since the Treaty was concluded, no one has taken advantage of the withdrawal clause. The attitude of the Big Two is evidence that in practice the Treaty rule has been modified. First thought of as cowardly in the extreme, as allowing any Party to withdraw at the least violation of the Treaty by another Party, or simply any other State, this rule has in fact become rigid and binding. Neither of the two Super-Powers

---

[25] F. V. Garcia-Amador, *La responsabilité internationale*, Report to the 8th Session of the CDI, A/CN. 4/96, 20 January 1956, pp. 78 and conclusions of the Afro-Asian Juridical Consultative Committee. Yasseen, *Annuaire français du droit international*, 1964, pp. 666–67.

[26] Cf. on the facts and legal difficulties presented by nuclear tests, G. Fischer, *L'Energie atomique et les Etats-Unis, Droit interne et droit international* (Paris, 1957), pp. 366 *ff*; G. Schwarzenberger, *The Legality of Nuclear Weapons* (London, Stevens, 1958), pp. 51 *ff*; N. Singh, *Nuclear Weapons and International Law* (London, Stevens, 1959), pp. 224 *ff*; Furet, op. cit., pp. 28–68.

[27] See: *La documentation française: La Convention de Vienne sur le Droit des Traités, Notes et études documentaires*, No. 3622, 25 September 1969; Deleau, "Les positions françaises à la Conférence de Vienne", *Annuaire française de droit international* 1969.

felt itself able to withdraw when the other committed a technical violation.

One might consider moreover if, arising out of the law established by the Moscow Treaty and the practice of States, there does now exist a customary norm applicable to all States, even non-signatories? A similar problem was examined by the International Court of Justice in 1969 in the *North Sea continental shelf* case.[28] The Court took into consideration the number of signatures to the Convention in question, the time which had elapsed since its signature and entry into force, the practice of States, and the extent to which they acted in the belief that they were legally bound by an obligatory rule of customary law. We know that the Moscow Treaty benefits from the signatures of almost the whole international community. Only two important countries remain outside but they are two out of the five Nuclear Powers. The Treaty only dates back to 1963, but it is undeniable that the period required to create a customary norm is much shorter today than in the past, even if it is only due to the accelerated rhythm of change in our world. The practice of States proves general respect for the ban laid down by the Moscow Treaty, but taking into account the attitude of China and France, is it possible, to quote the words of the Court, to describe it as "the practice of States, including those particularly interested . . . frequent and uniform in practice"? Suppose there does exist such a practice, is it "such as to establish a general recognition of the fact that a rule of law or a legal obligation is involved"? There is an element of subjectivity here that many good lawyers tend to minimise nowadays in order to limit the field of uncertainty and arbitrary interpretation.

On subjectivity, France can put forward a certain number of arguments. At the United Nations, the special committee appointed to study certain principles of international law was not able to reach unanimity about a proposition put forward by India and the UAR according to which States have not got the right to carry out nuclear tests.[29] But above all, the numerous protests made against the French nuclear tests of 1966 and 1968 do not seem to have called into question the legality of these tests in international law.[30]

American authors have referred, in order to justify the tests carried out in the past by the United States, to the principle of the "reasonableness" of the act. Behind this principle, which is distinguished from general legal rules, such as the freedom of the high seas, lie the old-fashioned ideas of self-protection, of the interests of the free world and other political notions that are inseparable from the cold war. It has been shown that even to resort

[28] ICJ *Reports of Judgments, Advisory Opinions and Orders*, 1969.
[29] Documents A/5746 (11/11/64) and A/AC 119/SR/35.
[30] *Revue générale de Droit international public*, 1966, pp. 1031–40; 1969, pp. 462–63.

to the principle of "reasonableness" leaves the legality of nuclear tests uncertain.[31] Yet it appears that in a legal system as decentralised and unintegrated as international law, the principle in question does present serious problems[32] owing to its subjective character, even when it is submitted to judicial opinion. The difficulties are even greater in other cases. This can be illustrated in a recent article according to which there has been in time past general agreement that the American tests were necessary and reasonable to establish a deterrent against the Soviet Union, but that once a balance has been struck, new national deterrents are superfluous. The author employs this argument to prove the illegality of the French nuclear tests.[33]

Really the basic principle at issue is the one according to which no State may exercise its power in such a way as to harm the interests of other States or other citizens. The French tests must be condemned in the light of this principle. As M. Charles Rousseau has aptly shown, the French government's attitude over the protests aroused by the tests contrasts with the position taken over the *Lotus affair* in 1927. At that time, France was opposed to the principle under which, in international law, any act which is not expressly forbidden is for that reason implicitly permitted.[34]

The French government replied to those States which had protested by proposing to send French experts who would prove the harmless nature of the tests.[35] It should at least have adopted the procedure laid down by the Treaty of 27 January 1967 on the principles governing the activities of States in the exploration and use of outer space. "If a State Party to the Treaty has reason to believe that an activity or experiment planned by it or its nationals would cause potentially harmful interference with the activities of other States Parties . . . it shall undertake appropriate international consultations before proceeding with any such activity or experi-

---

[31] Fischer, op. cit., Furet, op. cit.

[32] In spite of the limited use made by the Convention on the High Seas, 29 April 1958, "These rights as other rights recognised by the general principles of international law, are exercised by all States, taking reasonably into account the interest that the freedom of the high seas has for other States" (Article 2).

[33] D'Amato, *American Journal of International Law*, 1967, pp. 66–67.

[34] *Revue générale de droit international public*, 1966, pp. 1032–40. Repeated protests against the tests she had carried out led France on 20 May 1966 to modify her acceptance of the obligatory jurisdiction of the Hague Court and to refuse the Court's authority in disputes concerning activities relating to national defence.

[35] The French tests of July–August 1968 aroused a further round of diplomatic protest. Cf. *Le Monde*, 7–8, 9, 10 July, 6 and 27 August, 1968; *The Times*, 26 and 28 August 1968. Mexican experts detected in the atmosphere and in the sea traces of radioactivity they attributed to the French tests in the South Pacific. *Le Figaro*, 8 August 1968. See also Footnote 30.

ment."[36] Respect for the rights and interests of other States, ensured by appropriate international procedure, constitutes the best guarantee to each member of the international community for the protection of its own rights and interests. We can therefore only share the misgivings of a French deputy who in a written question asked the government to give up its tests, or at least to form a committee composed of French and foreign experts to ensure the necessary controls after these tests.[37] The French government ought even to have asked the Secretary-General of the United Nations to nominate a committee of experts for this purpose.

5. The meaning of the Treaty

This is perhaps the moment to indicate something of the scope of the Moscow Treaty and the conditions which enabled it to be negotiated. It was undoubtedly the Cuban crisis, the fact that the world went to the brink of nuclear catastrophe, that led the rulers of the Big Two to look for some basic common ground for agreement, even a limited one.[38] But public opinion also played a very important role. The dangers of radioactive fall-out had been constantly emphasised since 1954 by Nehru, the Japanese Diet, several of the developing countries, the British Labour Party, and numerous scientists—including 875 Americans who signed the Pauling Petition against nuclear tests in 1957.[39]

The weight of public opinion made itself felt all the time during the parliamentary work that preceded ratification of the Treaty in the United States. Secretary of State Rusk testified that the United States had taken into account "the instinctive impulse to put an end to pollution of the atmosphere and the earth" shown by the whole of humanity.[40] Professor Teller said that the United States could not carry out a greater number of tests in the atmosphere in 1961–1962 because public opinion would not have tolerated it.[41] According to Professor Brown (Director of Research in

[36] Article 9. This article also envisages that State Parties to the Treaty will pursue studies of outer space and the celestial bodies and will conduct their exploration in such a way as to avoid their harmful contamination and also adverse changes in the environment of the earth resulting from the introduction of extra-terrestrial matter. It can be noted also that according to a recent United Nations report by twelve distinguished experts: "as far as long range and long term fall-out is concerned, the radioactivity risk of so-called 'clean' weapons is about the same as that of less 'clean' ones". A/6858, 10 October 1967, para. 36.

[37] A written question addressed to the Prime Minister by M. Eugène Claudius-Petit, former Minister and P.D.M. Deputy for the Loire, *Le Monde*, 2 August 1968.

[38] Cf. A. Dean, op. cit., p. 58; J. Galtung, *Journal of Peace Resolution*, 1967, No. 2, p. 182.

[39] R. E. Lapp, op. cit., pp. 130–53.

[40] *Hearings 1963*, p. 11. See also p. 55.   [41] ibid., p. 440.

the Defense Department) the United States would find themselves at a serious disadvantage without the Treaty as they were more exposed than the Soviet Union to the pressure of public opinion protesting against radioactive fall-out.[42] Mr A. H. Dean, one of the Treaty negotiators, recalled that the newer nations were criticising the United States' lack of moral sense more and more severely, and he added: "as Jefferson said, since we have a decent respect for the opinions of mankind, even without a treaty I believe in two, three or four years, we would have to stop testing in the atmosphere".[43] The Generals, Commanders-in-Chief of the Army and Air Force also emphasised the importance of the political factor that world public opinion represented, which in their opinion had to be taken into account by all military chiefs when they were trying to evaluate the advantages and disadvantages of the Treaty.[44]

For its part, the Swiss Federal Council in its message dated 13 September 1963, dwelt on the role of international public opinion. "Because of the increasingly universal character of the Treaty, because of the justifiable hope that it will put an end to pollution of the atmosphere and of water, an abstention by Switzerland would not be understood, above all abroad. Switzerland's special position in the world would suffer if we wanted to stand on the sidelines by involving the legal and formal gaps in the Treaty."[45] Numerous Soviet texts could be quoted which stress the importance and effect of public opinion, qualifying the Treaty as "a step towards hopes held by world opinion . . . a step arising from care for the health of the Soviet people, for the health of all peoples".[46]

The Treaty reflects the fact that a certain balance in deterrent power now exists between the United States and the Soviet Union. Each contender has just about reached saturation point.[47] Both are faced with the paradoxical situation strikingly stated by the eminent scientist Herbert York; on either side military power is steadily increasing, while national security is steadily decreasing. According to Dr York, this dilemma can be solved neither by science nor by technology, only by political means.[48] The partial test ban was a first timid step towards such a solution.

How did this balance of power come about? In the United States, the Defense Secretary, the Army chiefs, and most scientists agreed that in the field of high-yield nuclear weapons, the Soviet Union had a slight edge over the United States. The test ban made it unlikely that the United

---

[42] ibid., p. 532.   [43] ibid., p. 818.   [44] ibid., pp. 398–99.
[45] Message from the Swiss Federal Council to the Federal Assembly, 13 September 1963, No. 8831, p. 6.
[46] Soviet Statement, 21 August 1963.
[47] Cf. on this subject E. Rabinowitch, *Bulletin of Atomic Scientists*, April 1963, p. 2.
[48] *Hearings 1963*, p. 762.

States could catch up. However, those responsible for American strategy rejected the need for such powerful weapons and preferred to stockpile weapons that were less powerful, but more sophisticated and available in greater numbers.

As far as the anti-ballistic missile is concerned, their tests have continued. But since the Moscow Treaty, it has become more difficult to study the effects of missiles fitted with nuclear warheads upon enemy missiles or upon defended launch bases.

On the other hand, the United States appear to be ahead of the Soviet Union in the underground testing of sophisticated tactical nuclear weapons. Now underground tests, which are still permitted, can help in the research of just this type of weapon. It could be said, and has indeed been said, that the Treaty prevents the United States from making progress in a field where they are behind, and virtually obliges the Soviet Union to catch up with the United States and begin a type of testing that they have not had much experience in up till now. But, as I stated before, it is not American strategy to follow the Soviet Union's example in adopting high-yield weapons. Also, without the Treaty, the Soviet Union could, according to Mr McNamara, develop its atomic arsenal more rapidly and more cheaply in the atmosphere. The fact that the Russians are now obliged to turn to underground testing will lose them time and involve them in extra expense.

Such was the situation in 1963. But nothing changes more quickly in our changing world than scientific and technical certainty and prospects. Since 1963 considerable progress has been made and it is possible today, more easily than could have been foreseen in 1963, to test very powerful nuclear weapons underground and to make new and decisive progress in the technology of these weapons. This is particularly true of different types of anti-missile missiles. It can therefore be said that hopes raised by the Treaty in this field have not proved very well founded.[49]

American diplomats and politicians had pointed out at the time the advantages the Moscow treaty gave the United States. This Treaty, it has been said, slows down and inhibits the development of super-weapons of destruction, reduces the danger of radioactive fall-out, prevents, to a certain extent, the spread of nuclear weapons, testifies to the peaceful character of American foreign policy and deprives the Communists of a propaganda weapon, opens up new possibilities of negotiation and ultimate agreement and, finally, diminishes tension between the two Super-Powers.[50]

Some of these arguments have also been valid for the Soviet Union,

[49] *SIPRI Yearbook of World Armaments and Disarmament*, 1968/69; pp. 246–49.
[50] Dean, op. cit., p. 83; *Congressional Record*, 23 September 1963, p. 16795 (Senator Dodd).

which in addition has had to take into account the German question and relations with China.

However, the partial test ban Treaty does not itself represent a step towards disarmament, even if it has been followed on both sides by a unilateral reduction in spending and force levels, as well as a tacit agreement by the Big Two, each holding itself up as an example to the other, to reduce their fissile material production in 1964. Above all, the partial test ban agreement was a symbol of *détente*,[51] a promise for the future of a possibility of agreement on nuclear weapons, a field which has upset international relations and the concept of war, and upon which until then it had proved impossible to agree. Nuclear weapons have now become the object, not the subject of foreign policy. The United States and the Soviet Union are now at last using the methods of traditional diplomacy in their bilateral relations.

By concluding a first Treaty, the Big Two have admitted, as Professor Shulman has shown, that their conflict is neither total nor absolute, that paradoxically the security of one is inevitably linked to the security of the other, and that in certain spheres, their interests coincide.[52] Mr Dean Rusk and several members of the Senate have shown that the United States and the Soviet Union have the same interest in avoiding nuclear war, in preventing the accidental explosion of a nuclear weapon triggering off a major conflict, in reducing pollution of the atmosphere, in delaying or inhibiting the spread of nuclear weapons, in strengthening *détente* and in restraining the armaments race in order to arrive at a reduction in military budgets.[53]

The Soviet Union also seems to adopt these arguments, which correspond to the doctrine of peaceful coexistence. A Soviet author has stated that two tendencies exist within the bourgeoisie of the capitalist countries—one aggressive and adventurist, the other moderate and sensible,[54] and he admits agreement is possible with the latter. The declaration of the Soviet government of 21 August 1963 seems to admit the existence of a sort of inevitable complicity between the possessors of nuclear weapons, when it mocks China's claim to make definitive judgements on the Great Powers' arms policy. "It is not a question of having a monopoly of talking about nuclear weapons by depriving others of this right, but in some people's mouths these declarations are meaningful whilst in others they are unwarranted."

---

[51] Cf. Radovanovic, "Les incidences du traité de Moscou", *Revue de la politique internationale*, 20 September 1963, pp. 5–7.
[52] *Hearings 1963*, pp. 798, 805.
[53] ibid., pp. 36, 65–66, 71–72; *Congressional Record*, 9 September 1963, pp. 15670-75, 10 September 1963, pp. 15678–69.
[54] Bourlatski, *Etudes soviétiques*, September 1963, p. 8.

However, the ratification debate which took place in the American Senate shows just how far the deterrent balance is a relative and political concept. Many military chiefs, as well as representatives who questioned everything yet were ready to accept the most unlikely information, gave a cold reception to the Treaty on the grounds that it would deprive the United States of certain advantages in the nuclear armament field.[55] This tendency always to want to overtake one's opponent by at least a short head, makes the armaments race inevitable and helps it along—as if it were not already propelled along by its own force of inertia. Thus President Kennedy had to give guarantees along these lines in order to get the Treaty ratified. In a letter dated 10 September 1963, he made the following promises: underground tests would be vigorously pursued; all precautions would be taken to enable the United States to begin tests in the atmosphere again if the Russians violated the Treaty; detection equipment and installations would be constantly improved and reinforced; the Treaty would in no way limit the right of the Commander-in-Chief, that is to say the President, to use nuclear weapons in case of need; the United States would take immediate measures if Cuba were to be used directly or indirectly to get round the Treaty or to make it inoperative; the Treaty would not change the status of the East German authorities; the programme for the development and perfection of nuclear weapons would be carried out energetically; and lastly, the United States would continue, through underground tests, their study and research into the use of nuclear explosives for peaceful purposes.[56]

6. The decline of bipolarity

The Moscow Treaty reflected, at the same time as it encouraged, the decline of bipolarity.[57] The two Super-Powers, by deciding to come to an understanding, took into consideration the chorus of world opinion and in particular that of the Third World. They, together with Great Britain, agreed to give up tests which, at the time, they alone were able to undertake. Within each bloc friction and contradictions got worse: between the United States and France, to a certain extent between France and Ger-

---

[55] This argument has been supported by J. H. McBride, op. cit., pp. 78–81; he feels the Treaty is unable to lessen political tension as the United States' aim is to defend the free world, and that of the Communists to destroy it. ibid., p. 120. This is a point of view which dates back to the most inflexible notions of the Cold War.

[56] *Congressional Record*, 11 September 1963, p. 15915. This statement and the pressures which produced it, explain the situation described in the passage to which footnote 49 refers.

[57] Cf. Jacobson and Stein, op. cit., pp. 500–501.

many, and between the Soviet Union and China. The message of the Swiss Federal Council confirmed that Switzerland's participation in the Treaty had no effect on her policy of neutrality, as "the group – in all probability a small one – of States opposed to the Treaty or remaining outside included States from both East and West". But if the rigidity of the blocs has lessened – in spite of the invasion of Czechoslovakia – it should not necessarily be assumed that the Big Two do not possess special political power nor that their mutual understanding is not necessary to international society as a whole.

7. The Treaty and non-proliferation

The Treaty forms the first official expression of the Soviet-American agreement on the necessity of preventing the dissemination of nuclear weapons. In his speech to the Nation on 26 July 1963, President Kennedy declared: "We have a great obligation – all four nuclear powers have a great obligation – to use whatever time remains to prevent the spread of nuclear weapons, to persuade other countries not to test, transfer, acquire, possess or produce such weapons". For his part, Mr McNamara, Secretary for Defense, testifying before the Senate Foreign Relations Committee, insisted on the dangers of the proliferation of nuclear weapons which would (i) increase the possibility of an accidental nuclear war because of the possession of nuclear arms by nations that had neither the means nor the technical knowledge nor the financial resources to apply the security, safeguard and control measures taken by the Big Two; (ii) increase the risk of a "small nuclear war" capable of causing a major conflict between the Big Two; (iii) introduce a factor of regional instability and upset the precarious balance of power at the regional level.[58]

In its notes of 31 July, 15 August and 1 September 1963, the government of the People's Republic of China accused the Moscow Treaty of trying to perpetuate the nuclear monopoly of the Big Three. The Soviet replies of 3 and 21 August and of 21 September show the importance attached to non-dissemination from the peace-keeping point of view. According to the note of 21 August "the danger of a nuclear war will increase with every new Capitalist State that possesses nuclear weapons. But it is impossible to expect the number of Socialist nuclear Powers to increase, whilst the number of nuclear States in the Imperialist camp remains the same. It would be, to say the least, naïve to suppose that it is possible to apply one policy in the West and another in the East, that one can on the one hand struggle against the equipping of West Germany with

[58] *Hearings 1963*, pp. 108, 145.

nuclear arms, against the dissemination of nuclear arms in the world, and on the other hand give these arms to China".

Let it be noted, however, that the Soviet decision not to give nuclear arms to China, not to help this country to manufacture them, was taken in 1959 and therefore independent of the Treaty. The latter only restricts the dissemination of nuclear arms. In his message to the Senate of 8 August 1963, President Kennedy expressed himself in these terms: "While the Treaty cannot wholly prevent the spread of nuclear arms to nations not now possessing them, it prohibits assistance to testing in these environments by others; it will be signed by many other potential testers; and it is thus an important opening wedge in our effort to 'get the genie back in the bottle' ".[59]

Even total agreement on a test ban is only a necessary precondition to non-proliferation – it is insufficient by itself.[60] Perhaps the Russians, who in 1958 had already expressed the hope that the prohibition of tests would prevent proliferation,[61] over-estimated the scope of the Moscow Treaty in this domain. During the 1963 negotiations, Mr Krushchev refused Mr Harriman's proposal to proceed to the immediate discussion of a Treaty on Non-Proliferation. He felt then that the stopping of tests ensured non-proliferation: as for the transfer of nuclear weapons by States that have them to those that are without, this could be examined later, he felt.[62] There is no doubt that the banning of nuclear weapons tests in the atmosphere and in outer space and underwater restricts proliferation. It is true that the signatories can carry out underground tests, but these demand large financial means, advanced technology and difficult preparation. Moreover, atomic weapons, above all simple ones, can be manufactured without tests taking place at all. Finally, the Moscow Treaty does not forbid signatories from obtaining atomic weapons by purchase, gift or other means.[63] A recent study shows that the United States also over-estimated the Moscow Treaty, if not as a psychological and political barrier, at least as a technological obstacle to proliferation.[64] Whence arose interest in a specific agreement concerning nuclear non-proliferation.

[59] *Hearings 1963*, p. 3.
[60] See D. G. Brennan (ed.), *Arms Control, Disarmament and National Security* (New York, Braziller, 1961), p. 244.
[61] A/L 247.
[62] A. M. Schlesinger, Jr., *A Thousand Days* (London, André Deutsch, 1965), p. 774.
[63] Cf. A. H. Dean, op. cit., p. 99.
[64] W. B. Bader, *The U.S. and the Spread of Nuclear Weapons* (New York, Pegasus, 1968), pp. 54–59. This author argues quite correctly that most countries are unable to carry out tests in the atmosphere without endangering their own population and those of their neighbours. In his opinion it is not certain either that underground tests are now more costly and difficult to carry out than others.

2. THE PROBLEM OF NON-PROLIFERATION

WE have seen that the problem of non-proliferation has preoccupied both Super-Powers for some time. Other countries are also paying attention to it. For example, in December 1961 the General Assembly of the United Nations in its Resolution 1665 (XVI) – also known as the Irish resolution – stressed the importance and significance of non-proliferation. It returned to the problem in Resolutions 1908 (XVIII) and 2149 (XXI). Resolution 2028 (XX) is worthy of special note. It says the future Treaty must (a) be free of escape clauses that might enable nuclear or non-nuclear powers to proliferate nuclear weapons, directly or indirectly, in any form whatsoever; (b) establish an acceptable balance of mutual responsibilities and obligations between nuclear and non-nuclear Powers; (c) mark a stage towards the achievement of general and complete disarmament, and, more particularly, nuclear disarmament; (d) contain acceptable and practical enforcement provisions; (e) not restrict the right of any group of States to conclude regional Treaties with a view to placing a total ban on nuclear weapons in their respective territories.

This resolution shows how non-proliferation is conceived less as an end in itself than as a means, a step on the road to disarmament. It helps to explain the difficulties met with during the drawing-up and adoption of the Non-Proliferation Treaty.

In this chapter, it is proposed to deal successively with terminology, historical development, and the arguments for and against non-proliferation.

I. TERMINOLOGY

It may be useful at the start of this chapter to say a few words about terminology. First a detail about two basic terms used here. The expression nuclear States refers to States that possess nuclear weapons, that is to say the United States, Soviet Union, Britain, France and China, and the expression non-nuclear States refers to all others.

The word proliferation, in its strict grammatical sense, covers the multiplication of nuclear arms without distinguishing the number of States that possess them. Attempts have been made to distinguish vertical proliferation (quantitative and qualitative increases in weapons held by nuclear States) from horizontal proliferation (increase in the number of countries holding nuclear weapons). We shall see that politically it is difficult to consider one of these ideas separately from the other. But only the second is actually covered by the Treaty. It boils down to a renunciation of nuclear weapons by non-nuclear States, and an agreement by nuclear States not to transfer nuclear weapons to States that do not have them. This second aspect is correctly called non-dissemination. The term non-proliferation is not sufficiently specific. We shall use it here because of its official connotation. It is possible to make a supplementary distinction between dissemination and diffusion. Diffusion takes place when a nuclear State deposits outside its frontiers nuclear weapons over which it retains control. The degree of control a nuclear State exercises over its weapons can in practice present complicated problems. The Atomic Energy Joint Committee of the United States Congress felt in 1961 that the control exercised by the United States over their nuclear weapons sited in Europe was not strict enough and President Kennedy immediately took steps as a result.[1]

II. POLICIES OF THE GREAT POWERS

During World War Two, the United States signed agreements with Britain, principally in June 1942, on 19 August 1943 and 19 September 1944.[2] Without going into detail, it can be said that these agreements, which have been subject to differing interpretations, envisaged fairly close military and commercial co-operation between the two countries. After the war, however, the United States sought to maintain their atomic monopoly. They said they would give it up only in exchange for an international control system. The Baruch-Lilienthal Plan put forward an extremely strict and elaborate control mechanism that corresponded neither to the structure nor the nature of international society, and in any case proved unacceptable to the Soviet Union.

The McMahon law, passed by the United States Congress in 1946, reflected America's wish to safeguard her atomic monopoly. It forbade the communication of military information abroad and imposed the same ban, as long as there was no international control system, upon information

---

[1] *Non-proliferation of Nuclear Weapons, Hearings before the Joint Committee on Atomic Energy*, on S. Res. 179, February–March 1966, p. 80 (referred to hereafter as *Hearings 1966*); cf. also on the two-tier system which is in operation at the present time B. Goldschmidt, *Les rivalités atomiques 1939–1966* (Paris, Fayard, 1967), pp. 243–44.

[2] Fischer, *L'energie atomique et les Etats-Unis*, pp. 243; M. Gowen, *Britain and Atomic Energy, 1939–1945* (London, Macmillan, 1964), p. 447.

capable of industrial use. So this law put a temporary stop to all exchanges of information and all co-operation between the United States and other countries, including Britain.

Britain then began to create, by herself, a civil and military atomic industry. So what did the American decision in 1946 actually mean? Some believe that in spite of appearances this decision encouraged nuclear proliferation,[3] for if the United States had communicated nuclear information to other countries, they would have been able to influence those receiving it towards purely peaceful ends.

Mr George Ball, an American diplomat who has played and still plays an important role, has a different view. In his opinion, President Truman's decision was a wise one and fulfilled the needs of non-proliferation. As it was, Britain never did have to establish an independent deterrent. She only got it thanks to American aid granted by Eisenhower and Kennedy.[4]

In any case, in 1954 and 1955, the McMahon law was amended so as to allow, under certain fixed conditions, the communication abroad of certain information about civil nuclear technology as well as the export of raw materials and equipment used in the industry for peaceful purposes. At the same time, the 1954 and 1955 amendments provided for the exchange of military information about nuclear weapons to the extent that it was necessary for carrying out defence plans and training staff for regional defence organisations. This limited and non-discriminative measure was perhaps not entirely compatible with a later non-proliferation policy. It was sufficiently vague to enable the United States to interpret it according to their policy needs.

In June 1958, the McMahon law was modified again to allow the transfer of nuclear information and materials as well as non-nuclear parts of atomic weapons to any allied nation having made substantial progress in its manufacturing capability of nuclear weapons. This amendment, which arose out of the special relationship with Britain, tended to favour her alone. It was difficult to reconcile with a policy of non-proliferation. In addition, it introduced into the alliance an element of discrimination, which was to cause friction and difficulty in the future.

From 1958 onwards, the United Kingdom received important aid in enriched uranium which was of benefit to her nuclear arsenal. In 1960, the United States decided to provide their partners with the Skybolt rocket, which proved useless shortly afterwards. Two years later at the Nassau

[3] This is the argument of Mrs Elisabeth Young, in her letter to *The Times* on 26 June 1968.
[4] G. W. Ball, *The Discipline of Power* (London, Bodley Head, 1968), pp. 95–108.

Conference the Americans agreed, under certain conditions, to supply Britain with Polaris submarines.[5]

Mr George Ball deplored these measures which went against non-proliferation and which in his opinion were the only reason why Britain was able to remain in the nuclear arms race.[6] The American diplomat's case is quite convincing and without any doubt Britain's creation of an independent deterrent influenced French atomic policy. It is worth noting that the United Kingdom, whose independent deterrent resulted in part from American assistance, remains more tied to the United States than France which did not benefit from such help. However, we must beware of too simple an interpretation; military technology does not explain everything; politics and the men who practice it are just as important factors. In any case, it might be surmised that an American refusal to help Britain's atomic arsenal would have had a different effect on that country's politics than it would have had for example in France.

Let us return now to the problem of the peaceful uses of atomic energy. Without going into technical detail, it will be recalled that the three materials with which it is possible to manufacture nuclear explosives are uranium 235, plutonium 239 and uranium 233. The latter is hardly ever used at present. Uranium 235, in order to be used in nuclear weapons, must be enriched by a gas diffusion process whose cost is very high. However, a new much cheaper separation process based on the high-speed gas centrifuge is at present the subject of research in the United States, in West Germany and in the Netherlands. Plutonium 239 is less costly than enriched uranium. Its manufacture demands natural uranium, one or more reactors and a chemical separation factory. The two materials can both be used for civil or military purposes.[7]

This very superficial explanation reveals the link that exists between technology for peaceful purposes and that necessary for the manufacture

---

[5] A French official commentator was quick off the mark to declare that the Nassau agreements "put an end to Britain's hopes of keeping a long-term independent nuclear deterrent". The submarines equipped with American Polaris missiles and British nuclear warheads were actually supposed to be available to a multilateral NATO force, now abandoned. Still, the United Kingdom retained the option of using this weapon independently, if its government "decided that her supreme national interest was at risk". A similar offer was made to France, which was refused. Cf. B. Goldschmidt, *Les rivalités atomiques 1939–1966* (Paris, Fayard, 1967), pp. 257–58.

[6] G. W. Ball, op. cit., pp. 95–108.

[7] Cf. L. Beaton, *Must the Bomb Spread?* (Penguin Books, 1966), p. 24 et seq. It is to be hoped that in a few years time super-regenerative reactors will become economic: they produce more plutonium than they use up. Cf. Goldschmidt, op. cit., p. 271.

of the bomb. As peaceful uses grow, increasing quantities of fissile materials become available, which can eventually be used for military purposes. We have seen that under the American law of 1954, information about civil technology and assistance in this field can be given by the United States to foreign countries, under certain conditions. The "Atoms for Peace" programme launched by President Eisenhower, was conceived in such a way as to enlist science and technology for political ends. Its originators wildly exaggerated the immediate economic possibilities of atomic energy.[8] It is true, however, that the programme was largely responsible for the increase in the number of countries holding fissile materials. Of course, the bilateral treaties concluded by the United States did provide for a control system. But this programme encouraged rivalry and competition, politically, economically and commercially, in a world where technology is now widely diffused.

It encouraged the transfer of knowledge and raw materials, even of manufactured products, which appears to be difficult to reconcile with the political objective of non-dissemination which has, however, been clearly and sincerely pursued by the United States. This at least is the opinion of some observers for whom the situation just described is one example among many of the lack of integration and cohesion in different aspects of American foreign policy.[9] For others, the atomic exports to which the United States consented have contributed towards non-proliferation: the States which benefited, forced to submit to a control system, did not bother to build certain plants, in particular for the production of enriched uranium (whose cost price is very high, it will be recalled).

The bilateral agreements concluded by the United States in the field of peaceful uses of nuclear energy carry detailed provisions about the control exercised by the United States. From 1956 onwards they envisaged the possibility of replacing this control by that of the International Agency. Since 1963 and above all since 1964 this bilateral system has tended in practice to be replaced by the international control of the International Atomic Energy Agency.

A recent study tries to prove that the United States only became at-

---

[8] On yet another point the 1955 forecast has proved wrong: only large nuclear power stations are viable and this has important consequences for developing countries. That is the opinion of a leading French authority. Goldschmidt, op. cit., p. 272. However, the British nuclear power industry is aiming at the construction and export of heavy water reactors which are more economically viable in small power stations and which correspond to the needs of the countries in question. Cf. *The Observer*, 28 July 1968.

[9] Cf. E. B. Skolnikoff, *Science, Technology and American Foreign Policy* (Cambridge, Mass., MIT Press, 1967), p. 43.

tached to the policy of non-proliferation from 1958 onwards.[10] But it appears in several ways that American non-proliferation policy, although unclear, goes back further than this. It is true, as the author of this study shows, that the "Atoms for Peace" policy tended to achieve non-proliferation by means of American control over the peaceful use of fissile materials, which then became international. At the same time, confidence was expressed, perhaps over-confidence, in the obstacle that access to a new technology presents. The amendments to the McMahon law of 1954 and 1955 were adopted under contradictory pressures; they mark the beginning of a doctrine which contrasts the idea of nuclear weapons control with that of the ownership or possession of these weapons. What this doctrine does is to set up a barrier against the creation of any new independent nuclear force, but to allow the supply of weapons, information and technology to nuclear forces already in existence. It also allows limited access by non-nuclear States to American nuclear weapons capable of being sited on their territory, and some training of members of their armed forces in the use of these weapons, as long as the United States retains control over the firing of these weapons.

These subtle distinctions between control and ownership of weapons, easy to establish at a technical level, were to create particularly complicated political problems, especially in so far as non-proliferation was concerned. Non-proliferation was seen in a new light when the French government announced on 11 April 1958 its intention to create an independent nuclear deterrent. It is true that according to Mr Ball, this decision was partly explained by that of the United States to amend the McMahon law again in 1958 and to reinforce the special relationship with Britain. But it appears that the creation of the French *force de frappe* was due to a whole host of other factors, mainly internal ones, and that the two decisions were linked to each other. In 1958, the United States were trying simultaneously to avoid proliferation, to appease the members of NATO by giving them a limited right of access to American nuclear weapons, and to exercise some control over Britain's nuclear armament, whose development appeared to them unavoidable. This was clearly full of contradictions and was to be the source of friction that can be detected more easily with the benefit of hindsight. But a policy, contrary to the belief of some people, is not a purely intellectual, logical exercise; it is rarely the result of a deliberate choice between radical alternatives. The United States, like many other countries, were trying in this case to reconcile a policy that was still rather vague, but that they had defined, with means that were not always appro-

[10] W. B. Bader, *The United States and the Spread of Nuclear Weapons* (New York, Pegasus, 1968), pp. 15–43, 101.

priate to the end in view. Washington, it must be understood, was faced with a new and and complex situation which might have developed along several different lines. It was the interplay of the different factors which determined the final course of events and the nature of future possible combinations that the United States was unable to define or influence to any real extent.

Soviet policy was not free from contradictions either, as we have already had occasion to observe above. These contradictions arose for exactly the same reasons. The problems which faced the United States within NATO – diffusion, proliferation, and discrimination – hardly faced the Soviet Union in its relations with its allies, except with China. And we know what happened. No other ally showed a desire for nuclear status.

As far as nuclear co-operation for peaceful purposes was concerned, the Soviet Union, in its bilateral Treaties, adopted different methods from those of the United States, since, on paper, it set up no comparable control system. But it did resort to indirect means; the regeneration of exhausted fuel is carried on in Soviet factories; the fissile materials supplied are only weakly enriched or concentrated; Soviet technicians are sent under a technical assistance programme to donee countries.[11] The Soviet Union supplied Peking with an experimental reactor and a cyclotron for exclusively peaceful uses of nuclear energy, under an agreement dated 15 October 1957. She helped China to build a gaseous diffusion plant, she trained Chinese technicians. There is no doubt that all this helped the Chinese to make their own bombs.[12] Canada built a research reactor for India, which has been in operation since 1960 and which is subject to no form of control; it is simply run under an agreement by which India will only use it for peaceful purposes. But, since that time, Canada's policy has changed. Since 1965, this large uranium producer has decided not to supply the material to foreign countries unless they undertake with proper verification to use it solely for peaceful purposes.[13] We shall return to this point.

It will be seen therefore that the development of a civil nuclear industry

[11] S. Rosen, "Proliferation Treaty Controls and the IAEA", *Journal of Conflict Resolution*, June 1967, pp. 168–175.

[12] Le Thanh Khoi, *Cahiers de l'ISEA*, February 1959, p. 22; Ball, op. cit., p. 201; Goldschmidt, op. cit., pp. 292–3.

[13] Statement by the Prime Minister in the House of Commons, 3 June 1965. In 1963, Canada signed an agreement with India for the supply of a nuclear power reactor to operate at Rajasthan, similar to the one at Douglas Point in Canada. Reciprocal bilateral guarantees were laid down to satisfy Indian sensitivity: by the Canadians for Rajasthan and by the Indians for Douglas Point. India was therefore consulted about the arrangements for the guarantees to be applied over 170 kilos of plutonium produced at Douglas Point and sold to France. Canada, *House of Commons, Debates*, 30 September 1968, Col. 545–6.

always facilitates the manufacture of atomic bombs. An example given by a well-informed author makes the point. The nuclear reactor built at Latina in Italy by the United Kingdom will produce 1,000 kilos of plutonium in ten years, a quantity sufficient to manufacture ten to twenty small bombs. According to the same author, three countries, West Germany, Japan and Canada, will have nuclear weapons in the near future. Following a short distance behind are Sweden, Italy and India. The same possibility is open during the next fifteen years, to Australia, the Netherlands, Belgium, Czechoslovakia, Israel, Brazil, Switzerland, East Germany and Poland.[14]

III. ARGUMENTS FOR AND AGAINST NON-PROLIFERATION

1. The Dissuasion Theory

One line of argument tries to justify proliferation by considering it simply as an extension of bilateral dissuasion and the balance of terror between the Big Two.[15] In the United States in particular there exists a school of thought that likes to state all the hypotheses of reciprocal dissuasion by employing games theory, logic that is abstract and often inhuman, and premisses that seem utterly unrelated to the complex realities of domestic and international society.[16] It is, however, interesting to observe that even the most fervent supporters of this line of thought are sometimes forced to admit that their arguments and deductions can just as well be used to support one solution as its very opposite.[17]

The balance of terror means that each adversary has the means to survive nuclear attack and to counter-attack by inflicting a punishment sufficiently severe to deter the other from attacking in the first place. Some go so far as to argue that this balance of terror is an essential factor in

[14] L. Beaton, "Nuclear Fuel for All", *Foreign Affairs*, July 1967, pp. 662–669. According to a recent estimate by the United States Atomic Energy Commission, the following countries will be able, five to ten years after having taken the decision, to perfect a fairly advanced atomic weapons system: Australia, Canada, West Germany, India, Italy, Japan and Sweden. Other States would take more time to arrive at the same result: Argentina, Austria, Belgium, Brazil, Chile, Czechoslovakia, Hungary, Israel, Netherlands, Pakistan, Poland, South Africa, Spain, Switzerland, UAR, Yugoslavia, *Non-Proliferation Treaty*, *Hearings before the Committee on Foreign Relations*, US Senate, 10, 11, 12 and 17 July 1968, p. 31 (Referred to hereafter as *Hearings 1968*).

[15] P. Gallois, *Stratégie de l'âge nucléaire* (Paris 1960); see also A. Beaufre, *Dissuasion et stratégie* (Paris, 1965).

[16] An admirable criticism of this school of thought has been made by P. Green, *Deadly Logic, the Theory of Nuclear Deterrence* (Ohio State University Press, 1966), p. 177, and *passim*.

[17] See for example H. Kahn, *On Escalation: Metaphors and Scenarios* (New York, Praeger, 1965).

preserving peace, since the awful character of nuclear weapons and their terrible effects make war impossible. Some even go so far as to argue that the supporters of nuclear disarmament are helping directly to perpetuate conventional warfare.[18]

Things are far from being as simple as this. A state of peace existed even during the period when the United States had a monopoly of atomic weapons. But, above all, the stability and balance essential to the idea of reciprocal dissuasion are constantly threatened by the armaments race and by the imbalance resulting from it.[19] The balance of terror can only be, at best, a state of fact which ought to be the starting point for the organisation of a definitive, stable peace. By itself, as an eminent American scientist has said, it is only a perversion of the noble idea of peace, a symbol of a world of institutionalised hate and mistrust, in which the best efforts of every nation are permanently devoted to the improvement of their own mechanics of mass destruction so as to match that of their rivals.[20] For his part, Mr McNamara, at that time Defense Secretary, expressed the same preoccupation on 18 September 1967: "There is a kind of mad momentum intrinsic to the development of all nuclear weaponry. If a weapons system works – and works well – there is strong pressure from many directions to procure and deploy the weapon out of all proportion to the prudent level required".

As we have already seen, increase in military power does not strengthen national security. In an interview given on 7 January 1967, M. Couve de Murville, a Minister in a government holding on to its nuclear deterrent, himself protested against the idea that the nuclear balance of terror was to be mankind's destiny.[21]

The fragility of this balance was clearly revealed by the new race which has started in the anti-ballistic missile field.[22] For some time, the Soviet

---

[18] See the debate between Messrs Beaufre, Bothoul, and Hamon, *La Table Ronde*, February 1967, pp. 71–88.

[19] See for example D. E. Lilienthal, *Change, Hope and the Bomb* (Princeton University Press, 1963), pp. 39–40.

[20] E. Rabinowitch, *The Dawn of a New Age, Reflections on Science and Human Affairs* (Chicago and London, University of Chicago Press, 1963), p. 138.

[21] *La Documentation française*, N.E.D., No. 3428–3430, 24 October 1967, p. 32. The recent report of the UN Secretary-General, drawn up with the help of twelve eminent experts, states: "Efforts made to maintain a state of nuclear dissuasion have demanded considerable resources and paradoxically, far from strengthening the feeling of security, they have sometimes created a feeling of insecurity. . . . In the absence of any common agreement, it is an endless race, which leads not to the establishment of a state of uniform security, but, as has been said, to periods of great insecurity alternating with periods during which relative security seems assured". A/6858, 10 October 1967, para. 80.

[22] A.B.M. = anti-missile missile.

Union has stated she has been setting up such a system, although its efficacy may be open to some doubt.[23] On 18 September 1967, Mr Mc-Namara announced the construction by the United States of a "light" system which, according to this statement, would protect the United States only against a Chinese nuclear attack. Some reservations have been made about this last point. Yet it remains a fact that it seems difficult to place limitations on the deployment of the A.B.M. system.

The Sentinel system of the Johnson administration was taken up again in March 1969 by the Nixon administration under a different name: Safeguard. But this now had different characteristics. It was no longer destined to form a barrier to a first Chinese attack, but to form part of the country's global defence system, that is to say to protect also against Soviet attack. In addition Safeguard was no longer supposed to form a barrier to nuclear attack upon certain cities (whose inhabitants, enlightened by the statement of experts who emphasised the doubtful efficacy of the system, made energetic protests against the initial project and the dangers they deduced to their own survival). Now it is regarded as a protective system for the Minuteman missiles as well as for administrative centres and important headquarters. At the beginning of 1970, President Nixon decided to go ahead with the second stage in the execution of this programme, which, it is to be feared, will tend, through its own power of inertia, to change from a "thin" to a more and more comprehensive system. The cost already threatens to exceed initial estimates of 5,000 million dollars (the cost of a full scale system being in the region of 50,000 million dollars).

A new weapon has made its appearance – the M.I.R.V. This is a rocket with multiple warheads, each one of which is aimed at a separate target. This weapon, now in process of development (the number of warheads can be constantly increased and the accuracy of the aim perfected) is a destabilising factor. It can only be detected for what it is (that is to say distinguished from an ordinary rocket) by observation satellites. It can also make it worthwhile to make a first strike, as one of the adversaries, at a certain stage of development, can be led to believe that it is more profitable to strike first with the M.I.R.V. which he already has, rather than build a reaction system that is viable and capable of withstanding the enemy's first strike. Thus a new armaments race emerges in the course of which each of the two Super-Powers has to keep on perfecting defensive and offensive weapons. Uncertainty over the range and capability of these weapons, some of which are completely new, threatens to intro-

[23] *The Economist*, 6 July 1968

duce a new factor of instability and tension into international relations.[24]

In any case, if either side felt completely protected from nuclear attack, the so-called balance of terror and the so-called "virtues" of dissuasion would not exist. Many other reservations could also be made about these two concepts. As Walter Lippman has shown, a great power, if faced with the choice between unconditional surrender and suicide "particularly if it is not absolutely fatal", will choose the latter.[25] Also, this dissuasion, this balance of terror, which is constantly challenged by galloping technical progress, can only exist in so far as (and this is still in doubt) the adversaries agree about and share the same basic concepts, such as nuclear parity, the extent of destruction that a nuclear counter-attack must cause to deter the adversary from striking first, and the qualitative and quantitative volume of weapons necessary to sustain a satisfactory counter-strike.[25a]

So the interest and importance of the bilateral negotiations between the United States and the Soviet Union, begun on 17 November 1969, on the limitation of offensive and defensive systems of strategic nuclear weapons becomes clear. Who would not support Resolution 2602 A (XXIV) of the General Assembly which calls upon the two Super-Powers, as a preliminary measure, to observe a moratorium on the testing and installation of new offensive and defensive strategic nuclear weapons systems?

2. Effects of an increase in the number of nuclear States

Some people will argue that the multiplication of States possessing nuclear weapons, by ensuring a more widespread deterrent, is a stabilising factor in the world. We have seen what it means in the context of relationships between the Super-Powers. The result of proliferation would be still more dangerous.[26] As an official of the Swiss Federal Political Department

---

[24] L. A. Frank, "A.B.M. and Non-Proliferation," *Orbis*, Spring 1967, pp. 67–79; R. L. Garwin and H. A. Bethe, *Scientific American*, March 1968, pp. 21–31; O. R. Young, *Bulletin of Atomic Scientists*, May 1967, pp. 35–42; and February 1968, pp. 16–209; L. W. Martin, ibid., May, 1967, pp. 43–46; R. L. Rothstein, *Foreign Affairs*, April 1968, pp. 487–502; Dyson, *Bulletin of Atomic Scientists*, April 1969, p. 31; Bethe, ibid., May 1969, p. 41; Fulbright, Rathyens, Bethe, York, ibid., June 1969, pp. 20, 23, 25, 27; Bothwell, ibid., October 1969, p. 21; De Volpi, ibid., January, 1970, p. 35.

[25] *Journal of Conflict Resolution*, September 1963, pp. 345–6.

[25a] See B. T. Feld, *Bulletin of Atomic Scientists*, January 1970, p. 7.

[26] On the arguments for and against see B. T. Feld in *Bulletin of Atomic Scientists*, May 1967, pp. 61–62; D. B. Bobrow, in ibid., December 1965, pp. 20–22; T. Read, *A Proposal to Neutralize Nuclear Weapons* (Centre of International Studies, Princeton University, 1960); by the same author, *Military Policy in a Changing Political Context*, ibid., 1964; A. Wohlstetter, "Nuclear Sharing", *Foreign Affairs*, April 1961; M. H. Halperin, *Contemporary Military Strategy* 'Boston and Toronto, Little Brown, 1967); by the same, *China and Nuclear Proliferation* (University of Chicago, Centre for Policy Studies, 1966); D.

has said, very much to the point: "Between two nuclear powers it's a game of chess, among four, it's bridge, among a dozen, it would be poker, roulette or any of those games controlled by chance."[27]

Dissemination means introducing into the equation many new independent variables.[28]

The present world, already bizarre, would be still more surprising, less predictable, more a prey to mathematical error. The Big Two, who now both accept certain identical rules, who have become accustomed to the same methods of calculation and prediction, would find their security threatened by the existence of others. There would be a greater chance of nuclear holocaust through accident, mathematical error, mistaken identity of the aggressor, or suicide attack.

Perhaps it would be a mistake to agree with Mr Krushchev, who used to argue in his day that possession of nuclear weapons bestowed wisdom and restraint. If you push this argument to its logical conclusion, other Powers ought to acquire these weapons to arrive at this happy state of affairs.[29] It is no less true that between certain States capable of reaching nuclear status there exist deep and, for the present, insoluble conflicts, and antagonistic feelings that are sharpened by the adversaries having common frontiers. These conflicts, these antagonistic feelings have no common measure with those that separate the Big Two. According to Mr Hermann

---

Healey in *Commentary*, January 1960, pp. 1–7; R. M. Rosecrance, *The Dispersion of Nuclear Weapons* (New York and London, Columbia University Press, 1964); H. Kahn in M. A. Kaplan (ed.), *The Revolution in World Politics* (New York, Wiley, 1962), pp. 337–40; K. Younger, "The Spectre of Nuclear Proliferation", *International Affairs*, January 1966, pp. 14–23; A. L. Burns, *Power Politics and the Growing Nuclear Club* (Centre of International Studies, Princeton University, 1959); by the same, "Can the Spread of Nuclear Weapons Be Stopped?" *International Organisation*, Autumn 1965, pp. 851–69; A. Buchan (ed.), *A World of Nuclear Powers?* (Englewood Cliffs, Prentice Hall, 1966).

[27] *Tribune de Genève*, 20 May 1968.

[28] The UN Secretary-General's report, already quoted, says: "As far as international security is concerned, it is very probable that any further increase in the number of States with nuclear weapons, or any new strengthening of existing nuclear arsenals would aggravate tension and instability in the whole world . . . If the number of nuclear Powers were to grow, regional tension would be greater, the danger of nuclear war breaking out accidentally, or by mistake, grows as the number of States having these weapons increases". A/6858, para. 82.

[29] To quote the Brazilian delegate: "Can it simply be that because a country possesses nuclear weapons it inspires more confidence than those which do not possess such weapons? Does having the status of a nuclear power mean that one is an internationally responsible person? If that were the case, it would be an excellent reason for taking the nuclear option". ENDC/PV. 310.

Kahn, proliferation can lead to blackmail and threats, surprise or anony-
mous attacks, the camouflage of nuclear strength and policy, the manufacture of primitive weapons which perhaps do not even need a complicated
infrastructure or logistical system, and to anarchy and lack of control in
international life.[30]

The fierce opposition of the Super-Powers to proliferation is an argument
that carries weight – the more so because they fear its effects not so much
as a danger to themselves or to their territorial integrity, but as a factor
of uncertainty affecting both international relations in general and their
mutual relationship in particular. Mr Dean Rusk showed, a short time
ago, that proliferation would add a new dimension to existing historical,
ethnic and territorial disputes. The decisions the United States would be
called upon to take when faced with a dispute would, he said, become
much more complex if the parties to the dispute were nuclear States.
Proliferation would also make the conclusion of arms control agreements
more difficult.[31] The appropriate security measures to prevent an accidental detonation are costly and complex, and not within just anybody's reach.
Also a conventional attack always leaves time for diplomatic negotiation:
it is not the same with a nuclear attack whose devastating results are
only too well known.[32]

3. The cost of nuclear armament

Supporters of proliferation feel that military technological development
is indispensable to progress in civil applications. This argument tries to
create a general abstract rule out of a fact. It is true that, chronologically
speaking, military technology preceded civil applications. But at the
present stage of development, there is nothing inevitable about this
process. It is easy to forget that some of the present nuclear powers are also
the most scientifically advanced ones. They have ample resources and can
develop military and civil applications in parallel. In other countries, the
situation is different, a choice is necessary; the investment, resources and
manpower available cannot support both categories of development.
Anyway the progress made in the exclusively civil field by West Germany,
Canada, Japan and Sweden, is a powerful reply to the argument we have
just been discussing. France, on the other hand, which has divided her
efforts between both fields, civil and military, does not appear to have had
brilliant success in either.

A recent United Nations report, drawn up by a group of twelve experts,

[30] H. Kahn, op. cit.
[31] *Hearings 1966*, pp. 4–5.
[32] *Hearings 1966*, pp. 88–89 (Mr McNamara).

tried to cost out the creation of a nuclear deterrent. It is obvious that the figures suggested are very approximate. They put the cost of the French nuclear military programme up to 1969 at some 8,400 million dollars whilst another author puts the figure up to 1968 at 15,000 million dollars.[33]

In any case it ought to be emphasised that any calculation ought to take into account several factors such as that: (a) any nuclear weapons programme always tends to go beyond the limits originally set; (b) technical progress makes necessary the constant revision of the manufacturing programme for vectors and missiles, the most expensive components of the nuclear armoury; (c) such armament has never freed a country from the need to develop its conventional armed forces, thus maintaining a double burden; (d) the cost estimate must take into account the financial, material and manpower resources diverted from other economic sectors, and the sacrifices thus imposed on the national economy – these sacrifices will be the greater, the less developed is the country.

The experts' report estimates the creation of a small nuclear force would cost 170 million dollars a year for nineteen years, and a medium-size one 560 million dollars a year. Now only six countries in the world, outside the five nuclear States, are capable of forming a small nuclear force without diverting a great deal of their technical resources from constructive activities, and these six might also find the resources necessary to establish a medium size nuclear force.[34]

4. Small States against Super-Powers

Other arguments are sometimes put forward to support proliferation. One is the reduced credibility of a nuclear umbrella held – but at what risk – by one of the Big Two over a non-nuclear State. On the contrary, a country having even a limited nuclear force has sufficient means to deter a Super-Power, since it could destroy one of the Super-Powers' cities and thus cause damage sufficiently important to constitute an unacceptable risk. Looked at in this way, the acquisition of a national nuclear capability forms a condition of political and military independence. Following on from this, a small or medium-sized power having atomic weapons can use them as a detonator to force their most important ally to use its own nuclear deterrent.

These arguments, stated very sketchily here, do not stand up to examination. The two Super-Powers have such a lead in the nuclear armaments field that no other country can catch up with them. Nothing could be more typical in this respect than the development of the French nuclear deter-

[33] Ball, op. cit., p. 131.
[34] A/6858, paras. 43 to 77.

rent whose creation goes back to 1958 and which, after having absorbed enormous amounts of money and effort, will, it is estimated, in 1975 have a capacity equal to one American B-52.[35]

Anyway the credibility of such a deterrent force is insignificant. It is inconceivable that someone capable only of maiming his adversary should expose himself to the possibility of complete and certain annihilation. If a Super-Power deems it necessary to put an end to a small or medium-sized State, it will employ all its resources, even at the risk of losing a hand or an arm. In calculating this, the other Super-Power's deterrent will weigh much more heavily. In fact a small or medium-sized State getting atomic weapons increases its chances of being totally annihilated by the use of all categories of nuclear weapons right from the start of the conflict.[36] The diffusion of these weapons poses new problems for the Super-Powers. It does not provide the means of achieving equality among the members of international society.

This is all the more true since the Big Powers' lead in the nuclear field could only be reduced if they decided by actual or tacit agreement to limit their deterrent to a minimum level. In this case we should have arrived at the basis of a disarmament policy that small or medium-sized States would simply be unable to refuse. This proves to what extent other countries depend upon the common policy of the two Super-Powers. Another example is no less convincing. If the Big Two decided to build a "light" A.B.M. system (and it is possible that such a system might be perfected before the possible entry into force of an agreement banning or limiting the construction of anti-missile missiles) the small or medium sized deterrent would become even more useless. Small and medium sized powers would moreover be unable to compete in an A.B.M. armaments race, which as we have seen is extremely expensive.

As for a small or medium nuclear force acting as detonator this seems quite improbable and in contradiction to the hypothesis put forward by supporters of proliferation. Logically, proliferation ought to induce the most powerful member of the Alliance to mistrust the acts of its nuclear allies and take precautions not to be dragged into nuclear war against its will. If a non-nuclear ally can no longer count upon a Super-Power's determination to risk suicide in order to come to its defence, there is no

---

[35] *Le Monde*, 11 July 1968. In July and August 1968, France tested an H Bomb. This is still in an experimental stage, has no real military scope and even in the best of foreseeable circumstances will not be operational for another ten years. *Le Monde*, 27 August 1968. France tested its first A Bomb in 1960 and its first thermonuclear weapon eight years later. The corresponding gap was four years for the Soviet Union and two and a half years for China.

[36] D. Vital, *The Inequality of States* (Oxford, Clarendon Press, 1967), pp. 164 et seq.

reason why it should do so for an ally which, having reached nuclear status, loses confidence for this very reason.

5. Relations between two small or medium nuclear States

We shall now examine what happens when a small or medium-sized Power's nuclear deterrent is aimed against a State in the same category. It must be observed first of all that proliferation is of necessity infectious, and that it is therefore a destabilising factor which in the final analysis jeopardises everybody's security. If, to take an absurd example, every country in the world, or a majority of countries, all became nuclear at the same time, the simultaneous and revolutionary character of such a change would lead to very serious imbalance. If, on the contrary, States become nuclear one by one, the imbalance will be no less dangerous, for a State which already has a minimum force might be tempted to destroy pre-emptively the nuclear installations that another State is constructing.[37] H. Kahn sums it up as he points out that, as a greater number of countries get hold of nuclear weapons, and come to fear escalation and flash-point more and more, the possibility of making advantageous gains by simple blackmail or by a combination of blackmail and a limited use of nuclear weapons, can grow considerably.[38]

In the case of two weak nuclear Powers, nuclear war can follow two possible courses. The one who fires first destroys his adversary and obtains a decisive victory. Or, a more likely theory, the aggressor is unable completely to destroy his adversary's deterrent, and both countries undergo nuclear devastation.

According to a more optimistic view (if you agree with the arguments of those who support proliferation), an increase in the number of States possessing nuclear weapons, by creating some sort of balance of power and by preventing nuclear war, would leave intact and would even increase the possibility of a conventional war.[39] If this is the end result, there is no point in passing through the stages of atomic development.

Proliferation makes any return to the *status quo* difficult. One of the reasons which appears to have made Britain decide to retain her independent nuclear deterrent is the attitude of France, who does not want to give up hers. The French seem to want West Germany to sign the Non-Proliferation Treaty. One could ask just to what extent France, in view of her own nuclear force, is justified in taking up such a position. Since West

---

[37] Such a possibility has been foreseen by Mr Dean Rusk, *Hearings 1966*, pp. 4–5.
[38] H. Kahn, op cit.
[39] In the interview already quoted, M. Couve de Murville said: "I should prefer to give conventional warfare a chance rather than leave it to nuclear warfare".

Germany obviously has no intention of relying on the French nuclear deterrent, by signing the Treaty she would – according to the spirit and logic of French strategy – increase her dependence on the United States. But it looks as if the French government prefers to be illogical rather than run the risk of a nuclear West Germany.

The arguments set out here show that proliferation carries considerable risks. Doubtless other arguments could be made against this view. But it seems a good idea to carry over to the diplomatic field the method of argument which, in the military field, conditions the arms race, that is to say always to take the least favourable hypothesis.[40] Such a method of reasoning, which leads to conclusions supporting those given here, is even more legitimate in the field with which we are dealing than in the context of the arms race.

Moreover it is obvious that until now atomic weapons have not strengthened the independence of any country which possesses them. Is Great Britain more independent than Yugoslavia or Romania? Was she able to use her atomic weapons over Suez?[41] As for France, she impresses the Third World by her independence in spite of her atomic arsenal, whose manufacture and testing produce unfavourable reactions, particularly in Latin America. The true yardstick of national independence at the present day is technical progress and economic strength.

The arguments of the supporters of proliferation end up by provoking and justifying fragmentation and anarchy within international society. Whilst the proliferators believe that no country can trust its ally over defence matters, some authors say that the non-proliferation agreement between the Big Two threatens to weaken and even break the links that unite each of these powers to their respective allies.[42] But in reality, as has been amply demonstrated, proliferation, just as much as non-proliferation, tends to multiply problems, for example within NATO.[43] The dis-

---

[40] Cf. D. R. Inglis, "Conservative Judgements and Missile Madness", *Bulletin of Atomic Scientists*, May 1968, pp. 6–11.

[41] A senior official of the French Atomic Energy Commission who defends the French independent nuclear deterrent is obliged to admit that Britain, a country with nuclear weapons, was the first to give in over Suez. He explains this by saying that the ties between Britain and the United States "were such that it was almost unthinkable for her not to bend immediately before the American veto". Goldschmidt, op. cit., p. 221. The Suez affair is clear proof that factors such as internal politics, foreign policy, public opinion, and economic imperatives prevail over military power.

[42] Ball, op. cit., p. 163, who stresses West German sensitivity; S. Hoffman, *Gulliver's Troubles* (New York, McGraw-Hill 1968), p. 134.

[43] W. C. Foster, "New Direction in Arms Control and Disarmament", *Foreign Affairs*, July 1965, pp. 587–601. Mr Morgenthau has summed up the obstacles to the nuclear alliance within which members swing between lack of confidence

appearance of the Cold War, the building up of *détente*, the growing diversity of the world, the breaking-up of ideologies, the multiplication of possible patterns of development, all these weaken alliances. All too often specialists look at events in the distorting mirror of a rigid system of concepts called the balance of power, bipolarity, polycentrism, etc. But in fact we are in the middle of a period of transition in which no proper system has yet emerged, in which the Super-Powers discover a certain common interest in their joint will to survive, in which the alliances of the Cold War are breaking up. The Big Two are far from being able to rule the world, but they are seeking to create a system of world organisation capable of safeguarding the *status quo* and their common interests.

---

due to the reduced credibility of the nuclear umbrella, and dissatisfaction because of the power of the nuclear member. Bipolarity is more and more difficult for other States to accept, the multi-nuclear alliance is only acceptable to Super-Powers, atomic proliferation among individual nations is a danger to peace. H. Morgenthau, *American Political Science Review*, August 1964, pp. 23–35.

3. THE DRAFTING OF THE TREATY

In Chapter 1, we emphasised the role played by public opinion in the conclusion of the Moscow Treaty. The radioactive fall-out caused by nuclear tests, the health risks involved, the warnings of leaders of the Third World and of numerous experts, all these explain the concern of public opinion and the influence it had to a differing degree in a great number of countries.

It was another matter over the Non-Proliferation Treaty which dealt with problems that at first sight were more abstract and had no immediate, direct connection with people's health. This is why in most countries public opinion has been much less interested in this second Treaty.

Having said this, we shall divide the chapter into two parts, devoted to the organisations within which the Treaty has been drafted, and to the meaning of the Treaty.

I. ORGANISATIONS

1. History

First a brief review of disarmament negotiations. The United Nations Charter only went as far as to entrust the General Assembly with the study of the principles governing disarmament and arms control[1] whilst the Security Council was given the task of drawing up plans for the creation of an arms control system.[2] During a first phase, disarmament negotiations took place under the aegis of the Security Council. In January 1946, the General Assembly created the Atomic Energy Commission to include all member States of the Security Council as well as Canada then not a member. On 13 February 1947, the Security Council established a Commission for conventional armaments. In January 1952, the General Assembly created a single Disarmament Commission comprising the members of the Security Council plus Canada. In 1953, following a French proposal, a sub-committee of the Big Five was established to facilitate negotiations in a less crowded, calmer atmosphere. In 1957, in spite of Soviet opposition, the General Assembly by its Resolution 1150-(XII) appointed a 25-member Disarmament Commission. In 1958, by

[1] Art. 11. [2] Art. 26.

Resolution 1252-(XIII), this body was further enlarged and became a plenary committee of the General Assembly, which, however, did not meet until 1965.

In 1959 the Big Four agreed to create a Committee of Ten on Disarmament (five countries from the East and five from the West) whose existence came to an end when the Soviet Union left it on 27 June 1960.[3] On 21 September 1961, the United States and the Soviet Union announced to the United Nations that they had agreed on a common declaration of principles upon which disarmament negotiations would be based. On 13 December of the same year, the two countries decided to form an 18-member Disarmament Committee in which were represented 5 Eastern countries, 5 Western, and 8 non-aligned. This committee is not a United Nations body but its creation has been approved by the General Assembly.[4] The Committee of 18 originally really only had 17 members as France has always refused to occupy the chair reserved for her. In 1969, the Committee was enlarged. New admissions were two allies of the United States, two Eastern bloc countries and four non-aligned States including Pakistan (which is a State belonging to a military pact).

2. The role of the General Assembly

The history that has been retraced, although only in outline, does show that within the United Nations, disarmament problems tended more and more, particularly from 1954 onwards, to become the prerogative of the General Assembly, which in that year passed its first important resolution in the disarmament field. This growing responsibility of the General Assembly was exercised at the expense of that of the Security Council whose role under this heading became insignificant.[5]

Although the Committee of 18 is not an organ of the United Nations, it presents annual reports to the General Assembly, which in its turn recommends, encourages and exhorts. The Big Two are not insensitive to these appeals, even when they are not disposed to follow them up. A recent fact illustrates this point: before the Committee adjourned on 14 December 1967, there was a discussion on whether to present a very short report to the Assembly or if, as eight non-aligned countries asked, the documents before the Committee ought to be appended. The Big Two fought bitterly and successfully to avoid giving the Assembly the chance of pronouncing upon

---

[3] Cf. B. G. Bechhoefer, *Post-War Negotiations for Arms Control* (Washington, Brookings, 1961).

[4] Resolution 1722 (XVI).

[5] A. Lall, *Modern International Negotiations* (New York and London, Columbia University Press, 1966), pp. 107–110.

these documents and exercising a moral pressure which was obviously felt to be quite powerful.[6]

It is a fact that as soon as disarmament negotiations take a practical and serious turn, they become the prerogative of the Big Two. The problem is then to find a formula satisfactory both to them and to the others which allows negotiations to be organized within a small committee, in the presence of countries in which both Super-Powers have confidence. In its Resolution 1660 (XVI) the General Assembly had invited the Big Two to agree on the composition of a negotiating body, and to submit a recommendation to this effect. Agreement was reached on this and communicated to the Assembly, which then by its Resolution 1722 (XVI) made "its own the decision reached by common accord". It thus recognised and officially confirmed that the Big Two had taken a decision. It is important to remember this, as well as the predominant part played in this process by the Big Two. The Assembly can exert pressure upon the Committee, make recommendations to it, and help it by calling on States to ratify Treaties it has drawn up. The United Nations also provide meeting premises, staff and necessary services. But that is the limit of the United Nations' contribution. In 1969, when the Big Two decided to add eight new members to the Geneva Committee, certain countries, Mexico among them, criticised the procedure, saying that as far as the admission of new members was concerned, the function of the Big Two ought to be limited to making recommendations to the General Assembly. This does not appear to be the legal and political position. As in 1961, the Assembly limited itself, by its Resolution 2602A (XXIV), to make "its own the decision reached by common accord".

Yet on 19 December 1967, the General Assembly did decide to keep on its agenda the question of non-proliferation of nuclear weapons. At the same time, it invited the Committee of 18 to continue its work and submit a complete report before 15 March 1968.[7] This report was duly presented. The General Assembly began to examine the question in April, in its First Commission, and passed its Resolution 2373 (XXII) on 12 June 1968.

So the General Assembly was called upon to approve a text that had been drawn up outside. It did not take part in negotiations in the traditional sense and indeed this is not its role. Negotiation, to quote a good definition, consists basically of communicating and perceiving intentions that have been more or less clearly formulated.[8]

---

[6] ENDC/PV. 353 and 354.
[7] Resolution 2346A (XXII).
[8] T. C. Schelling, *Arms and Influence* (New Haven and London, Yale University Press, 1966), pp. 136–137.

Yet it is true to say that the Assembly showed that it was not prepared simply to rubber-stamp the text submitted. As the President of the First Commission said, no other disarmament debate attracted so many speakers from medium and small powers. A great number of these regretted what they felt was the discriminatory character of the Treaty which made a distinction between nuclear and non-nuclear States. These United Nations members, reflecting the depolarisation, the centrifugal trend that marks international relations at the present time, were rather hesitant to ratify an agreement which was in effect only a compromise between the Big Two. In so far as the latter have a definite common interest in concluding an agreement, the other States whose signature will make it meaningful and give it weight, are conscious of an increase in their bargaining power. It is understandable that they should take advantage of this, all the more so because some of them are in a special situation.

The same trend appears in the resolutions adopted by the General Assembly in 1966 and 1967, when it was decided to call a conference of non-nuclear States in Geneva at the end of August 1968. According to one of those who drafted the 1966 text, the aim of this conference was to persuade non-nuclear States to define a common point of view and thus begin a fruitful dialogue with the nuclear powers.

This was an attempt to form a club of non-nuclear countries. Several of them felt that the General Assembly ought to put off its decision on the Treaty until after the meeting of the Conference due to be held on 29 August in Geneva.[9] Others on the contrary felt that it was wrong to contrast the two categories of States, and that the Treaty might offer a fruitful basis for discussion at the Geneva conference which would have the chance to put forward firm proposals for the implementation of the provisions adopted.[10]

Yet another consideration came into play in the General Assembly. The African countries tried unsuccessfully to barter their support for the Treaty against Big Power support for their proposals on South-West Africa.

In any case, during this debate, what stood out was the desire of all the small countries to play a full part in drafting the parts of the Treaty which concerned them as well.[11] One of the States which, while criticising the Treaty, said it wanted to vote in favour of it, asked the Big Two to revise their proposals. "That would be more than an elegant gesture on their part.

[9] See for example A/C. 1/PV. 1567 (Mauritania), 1568 (Dahomey) and 1562 (Ruanda).
[10] For example A/C. 1/PV.1566 (Pakistan) 1569 (Iraq) and 1571 (Soviet Union).
[11] See for example A/C. 1/PV. 1566 (Uganda).

Such an act would give more meaning to our meeting together here, in an Organisation of sovereign, equal Nations."[12]

This request was finally granted if only because the Super-Powers wanted to get the largest number of votes for their proposal. So the Treaty preamble was strengthened by the addition of an extra paragraph by which both the States Parties resolved to take effective steps towards nuclear disarmament; they emphasised their obligation not to resort to the threat or use of force.[13] Article 4 was modified so as to impose a real obligation in the field of peaceful uses and this obligation refers not only to the exchange of scientific and technological information, but also to that of equipment and material. This co-operation had to take place – and this was another new provision – "taking duly into account the needs of the developing regions of the world." Article 5 was revised as well. A more international character was given to the conditions under which non-nuclear countries might benefit from the advantages accruing from peaceful applications of nuclear explosions.

In addition, the draft resolution about the Treaty was itself amended: one of the paragraphs in the preamble was completely taken out.[14] The second paragraph was modified and the fourth one, an entirely new paragraph, was introduced in order to emphasise co-operation in the field of peaceful uses. The sixth paragraph in the resolution preamble was also new. Finally, in the first point of the Resolution proper the Assembly "welcomes" the Treaty, whilst according to the draft made by the Big Two, it claimed authorship .[15] So the Resolution, as it was finally adopted, satisfied both small and medium Powers. At the same time compared to the initial draft, it shows much less enthusiasm and even a certain reserve towards the Treaty. Thanks to these modifications, the Resolution was carried by 95 votes to 4 with 21 abstentions.[16]

[12] A/C. 1/PV.1565 (Ceylon).
[13] The last paragraph of the preamble is new and was added during the Assembly debate.
[14] The clause in question is as follows: "convinced that the Non-Proliferation Treaty, the proposal for which is appended to the Committee's report, will constitute an effective measure to stop the diffusion of nuclear weapons."
[15] The Assembly used the same formula of "welcome" for the Treaty on the principles governing the activities of States in the exploration and use of outer space.
[16] Those voting against were: Tanzania, Zambia, Albania and Cuba. Those abstaining were: Guinea, India, Malawi, Mali, Mauritania, Niger, Portugal, Ruanda, Saudi Arabia, Sierra Leone, Spain, Uganda, Algeria, Argentina, Brazil, Burma, Burundi, Central African Republic, Congo (Brazzaville), France, Gabon. A/PV. 1672. The following countries signed: Afghanistan, Austria, Bermuda, Bolivia, Botswana, Bulgaria, Ceylon, Republic of China, Colombia, Costa Rica, Cyprus, Czechoslovakia, Dahomey, Denmark, Dominican Republic, El Salvador, Finland, Ghana, Greece, German Democratic Republic, Haiti,

It is worth noting, however, that these modifications were made after confidential negotiations and that, contrary to habit, no formal amendment was put forward during the Assembly debate.

A State which voted for the resolution did not thereby take upon itself the legal or even moral obligation to sign or ratify the Treaty.[17] In any case an important fact remains; the wording which has been described by the Super-Powers as such a delicate compromise that it was impossible to change it, was modified, even if not in its essential points. The public debate in the First Commission was not the only means of pressure. A negotiating Committee designated by the Latin American group, and comprising Mexico, Chile and Colombia, made contact with the representatives of the Soviet Union and the United States and put certain suggestions to them.[18]

The Assembly majority went much further in 1969 when it referred back to the Geneva Committee a Treaty drafted by the Big Two on the Denuclearisation of the Sea-Bed and the Ocean.

3. The Geneva Committee

Let us return now to the Geneva Committee. Its composition owes something to the idea of the Troika put forward at one time by the Russians. It appears they had nominated five non-aligned States in 1966: Ghana, India, Indonesia, Mexico and the UAR. The Western nations then asked for and succeeded in getting the non-aligned increased to eight: India, Mexico, the UAR and five other countries which appeared less anti-Western: Brazil, Burma, Ethiopia, Nigeria and Sweden.[19]

It is worth noting that from the time it was created in 1961 until 1969,[19a] the Committee membership remained unchanged, and this situation was criticised in an American report.[20] Also the structure of the Committee, although quite different, set the future pattern for subsidiary organisations

---

Honduras, Hungary, Iceland, Iran, Ireland, Ivory Coast, Jordan, Kenya, South Korea, Laos, Lebanon, Liberia, Malaysia, Mauritius, Mongolia, Morocco, Nepal, New Zealand, Nicaragua, Nigeria, Norway, Panama, Paraguay, Peru, Philippines, Poland, Romania, San Marino, Senegal, Somalia, Togo, Tunisia, USSR, United Kingdom, United States, Uruguay, Venezuela, South Viet-Nam.

[17] See the speeches made by the delegates of Sweden and South Aírfca: A/CI/PV.1579.
[18] See ibid: speeches of the representatives of Colombia and Uruguay.
[19] Jacobson and Stein, *Diplomats, Scientists and Politicians*, 1965, pp. 356–58.
[19a] When eight new members were appointed: Japan and the Netherlands; Hungary and Mongolia; Argentina, Morocco, Pakistan and Yugoslavia.
[20] *Bulletin of Atomic Scientists*, January 1967, pp. 38–42.

of the General Assembly operating in the economic field.[21] Thus the Council of the United Nations Development Programme comprises 37 members, 19 of which are developing countries; the corresponding figures for the Council of UNCTAD are respectively 51 and 31 and for the Council of UNIDO 45 and 25.[21a]

So real interest groups are represented, according to a quasi-parliamentary formula.[22] The principle of parity among the three groups is not respected.

Yet the Geneva Committee is a political, not a technical or economic body, like the previously quoted examples. The common factor of the largest single group is not under-development but non-alignment, which implies more diversity. According to Brazil, the expression "non-aligned State" has a particular meaning as far as it is concerned: it indicates that she belongs neither to NATO nor to the Warsaw Pact and is meaningful only within the limits of Brazil's participation in the work of the Geneva Committee.[23]

The Committee, we have seen, is not a United Nations body. Most likely the Big Two thought that owing to the non-stop growth in membership of the United Nations, it would be difficult to create within the UN a body that was at the same time restricted and representative.[24] It could also be that the United States, having agreed to accept the Troika formula, did not at that time want it to become a UN precedent.

The Committee sits in private and the transcripts of its work are only available after some delay. From the beginning, meetings were held in conference in official plenary Committee; some time later, a small committee consisting of the three nuclear members was appointed.[25] According to one school of thought, the Committee ought both to publicise its work more and split up into proper working groups.[26a]

As we have seen, the Committee has no budget of its own, its administrative staff and services being provided by the UN. When the Committee wants to carry out an enquiry or obtain a report it addresses itself to the United Nations. Thus in 1968, "the Committee agreed to recommend that the General Assembly ask the Secretary-General to appoint a group of

[21] Cf. W. M. Kotschnig, *International Organization*, Winter 1968, pp. 16–43.
[21a] The division of seats in these three Councils also follows the Troika principle, but the developing countries have a majority. Note that in the Geneva Committee the neutral group includes one developed country – Sweden.
[22] G. Fischer, *Annuaire français de droit international*, 1966, pp. 239–40.
[23] ENDC/145.
[24] L. S. Finkelstein, *International Organization*, 1962, pp. 1–19; C. S. Manno, ibid., 1965, pp. 39–41; D. S. Cheever, ibid., pp. 463–83.
[25] See for example ENDC/1 and Add. 1.
[26a] *Bulletin of Atomic Scientists*, January 1967, p. 40.

experts to study the effects of the possible use of chemical and bacteriological methods of warfare."[26b]. It is worth mentioning also that States,
whether or not they are UN members, can communicate in writing with the
Committee but cannot make verbal representations nor send observers to
meetings.

The basic task of the Committee is to reconcile the positions of the two
Super-Powers, to help them to understand each other better, and to promote their agreement. The creation of permanent Co-Chairmen and the
Committee's rules of procedure illustrate this. [26c] When in 1969, the
Co-Chairmen decided to add eight new members to the Committee,
certain representatives rebelled against a procedure that presented them
with a *fait accompli*. There is, it appears to the author, no legal obligation
for the Co-Chairmen to consult the Committee over such a question. But
on the political and diplomatic level it is evident that even in their own
interest, the Co-Chairmen ought to show a little more regard for the other
members of the Committee.

As it has no rapporteur, the Committee has two Co-Chairmen: the
Soviet and American delegates. It has been suggested that lawyers who
care about efficiency and good organisation ought to regret the creation of
Co-Chairmen and the absence of a rapporteur.[27] This legalistic view seems
rather too narrow. In fact the appointment of Co-Chairmen was due to the
initiative of Canada and India. The precedent was the Geneva Conference
of 1954 on Viet-Nam, as well as the declaration and protocol on the
Neutrality of Laos of 23 July 1962. In these two cases, the Co-Chairmen
(Britain and the USSR) were considered to belong to countries not
immediately involved. On the other hand in the Geneva Committee the
Co-Chairmen belong to directly interested States who assume the main
responsibility for world security. Without their agreement, nothing can be
accomplished in the field of disarmament. The almost permanent contact
they are forced to keep with each other is all the more welcome in that they
have to report to the Committee which in turn starts new negotiations in
case of difficulty and prevents a break in relations or even recesses that
last too long.[28] So it is quite clear that common, routine solutions are no use

---

[26b] ENDC 236, p. 5.
[26c] For example: "The co-chairmen will consult each other and the other delegations, if necessary, to help the official and semi-official tasks of the Committee."
ENDC/1.1962.
[27] A. Martin, *Legal Aspects of Disarmament* (London, British Institute of International and Comparative Law, 1963), p. 5.
[28] A. H. Dean, *Test Ban and Disarmament* (New York and London, Harper and
Row, 1966), p. 37; A. Lall, op. cit., p. 17; A. Gotlieb, *Disarmament and International Law* (Toronto, Canadian Institute of International Affairs, 1965),
pp. 63–67.

in new or exceptional situations. In the present case, the appointment of two Co-Chairmen with vested interests, and the absence of a neutral rapporteur, were necessary because of special conditions, the relative strength of the forces involved, the importance of the questions being dealt with, and their vital significance for the two Super-Powers.

No vote is taken within the Committee: decisions are made by general assent. During the drafting of the Treaty many amendments were tabled and discussed. The Co-Chairmen chose those which seemed acceptable to them.

4. The role of the non-aligned States

It is worth noting, in the first place, that the two groups of "aligned" States are by no means monolithic. Romania among the Eastern bloc countries, and Canada among allies of the United States, are particularly prone to take an independent line. Having said this, the role of the non-aligned States is in some respects that of mediator and is strengthened by the influence they have over the majority of members of the General Assembly.

As the Swedish delegate has observed, when the two Co-Chairmen are deadlocked, the non-aligned members can put up their own proposals even if at first sight these are unacceptable to the Super-Powers.[29]

Of course the eight (who are now twelve) do not all have the same means at their disposal to contribute towards the work of the Committee. Sweden in particular has brought some remarkable technical efforts to bear upon such subjects as the detection and identification of underground nuclear tests – Mrs Myrdal, in a lecture given in Geneva on 14 March 1968, recalled that the memorandum presented by the eight on 16 April 1962 torpedoed proposals for verifying the banning of tests in general under which two thousand million dollars would have had to be invested in control machinery, five hundred million dollars spent every year on running expenses, and thousands of experts stationed over every part of the world.

Yet the non-aligned States are still only a diplomatic group,[30] not very tightly organised, in spite of the fact that they meet regularly once a week.[31] In April 1962, just as much as in April 1963, a more united and determined attitude by the eight would perhaps have made possible the conclusion of a complete Test Ban Treaty.[32]

[29] ENDC/PV.5.
[30] M. S. Ahmed, *The Neutrals and Test Ban Negotiations* (New York, Carnegie Endowment, Occasional Paper no. 4, 1967), p. 8.
[31] ENDC/PV.365.
[32] Ahmed, op. cit., pp. 64 *ff*, 74; A. S. Lall, *Bulletin of Atomic Scientists*, December 1967, pp. 33–34.

In any case the essential part of the Moscow Treaty was negotiated in that city in July 1963 between the three nuclear Powers and it was not presented to the General Assembly before signatures were invited.

Senator Mundt observed that the Moscow Treaty was an exceptional document in that it had been drawn up by the Big Three who, after having reached agreement, called on other States to recognise it, to support the Treaty and to subscribe to it.[33] It cannot be denied that the Big Three tried, in a field where their technical superiority gave them the power of decision, to legislate for all other States, without the latter having had a chance to participate in the drafting of the legal norms which they were called upon to support. A curious situation resulted; the provisions of the Treaty are imprecise and only the three original Powers have access to records of the preparatory work and are able to clarify the meaning of ambiguous passages, if they so desire.

As far as the Non-Proliferation Treaty was concerned, it was noticeable first of all that Britain's role was far less prominent than during the 1963 Moscow negotiations. Also the influence of the Geneva Committee was much more important and negotiations within this body much more realistic. Many amendments were put forward by members of the Committee. The Eastern and Western blocs did not divide along rigid lines; members of either side, as for example Romania and Italy, made proposals and took up positions quite out of line with those of the Co-Chairmen. Non-member States submitted memoranda to the Committee – principally Switzerland, Spain and West Germany. In addition the United States kept NATO regularly informed of the progress of the work.[34] They were also in contact with the Euratom Commission, and had long and difficult negotiations with West Germany.

The Committee carries on negotiations on the basis of proposals presented by the Big Two. The first Treaty draft was presented by the United States on 17 August 1965.[35] The Soviet draft was given directly to the General Assembly on 24 September 1965.[36] On 24 August 1967 the United States and the Soviet Union put up two identical proposals, which did not yet include provisions about controls.[37] On the same day, the American delegate said the proposal was "recommended for discussion and negotiation by the Committee of 18, and for examination by all governments," and that "all governments would wish to examine the improvements that might be suggested here."[38]

[33] *Congressional Record*, 23 September 1963, p. 16815.
[34] Cf. *Hearings 1968*, p. 5.
[35] ENDC/152
[36] A/5976.
[37] ENDC/192 and 193.
[38] ENDC/PV.325.

On 18 January 1968 two identical drafts were tabled, in complete and revised form.[39] This text included an Article about control, and at the same time incorporated eight of the amendments proposed by members of the Committee. When he presented this draft, the American delegate declared: "the discussions which have taken place here since this proposal (of 24 August 1967) was presented, provide ample evidence in my opinion that it was not presented on a take it or leave it basis."[40]

Followiqg renewed criticism the two Co-Chairmen agreed on 11 March 1968 to modify their text on three points.[41] In accordance with a Swedish amendment, a new paragraph was brought into the preamble about the stopping of all nuclear tests. Anglo-Swedish proposals were taken into account in Articles VI (Disarmament) and VIII (Review conferences). We have also seen how new modifications took place as a result of the General Assembly debate.

However, the initial project, in its essentials, was not modified. Mrs Alva Myrdal (Sweden) was somewhat bitter and disappointed when on 30 May and 3 October 1967 she asked the Committee of 18 for full rights for non-aligned members of the Committee to propose and support amendments and to take full part in the negotiation and drafting of the Treaty. Even if she did obtain some satisfaction and if the number of amendments accepted was impressive, the two Super-Powers kept their position intact on essentials. Articles I, II and III remained unchanged and the explanations of the two Co-Chairmen were hardly sufficient to clarify the text, or the intentions of those who drafted it. The British delegate, in order to discourage a flood of minor amendments, said the text of Articles I and II was the result of such complicated negotiations and established such a delicate and fragile balance that it was impossible to touch it.[42] So the Brazilian delegate was perhaps not so far from the truth when he said the Treaty was "basically a bilateral agreement between the two Super-Powers as to the maximum number of reciprocal concessions that it was possible to make in reply to some of the demands and suggestions of non-nuclear countries".[43]

Several provisions of the Treaty represent an extremely delicate coincidence of ulterior motives between the two Super-Powers, that they themselves were not anxious to formulate clearly. The simple existence of the agreement seemed to be more important than its shape and drafting. A

[39] ENDC/PV.192/Rev. 1 and 193/Rev. 1.
[40] ENDC/PV.357.
[41] ENDC/224 and ENDC/PV.376.
[42] ENDC/PV.337.
[43] A/C.1/PV.1560.

Soviet diplomat is reported to have said about the January 1967 Treaty on Outer Space (whose text is also very ambiguous): "first we have decided to sign the Treaty; the interpretation will come later."[44] In any case, the meaning of certain provisions in the Non-Proliferation Treaty can only be explained by the Co-Chairmen. This is why the Canadian delegate said he was happy with the interpretation given by the American Co-Chairman to the first paragraph in Article III, the wording of which was much narrower than the explanation given by one of its authors, and he asked the Soviet Co-Chairman to confirm this interpretation.[45]

Thus the Geneva Committee and the way it works can be legitimately criticised and is open to reform. Yet we are hardly in agreement with the position recently adopted by the French cabinet. According to the communiqué published on this occasion, France wants disarmament negotiations limited to the five nuclear states. In addition, the communiqué claims that the Geneva Committee is practically dispossessed and has no further part to play.[46]

As M. Jules Moch aptly wrote, "it is not realistic to suggest talks only between the five nuclear Powers, firstly because all States, large and small, are interested in disarmament; secondly because to try and make Peking talk to Moscow and Washington amounts at the present time to deferring all contact".[47] Doubtless the Geneva Committee is not yet fully playing its proper role. But the superficial account we have just given does show that its importance and influence have been growing all the time since 1963. It was able to take part in the drawing up of the agenda, which was supposed to he the task of the Co-Chairmen alone. At the same time the role of the United Kingdom, a nuclear State, has been diminishing all the time. One might well ask why a country like France or the United Kingdom should contribute more wisdom, experience, competence or knowledge than Sweden or Canada on such questions as the use of nuclear explosives for peaceful purposes, anti-missile missiles, the total Test Ban, etc. The contemptuous attitude adopted by France towards small and medium powers is deeply harmful to her real interests and has a boomerang effect, for whatever she does, she does not belong to the same category as the two Super-Powers.

Of course, every non-aligned member does not contribute to the progress of the Committee's work in the same way. But it does not appear that the answer lies in a change in the structure of the Committee or even in the extra members appointed in 1969. It would be enough for the non-

[44] W. C. Clemens, Jr. *Bulletin of Atomic Scientists,* November 1967, N.27.
[45] ENDC/PV.358.
[46] *Le Monde* 25 July 1968,   [47] ibid., 31 July 1968,

aligned members to concert their activities to a greater extent and try more effectively to draw up common policies and support them by jointly arrived at methods.[48] Work in small sub-committees can be very effective.[49] And the Committee ought to have its own budget, and set up groups of experts working quite publicly, who would help and support member States of the Committee. The experts ought to be able to be chosen without taking nationality into account. The Committee ought to have the benefit of more publicity in its work, and itself ought to endeavour to obtain more and more explanations and precision from the Co-Chairmen.

It would in any case be presumptuous, unrealistic, and vain to expect France alone (for China is not prepared to take part) to be able to exercise more influence over the Super-Powers than the Eight or Britain. By occupying its seat at the Committee table, by joining forces with other States, France will best make its voice heard.

II. THE IMPORTANCE OF THE TREATY

The importance of the Treaty as an instrument capable of consolidating agreement between the Big Powers and contributing to the organisation of international society is illustrated by recent history.

From 31 October 1958 until the end of August 1961 the United States, Britain and the Soviet Union suspended all nuclear tests. The last of these three countries began testing in the atmosphere again in September 1961. This reveals the fragility of a precarious and temporary moratorium based on unilateral declarations and revocable at any time which, just because of these characteristics, helped to prolong an atmosphere of suspicion and mistrust between the protagonists. The Treaty, although it was very flexible and easy to denounce, introduced a completely new element. Secretary of State Dean Rusk referred to it: "There is a difference, I believe, between a solemn Treaty solemnly entered into, and in the case of this Treaty, endorsed by the signatures and the adherence of almost every nation in the world, on the one side, and the kind of moratorium which we had between 1958 and 1961. That moratorium was based, in effect, upon unilateral declarations. It was not a contractual relationship between the Parties".[50]

---

[48] It is regrettable for example that the UAR and Nigeria should have decided to put forward separately and without really having discussed the matter with the six other neutrals, amendments that were differently formulated and which basically set out – quite legitimately – to ensure that persons, companies and public and private organisations should comply with the aims and provisions of the treaty. ENDC/197 and 202.

[49] See later chapter 9.I.1.   [50] *Hearings 1963*, pp. 52–53.

The Soviet government for its part, in its statement dated 21 August 1963, took the same point of view: "The authors of the Chinese statement seem to argue that if there were no Test Ban Treaty, there would be no tests, given that the United States government would be unlikely to start them again without good reason. But that is just absurd. It is the same as trying to argue that there would be no criminals if States did not have Laws".[51]

Both sides therefore were anxious to stress the importance of the Treaty and of Treaty relations as apart from unilateral promises – even if they did coincide. It may not be a compliment paid by vice to virtue, but it is certainly one that politicians and diplomats pay to the Law.

The same conclusion emerges from the drafting of the January 1967 Treaty on Outer Space. The General Assembly in its Resolution 1962 (XVIII) issued unanimously in December 1963 a certain number of principles governing this matter. But a resolution, even if it is unanimous, does not have the restraining power or offer the security of a Treaty. The Resolution, which is not without legal value, prepared the way for the real instrument of international legislation – the Treaty, whose legal, political and psychological superiority was evident.[52]

During the drafting of the Non-Proliferation Treaty, and faced with long-drawn out and difficult negotiations, Italy had presented a proposal on 14 September 1965[53] which came to be called the Fanfani plan. It was for a declaration of unilateral renunciation of the acquisition of nuclear weapons, which would have lasted for a fixed limited period. A State signing the declaration would have accepted the application of the guarantees of the IAEA to its nuclear activities. Each signatory would also have made the entry into force of its undertakings contingent upon the signature of "similar declarations" by a definite number of States.

This idea, which was never seriously discussed, was characterised by its great instability and fragility. Only non-nuclear States would have been called upon to sign the declaration. The nuclear Powers promised nothing, which reduced the credibility of the system. The declarations would in fact have been conditional and their coming into force thus would have been of secondary importance.[54] The fact that only non-nuclear States

---

[51] *Documents, supplément à Etudes Soviétiques*, No. 186, September 1963, pp. 3–4.
[52] M. Lachs, "The International Law of Outer Space," *Recueil des Cours de L'Académie de Droit International de La Haye*, vol. 113, 1964, pp. 95–99; W. C. Clemens Jr., *Bulletin of Atomic Scientists*, November 1967, pp. 24–28; J. E. S. Fawcett, *International Law and the Uses of Outer Space* (Manchester University Press, 1968), pp. 1–16.
[53] ENDC/157.
[54] The Italian delegate had recognised the difficulty of co-ordinating the adhesions of different countries. ENDC/PV.232.

were interested in the declaration meant that they would have lost a good deal of the bargaining power that they had in the context of negotiations for a general Treaty. Their undertakings were not going to last long. Lack of stability and certainty would have been the most likely result. The Italian delegate in fact explained recently that his country's proposal was essentially provisional in character, and that its aim was to allow negotiations to take place in a more relaxed, less hasty atmosphere.[55]

The reason why the Treaty was so much better than unilateral declarations emerged from the General Assembly debate. By means of identical declarations made to the Security Council, the Big Three nuclear Powers had promised to come to the help of any non-nuclear State Party to the Non-Proliferation Treaty which was the victim of aggression or the threat of aggression involving the use of atomic weapons. This guarantee, which in general was considered insufficient by non-nuclear States, was mainly criticised for its unilateral character and because it was not an integral part of the Treaty.[56]

So it is clear that the attitude of certain countries which for different reasons did not intend to sign the Treaty while making a unilateral declaration renouncing nuclear weapons, could not possibly help to provide the sort of security resulting from a proper Treaty relationship and mutual obligations between the Parties.

Some observers feel that perhaps with the exception of the Moscow Treaty which reduced pollution of the atmosphere, Treaties are not the right way to resolve major problems between the Super-Powers. According to this way of thinking, in order to avoid any possible obstruction in the United States Senate, it is preferable for the Super-Powers to carry out similar decisions in co-ordination with each other.[57]

This opinion hardly carries much conviction. In some countries such as Canada, where politicians were the group most opposed to the acquisition of a nuclear force,[58] the conclusion and ratification of the Treaty enabled public opinion to be informed and moulded. This was also the case in the United States where, after the signature of the Moscow Treaty, public opinion became more favourable to it, as a measure that had actually been

---

[55] A/C.1/PV.1565. According to an Italian author, the moratorium established through unilateral declarations was a means of exerting pressure for the rapid conclusion of a satisfactory Treaty. A. Albonetti, *Survival*, July 1967, pp. 223–26.

[56] See for example A/C.1/PV.1580 (Barbados) 1582 (Spain and Algeria).

[57] J. S. Stone, *Strategic Persuasion, Arms Limitations through Dialogue* (New York and London, Columbia University Press, 1967), pp. 85–87.

[58] J. Laulicht, "Public Opinion and Foreign Policy Decisions," *Journal of Peace Research*, 1965, No. 2, pp. 147–160.

taken, than certain policy-makers had feared.[59] In other countries the existence of the Treaty might constitute a powerful means of moral and political pressure to get reluctant governments to sign. It would most likely mobilise public opinion which, in its turn, would react upon governments. Anyway, those were the hopes that were expressly stated by two American leaders.[60]

One author showed some scepticism about the scope of a non-proliferation Treaty. In his opinion, the United States ought to dissuade countries with the means of becoming nuclear from doing so, by means of bilateral talks.[61] Without going to the opposite extreme of a legalistic view, we believe that this view is based upon a total misunderstanding of the psychological and political effect of the multilateral Treaty as a factor in world stability. Also, it must not be imagined that efforts to conclude a non-proliferation Treaty were not accompanied by a series of private negotiations and discussions. According to one well-informed author, India has had the capacity to carry out a nuclear explosion since the end of 1964. She wanted to go ahead (it was an explosion for peaceful purposes) and was only prevented from doing so by the joint pressure of the United States and the Soviet Union.[62]

An interesting debate took place in the Foreign Relations Committee of the United States Senate. One of the members asked for negotiations for nuclear aid agreements for peaceful purposes, for example with Spain, to be used to secure this country's promise not to sell natural uranium abroad except under international supervision. The State Department showed the limitations of such a measure in a competitive world. The United States supplied a reactor and enriched uranium to Spain, under the control of the International Agency. Part of the Spanish uranium will be used in this reactor and therefore be under supervision. But it would have been very difficult to go beyond this and demand the supervision of Spanish exports.[63] Mr Foster, the disarmament representative, for his part, recognised that it was diplomatically difficult to achieve non-proliferation through American pressure.[64] Diplomatic action "according to the opinion of all

[59] See Fischer, *Annuaire français de droit international*, 1963, p. 12; J. N. Rosenau (ed.), *Domestic Sources of Foreign Policy* (New York, Free Press, 1967), pp. 129, 153.
[60] W. C. Foster, "New Direction in Arms Control and Disarmament", *Foreign Affairs*, July 1965, pp. 587–601; *Hearings 1966*, p. 28 (Dean Rusk).
[61] S. Hoffman, *Gulliver's Troubles* (New York, McGraw-Hill, 1968), p. 134.
[62] M. Edwards, "India, Pakistan and Nuclear Weapons", *International Affairs*, October 1967, pp. 655–63.
[63] *Hearings 1966*, pp. 11–12, 29–30.
[64] One author proposed extra economic and military aid to countries it was considered desirable to prevent becoming nuclear. But he himself doubted whether the US Congress was sufficiently generous. L. A. Frank, "ABM and Proliferation", *Orbis*, Spring 1967, pp. 67–79.

those I know, is not as effective as a Treaty, which would be an outward, visible public commitment under international legal restrictions that the countries would not go this route (of proliferation) which we think is disadvantageous to every nation in the world".[65]

The adoption of the Non-Proliferation Treaty has already won round some waverers and even some opponents. For example, Romania voted for the Treaty and signed it in spite of the fact that it had been one of the Treaty's strongest critics and at the Sofia meeting in March 1968 had requested that the signature of the Treaty be at least postponed until the end of the Viet-Nam war. West Germany and Japan signed. But the United States expected the Treaty's coming into force would convince those who refused to be won over and tried for their part to hasten the process. President Nixon said at the beginning of 1969: "I believe if we carry on insisting, particularly in public, on trying to get others to follow our example, it will not help us to succeed in our aim. All these governments are sovereign. Each has its own political problems. I believe in the end most of our West European friends will follow our example. I shall try and persuade them, but I shall certainly not try to use blackmail or brute force to bring them round to our point of view . . ."[66] A few days afterwards, Secretary of State Rogers followed this up by saying: "We would do everything we reasonably could to persuade other States to sign."[67]

Those who are constitutionally opposed to Treaty signing, who say that conditions are far from being propitious for a non-proliferation agreement to work, have, in the author's opinion, a false idea of current international relations. They seem to adopt the motto "all or nothing at all". The struggle against proliferation is only one phase of a long term effort to organise the world in a realistic way. Even if the Treaty does not receive the hoped-for membership, even if it does not prevent all proliferation in the future, it is none the less a valuable attempt at organisation and shows that in spite of existing tensions the Super-Powers are capable of agreeing upon extremely important questions. They are continually being forced to redouble their efforts in varying directions and by different means – including in the first place Treaties – which can only end in success. They are concerned with limiting risks, manipulating, containing, watching over, supervising countries which might become possessors of nuclear weapons.[68]

---

[65] *Hearings 1966*, p. 45.   [66] *Le Monde*, 8 February 1969.
[67] *Non-Proliferation Treaty, Hearings before the Committee on Foreign Relations*, U.S. Senate on Executive H, 90th Congress, second session, Part 2, February 18 and 20, 1969, p. 370 (referred to hereafter as *Hearings 1969*).
[68] Cf. F. C. Ikle, "Nth Countries and Disarmament", *Bulletin of Atomic Scientists*, December 1960, pp. 391–94; J. J. Stone, "On Proliferation", ibid., November 1965, pp. 15–18.

None of this will eliminate the contradictions between the Big Two nor those which exist between them and other countries. But it is right to encourage and praise any development which might lead towards a more rational and peaceful organisation of the world. The Non-Proliferation Treaty, even if it has not achieved all its aims, does mark an important milestone along this road.

4. THE BAN ON THE TRANSFER, RECEIPT AND MANUFACTURE OF NUCLEAR WEAPONS

THE nub of the Treaty is in Articles I and II which are inspired by the letter and spirit of the internal legislation of the United States.[1] Nuclear States undertake not to transfer nuclear weapons or other explosive nuclear devices – or the control of such weapons or devices – to anybody else, either directly or indirectly. They will not assist a non-nuclear State in any way to manufacture or acquire such weapons or devices, nor to gain control over such weapons or devices. Non-nuclear States similarly undertake to give up the acquisition, manufacture and control of such weapons or devices or any outside help with this aim in view.

We are going to examine the meaning of certain terms, the undertakings of the parties, the importance of the distinction between the two categories of States, and finally West Germany and nuclear arms.

I. THE MEANING OF CERTAIN TERMS

1. "Nuclear Weapon"

The Treaty remains silent over the meaning of this expression and its definition. Once more we must recall that only the Big Two can interpret the above-mentioned articles with full knowledge of their implications. The United Kingdom delegate has already warned the Geneva Committee against any attempt to modify the text of Articles I and II, which were the result of long discussions which led to a simplified, shortened form of words. It is another case of coincidence of unexpressed motives and it can be questioned whether the authors wanted to explain the different elements involved.

According to an American proposal of 21 March 1966, a definition of nuclear weapons should have figured in the final text of the Treaty.[1a]

As we shall see later on, the Treaty for the Denuclearisation of Latin America includes an article defining nuclear weapons. The same is true of

[1] *Hearings 1969*, p. 356.
[1a] ENDC/152/Add. 1 and Annex III.

Annex II of Protocol Number III of the Paris Agreements of 23 October 1954.[2]

According to a Swiss memorandum, "Articles I and II of the draft contain some notions which ought to be defined in order to clarify the undertakings involved".[3] And, according to the Swiss government, whose interpretation here seems quite correct, "the expression 'manufacture or otherwise acquire nuclear weapons or other nuclear explosive devices' does not cover the exploitation of uranium deposits, the enrichment of uranium, the extraction of plutonium from nuclear fuel, the manufacture of fuel elements or heavy water when these processes are carried out for civil purposes".

Nuclear-propelled ships (including submarines) are not nuclear weapons.[4] It must be recalled, however, that according to the Franco-American agreement of 7 May 1959, the United States only agreed to supply enriched uranium to France for a land prototype of a submarine engine.[5]

So it was bombs and nuclear warheads that were covered by Articles I and II and not vectors.[6] On the contrary the expression "nuclear weapons" can refer just as well to offensive as to defensive weapons. Some American experts and Congressmen have deplored this. They have felt that if an anti-missile missile system can be produced that really works and is only for defence, the United States ought to be able to transfer it to others.[7] This is clearly an illusion. No weapon has a purely defensive or offensive

---

[2] This is the definition:
(a) An atomic weapon is defined as any weapon which contains, or is designed to contain or utilise nuclear fuel or radioactive isotopes and which, by explosition (sic) or other uncontrolled nuclear transformation of the nuclear fuel, or by radioactivity of the nuclear fuel or radioactive isotopes, is capable of mass destruction, mass injury or mass poisoning.
(b) Furthermore, any part, device, assembly or material especially designed for, or principally useful in, any weapon as set forth under paragraph (a) shall be deemed to be an atomic weapon.

[3] ENDC/204.

[4] See *The Times*, 16 March 1968 and *The Economist*, 23 March 1968; *Hearings 1966*, p. 79; *Hearings 1968*, pp. 64–66.

[5] B. Goldschmidt, *Les rivalités atomiques 1939–1966* (Paris, Fayard, 1967), pp. 242–43. France, on the contrary, hired two tons of enriched uranium to Italy to supply fuel for the reactor of the nuclear warship *Enrico Fermi*. The United States refused to supply this fuel because of the military character of its use. *Le Monde*, 27/28 October 1968. The French decision does not constitute a legal violation of the Non-Proliferation Treaty (which by the way was not in force at that time), but it marks a slip in standards and has a unilateral character which has unpleasant connotations. In a field such as this, it is difficult to understand why there was no consultation with the United States and Britain before a decision was made.

[6] *Hearings 1968*, p. 5.

[7] ibid., pp. 181 et seq.

character. In any case every technological advance in the defence field causes another in the field of attack. Besides, the Treaty does not prevent a nuclear State from placing atomic weapons on the territory of a non-nuclear State, on condition that it keeps them under its protection, in its possession and under its control.

2. "Indirectly"

Let us continue the explanation of Article I. To understand the term "indirectly" it is useful to refer again to the Swiss memorandum (whose interpretation is not of course final and authentic): "the Swiss authorities consider that the term indirect refers to the supply of arms, explosives or technical assistance for military purposes carried out through a third State, whether or not party to the Treaty".

3. "Explosive"

As far as the term "explosive" is concerned, we shall have the opportunity to discuss it in more detail in another chapter. It is sufficient to note here that what is meant are devices for excavating or canal digging, etc., which, because of the present state of technology, cannot be distinguished from nuclear weapons. The Italian delegate observed that the provision about explosives must be interpreted with a saving clause understood *rebus sic stantibus*. As a result, the ban ought to disappear automatically on the day that technical progress enables explosives to be manufactured that are quite distinct from nuclear weapons.[8]

4. "The diffusion of nuclear weapons" and the term "control"

In contrast to the Denuclearisation Treaty of Latin America, the Non-Proliferation Treaty does not ban the storage or the installation of nuclear weapons by a nuclear State on the territory of a non-nuclear State, so long as the nuclear State retains the ownership or control of these weapons. This is the difference therefore between denuclearisation and non-proliferation.

According to a definition which appeared in the American draft of 21 March 1956, but which is not in the actual Treaty, the term "control" means "the right or ability to fire nuclear weapons without the concurrent decision of an existing nuclear weapon state". It was explained at the time that such agreement had to be explicit and contemporaneous; in other words, it could not consist of a general authorisation given in advance.[9]

[8] A/PV.1672.
[9] *Hearings 1966*, pp. 113–14.

Yet several States have seriously criticised this authorisation by means of which nuclear States can continue to keep atomic weapons on the territory of non-nuclear States. They have also protested against the fact that nuclear States can continue to train experts from the armed forces of non-nuclear allies, with a view to using nuclear weapons.[10]

The change in Soviet policy since 24 September 1965, the date on which she presented her own draft Treaty, can be measured. Article I of this Treaty forbade the nuclear Parties to entrust the installation or use of nuclear weapons to units or members of armed forces of non-nuclear States, even if these units or members of armed forces had been placed under the command of any form of military alliance. By means of this article, the Soviet Union resisted any access[11] by West Germany to nuclear weapons. But she had to abandon her original position on this point.

According to American interpretations, the control of nuclear armaments is not affected by an organisation such as "a nuclear planning group under which members of NATO get together and make contingency plans as to what they will or will not do. I think control in this sense means the ability actually to push the button". But control is not affected either if the non-nuclear country where nuclear weapons are sited by a nuclear State has the right of veto (or a right of negative control) over the use of these weapons, so long as the nuclear State keeps its right of positive control.[11a] This must lead us to accept the definition quoted above only with certain qualifications.

II. THE UNDERTAKINGS OF THE PARTIES

1. Non-nuclear States and their obligations

We begin with this question as it is the one which raises least problems. Article II, in contrast to the corresponding provision in the Treaty on the denuclearisation of Latin America, does not include an undertaking by non-nuclear States not to assist, encourage or induce any other non-nuclear State whatsoever to manufacture or to acquire nuclear weapons or explosive nuclear devices.[12] The UAR proposed to add to the last phrase in this article an amendment in these terms: "not to help, encourage or

---

[10] ENDC/PV.370 (India); A/C1/PV.1571 (Algeria). See also later chapter 5.IV.1.
[11] On the history of the dissociation of the concepts of ownership and control on the one hand and access on the other, as seen in American policy since 1958, cf. W. B. Bader, *The US and the Spread of Nuclear Weapons* (New York, Pegasus, 1968), pp. 37–38.
[11a] *Hearings 1969*, pp. 357–358.
[12] There are States without nuclear weapons which are sufficiently technologically advanced to be able to start manufacture at any time and help others to do so.

induce in any way any State whatsoever not possessing nuclear weapons, to manufacture or acquire in any other way nuclear weapons or other explosive devices or the control of such arms or such explosive devices."[13] In fact Article II forbids any non-nuclear State Party to the Treaty to receive or to seek any help whatsoever to manufacture nuclear weapons. The question arises therefore in relations between a non-nuclear State Party to the Treaty and a non-nuclear State which does not adhere to it. According to the delegates of the Super-Powers, a non-nuclear State Party to the Treaty must not help any other non-nuclear State whatsoever to manufacture nuclear weapons. It would moreover have no interest in gaining for another advantages that it had itself waived. If it were to do so, there would be a strong presumption that it was acting indirectly on its own account and that it was violating the Treaty.[14] The UAR's amendment was therefore not adopted. The control provisions in Article III (2) would also make it ineffective.

On the other hand, there is nothing to prevent a non-nuclear State Party to the Treaty from helping (particularly by supplying nuclear materials) a nuclear State to manufacture atomic weapons. This omission is glaring. It may be recalled that Canada, a leading producer, since 1965 has refused to sell uranium except by means of contracts covered by clauses on peaceful use and control.

2. Nuclear States

According to the Treaty, nuclear States are those that have manufactured and exploded a nuclear weapon or other explosive nuclear system before 1 January 1967.[15] This amounts to recognition and safeguard of the *status quo*, the nuclear status of the United States, the Soviet Union, Britain, France and China. China, however, as is well known, is opposed to the Treaty which, in its opinion, expresses the collusion and agreement of the Big Two against revolutionary movements in general. According to China, proliferation is desirable when progressive nations do it.[16] As for France, her position is more complex. On 28 September 1966 before the General Assembly, M. Couve de Murville limited himself to a show of scepticism as to the chances of concluding a Treaty.[17] Yet on 4 November France voted in favour of the Resolution on non-proliferation (2149–XXI). On 3 November 1966, in the National Assembly, the Foreign Minister said the

[13] ENDC/197.
[14] ENDC/PV.370; see also ENDC/PV.338 (Canada).
[15] Art. IX (3).
[16] M. H. Halperin, *China and Nuclear Proliferation* (The University of Chicago, Centre for Policy Study, 1966).
[17] *La documentation française*, N.E.D., No. 3384 to 3387, 29 April 1967, p. 147.

government was not at all favourable to the dissemination of nuclear weapons but that it was not in favour either of "the perpetuation of atomic armaments". He remarked that non-dissemination was not a disarmament measure.[18] M. Couve de Murville repeated the same ideas in his interview to the ORTF on 7 January 1967[19] and in another published in *Jours de France* on 28 January 1967.[20] In the first of these he admitted "there is no advantage, there is even a great danger that more and more countries may manufacture nuclear weapons". But he added: "I cannot myself believe that it is less dangerous for a large country like the United States, Soviet Russia, and later, China, to have the means of destroying the world than to see small countries possessing arms which would only be capable of reaching their immediate neighbours."[21]

It is difficult to follow the logic of this argument. No one pretends that the Non-Proliferation Treaty is a disarmament measure but it can help disarmament. Also international relations, today more than ever before, are not amenable to an "all or nothing at all" policy. It is possible to speculate that France's attitude, like China's, might be motivated by fear of a Soviet-American condominium. This is what seems to emerge from a speech made to the Assembly on 20 April 1967[22] by M. Pompidou who did not seem to realise that the danger he depicted was that of a bipolar world which already belonged to the past. The two Super-Powers even if they were to join forces could not impose their will upon present day international society (which incidentally shows the limited political value of nuclear weapons). Again, their agreement cannot and ought not to be necessarily regarded as a desire to dominate nor as an occurrence that is

---

[18] ibid., p. 198.

[19] *La documentation française, N.E.D.*, No. 3428 to 3430, 24 October 1967, pp. 31–33.

[20] ibid., 53–54.

[21] The French Cabinet stated on 13 June 1968: "This Treaty will probably be adopted by this Assembly but without enthusiasm, with none of the unanimity hoped for by its authors, and in a climate such that France's position will be better understood. This Treaty solves no problems, it simply confirms the vast nuclear power of the United States and the Soviet Union. What France wants is real disarmament which implies the destruction of stocks, the control of weapon manufacture and the control of vectors". *Le Monde*, 14 June 1968.

[22] "Let us not be asked to approve a system under which the two great powers with a surplus of nuclear weapons – the United States and the Soviet Union – organise the disarmament of the others for that is firstly a mockery of disarmament and secondly a fundamental danger to peace. This system would oblige all disarmed countries to separate into two blocs, each huddling under the protective wing they had chosen; sooner or later this situation would lead us to an evil confrontation that would be fatal to humanity". *La documentation française, N.E.D.*, No. 3428 to 3430, 24 October 1967, p. 85. See also in the same line of thought, M. Messmer's statement of 23 January 1968.

harmful to the interests of other powers. The French position seems completely at variance with the real facts.[22a]

Certain countries felt that the membership of China and France was essential.[23] The General Assembly in its Resolution 2373 (XXII) for its part expressed the hope "that adhesions to the Treaty will be as numerous as possible both by nuclear and non-nuclear weapon States". In a more realistic way, Finland observed that China and France will no doubt not adhere to the Treaty but that having done nothing up till now to contribute towards dissemination, they will probably maintain this attitude in the future.[24]

The French delegate to the General Assembly took this very line. France, he said, did not want either to condemn or to advocate the conclusion of the Treaty, but understood perfectly that non-nuclear States should give up the nuclear option under the conditions laid down by the Treaty. France did not desire dissemination and considered that nuclear States ought not to encourage it in any way as it would be contrary to the interests of the whole world. "No country that has the terrifying responsibilities resulting from the possession of these weapons will ever agree to share them with others. For its part, France, which will not sign the non-dissemination Treaty, will behave in future in this field exactly like States which do decide to adhere".[25]

This statement illustrates the importance and influence of the Treaty, since a State as reticent as France feels it has to behave as if it had signed. But at the same time the French attitude is singularly illogical. If you intend to respect rules drawn up in common, why not adhere to the rules of the Treaty and so give the Parties that feeling of security and mutual confidence that only such an adhesion can bring and consolidate? Here again can be seen at one and the same time the inconveniences of a unilateral declaration, and an attitude that is incompatible with the demands of the satisfactory organisation of international society.

3. Information

The Malaysian delegate said that Article I must not be used to deprive non-nuclear States of information and supplies under the pretext that it might help them to perfect nuclear weapons or explosives.[26] It is worth recalling, in reference to this, the Soviet draft Treaty of 24 September

---

[22a] Whatever opinions are held about the value and the future of an independent French nuclear force, it is already clear that in the field of peaceful applications France decided in 1969 to abandon a purely national policy and to buy certain types of reactors from the United States.

[23] See for example A/C1/PV. 1562 (Kenya).

[24] A/C.1/PV.1559.   [25] A/PV.1672.   [26] A/C.1/PV.1563.

1965 (Article I) which forbade nuclear States communicating to non-nuclear States "any kind of manufacturing, research or other information or documentation which can be employed for purposes of the manufacture or use of nuclear weapons". The United States, for their part, were unfavourable to an Irish proposal made at the UN General Assembly in October 1960 for the banning of information capable of being used for the production of nuclear weapons. At the time the United States wanted to keep its options open.[27] Now Article I imposes on nuclear States the obligation not to assist, encourage, or induce a non-nuclear State in any way to manufacture nuclear weapons. It is clear that this provision forbids the transfer of information concerning the manufacture of nuclear weapons. But contrary to the Soviet proposal, it does permit the communication of information about the use of these weapons.

As we shall see later, the Treaty insists on the development of nuclear technology for peaceful purposes and on the help that nuclear States should provide in this field to other States. Now as is well known, certain techniques are used in military manufacture just as much as in civil production. Yet it is relatively simple to distinguish between this sort of information and the sort which ought to be kept secret about the creation, plans and internal structure of nuclear weapons. On this point there are precise rules in American legislation. In a very few doubtful cases, the Treaty provisions about control and safeguards ought to allow a liberal attitude to be adopted towards non-nuclear States party to the Treaty.

4. The problem of entities other than States

The completely hypothetical possibility of a nuclear State assisting organisations or entities other than States to acquire nuclear weapons has been raised.[28] The UAR mentioned another omission and proposed, to fill the gap, an amendment by means of which nuclear States would promise to take appropriate measures to ensure that "persons, companies, public or semi-public or private undertakings or organisations under their jurisdiction, engaged in nuclear activities should not commit acts prohibited by Article I".[29] A similar proposal was made by Nigeria.[30] But the

---

[27] Cf. XVth session of the General Assembly, Point 73 of the Agenda, and also Resolution 1576 (XV). See also Bader, op. cit., pp. 41–42, 47.

[28] A/C.1/PV.1575 (Malta).

[29] ENDC/197 and ENDC/PV.340.

[30] This is the proposal: "Each party to the present Treaty must take the necessary legislative and administrative measures to ensure that all organisations working on atomic energy developments on the territory under its jurisdiction act in conformity with the aims and provisions of the Treaty". ENDC/PV.202.

Canadian delegate thought this detail was unimportant and that the wording of Article I covered the possibility raised by the UAR delegate.[31]

Note that the 1963 Statement and the 1967 Treaty on Outer Space say that States are responsible internationally for activities carried out in space by non-governmental entities. As has been observed, in this case, contrary to the general rule, any national activity is regarded as the action of the State.[32] But in the nuclear field the State controls all manufacture and possesses all weapons. In any case, the United States, like the Soviet Union, declared that the text of the Treaty covered the UAR's amendment, according to their interpretation.[33] However, taking into account the growing role of the private sector in the nuclear field, the proposal by the UAR and Nigeria would have been worthy of adoption. But these two countries failed to join forces or to convince the six other non-aligned States which are members of the Geneva Committee. This example shows again how the non-aligned States must reach better general agreement and stick together more.

5. Help by a nuclear State to another nuclear State

According to Article I each nuclear State party to the Treaty undertakes not to transfer to any recipient whatsoever nuclear weapons or other nuclear explosive devices. The ban covers even transfer to another nuclear State. It also applies to transfers to peace-keeping forces, created by the UN under Article 43 et seq. of the Charter.[34]

Article I forbids a nuclear State party to the Treaty to assist, encourage or induce a non-nuclear State (party to the Treaty or not) to manufacture or acquire nuclear weapons, etc. In this latter case, only non-nuclear States are affected. Yet the case could be imagined of a State that is already nuclear asking the assistance of a more advanced nuclear State in order to manufacture more sophisticated weapons. The United States delegate

[31] ENDC/PV. 338.

[32] M. Lachs, "The International Law of Outer Space", *Recueil des Cours de L'Académie de Droit International de la Haye*, vol. 113, 1964, pp. 74–76. Yet Article 21 of the ILO Convention ought to be noted, which establishes State responsibility for private "recognised" organisations.

[33] ENDC/PV.370. The American delegate said specifically: "Nuclear weapons programmes in States possessing nuclear weapons, are under government control. Such control is essential for national security is directly at stake. No government which wants to remain a government can let go of this control. For example, as Mr De Palma emphasised at our meeting on 22 February, United States legislation already forbids any divulging of information about explosive nuclear devices. (ENDC/PV.369 para. 38) In addition, it forbids private organisations or individuals in the United States, from developing, manufacturing or acquiring explosive nuclear devices".

[34] Cf. *Hearings 1968*, p. 88.

declared "there is no real or important risk" of nuclear States helping other nuclear States to perfect their nuclear armoury.[35]

Perhaps it might be useful here to recall the precedent of the Moscow Treaty. According to Article I (2) no party to this Treaty may assist a State, whether or not a Party to the Treaty, to carry out tests in forbidden environments. A letter from the State Department on 17 August 1963, addressed to the Chairman of the Senate Foreign Relations Committee, summarises the American position as follows.[36] The United States will refuse to supply material or equipment usable in nuclear weapons, or information concerning the creation or manufacture of such weapons, to any State which, whether or not it has signed the Treaty, and whether or not affected by the previously quoted provision of the McMahon law, carries out or proposes to carry out tests banned by the Treaty. Co-operation in the field of peaceful uses of nuclear energy is not affected by the Treaty, since bilateral Treaties concluded in this field by the United States provide that material equipment and information supplied may not be used for military purposes. This ban is guaranteed by a control system set up by those bilateral Treaties.

It even appears that President Kennedy had offered the French government to supply it with all information obtained from tests in the atmosphere if it would itself give up such tests. This offer left France with the possibility of carrying on underground tests. It was considered to be incompatible with French independence.[37]

But even at the time the Moscow Treaty was ratified, it was seen that the ban raised some complicated practical problems. Suppose that the United States, under a bilateral agreement, supplied nuclear material to a country that carried out or wanted to carry out tests in forbidden environments. The country in question, if it already manufactured these materials, could devote an increased quantity of its own production to weapons tests. However, according to the Chairman of the American Atomic Energy Commission, the supply of nuclear material for peaceful purposes would not in this case be contrary to the provisions of the Moscow Treaty.[38]

In any case, since the signature of the Moscow Treaty no military assistance appears to have been provided by the United States to France.[39]

---

[35] ENDC/PV.369.
[36] *Hearings 1963*, p. 976.
[37] A. M. Schlesinger, Jr, *A Thousand Days* (London, André Deutsch, 1965), pp. 856, 914 et seq.
[38] *Hearings 1963*, pp. 264–65.
[39] Note that the agreement on the supply of enriched uranium to France for a land-based prototype submarine engine dates from 7 May 1959. According to

In the field of nuclear collaboration for peaceful purposes, the United States tried to keep multilateral control, if possible, over supplies meant for France. Undertakings were even demanded from France about the exclusively peaceful use of computers supplied by the United States.[40] Canadian policy on uranium deliveries, subject to controls and for exclusively civil purposes also affects France and is certainly influenced by the United States.[41]

Thus the American attitude is fairly consistent towards France who did not sign the Moscow Treaty and will not sign the one on non-proliferation. Aid to Britain in the civil field is also subject to control. There remains the problem of American assistance to British nuclear armament. It appears this assistance has now been reduced and that it consists mainly of vectors which are not in themselves nuclear weapons.[42]

Recently the prospects of Franco-British nuclear collaboration in the military field have been discussed. In a letter to *The Times* on 20 October 1968, Sir Michael Wright showed that such collaboration might lead Britain to violate the Moscow Treaty, the Anglo-American Agreements of 1958, and the Non-Proliferation Treaty. As far as this last Treaty is concerned, it would not be violated by such collaboration in so far as this meant a true integration of the two nuclear forces. M. Léo Hamon had envisaged another form of collaboration: "Could we not in so far as is possible, link the French nuclear force to the only other nuclear force in Western Europe, the British, so as to make them the nucleus of a system of co-operation that is flexible and respects the identity of the different forces? And add to them the forces of countries which through necessity

---

Mr Goldschmidt himself, who complained of American pressure, the agreement gave France several years' headway in the construction of a nuclear engine. Another agreement, on 27 July 1961, enabled French troops in Germany to be provided with tactical nuclear weapons under the "master key" plan. This agreement came to an end with the withdrawal of France from NATO.

[40] *New York Times*, 22 and 23 October 1966; *Le Monde*, 22 October 1966.
[41] B. Goldschmidt, op. cit., pp. 278–79, 288.
[42] According to the Americans, the drafting of Article I is due to the efforts of the United States, which wanted a text similar to their own internal legislation which would allow them to continue the "special relationship" with Britain. According to official statements this relationship does not extend to the transfer of nuclear weapons or the control of these weapons to Britain, but to scientific exchange and close co-operation. Now this is the only exchange permissible under the Treaty between one nuclear State and another. *Hearings 1968*, p. 89; *Hearings 1969*, pp. 355–56. But under the Anglo-American Agreements of 1958, London received fissile materials destined for military use or research. It appears to us that the continuation of these Agreements, after the entry into force of the Non-Proliferation Treaty, would be contrary to the provisions of Article I.

or choice have limited themselves to conventional armament, as a necessary complement to ensure equilibrium in a transformed world?"[42a] Strictly speaking, such collaboration would not be incompatible with the Treaty, to the extent that it would not imply the transfer of nuclear weapons or of their control. But one would have to be extraordinarily optimistic, not to see that such collaboration would postpone any solution to the problems of European nuclear collaboration and of the participation of West Germany which figure among the essential questions settled by the Non-Proliferation Treaty and, hence, through the Treaty, by the two Super-Powers. We shall return to this question. But let us note here that in a speech made in London on 19 May 1969, Herr F. J. Strauss, then West German Finance Minister, foresaw the fusion of the French and British nuclear forces and the creation of a European nuclear central organisation taken over later by a European Federal State.[42b] Doubtless M. Hamon's idea was different, but the appetites which would be sharpened by its achievement and the objective consequences flowing from it appear to us quite formidable.

III. THE IMPORTANCE OF THE DISTINCTION BETWEEN THE TWO CATEGORIES OF STATES

It will be observed that if non-nuclear States, by signing the Treaty, make an important pledge which affects their foreign and military policy, it is quite otherwise for nuclear States. The latter take on no new obligation. None intended to transfer nuclear weapons to a non-nuclear country. The nuclear powers see the Treaty as a means firstly of freezing the present situation and secondly of forestalling any pressure which might be directed against one of them by one or several non-nuclear States wishing to acquire nuclear weapons.

An American author has asked what interest the Super-Powers had to give up a right (the transfer of weapons) they never had any intention of exercising.[43] The answer is that the Treaty offers safeguards that are vastly superior to simple common intent. It also enables the promises of non-nuclear States to be formally recorded. It establishes mutual rights and obligations which, it must be hoped, open new prospects of international co-operation.

It remains a fact that Articles I and II, like many other provisions in the Treaty, mark the inequality between the Parties, nuclear States on the one hand, non-nuclear on the other. The first only renounce the transfer of

---

[42a] *Le Monde,* 7 December 1968.
[42b] *The Times,* 20 May 1969.
[43] S. Hoffman, *Gulliver's Troubles,* pp. 133–35.

nuclear weapons to the second whilst the latter renounce any nuclear military option. This inequality and disproportion were the cause of the loudest protests and widest criticism on the part of non-nuclear States. It would be difficult to give an exhaustive account and we must be satisfied with a superficial sample. Certain countries, such as Cuba, questioned the whole concept of the Treaty, and felt that it dealt with a hypothetical risk. The authors of the Treaty, they alleged, disregarded the danger of classical warfare, the development of imperialist concepts of local warfare and special warfare directed against the peoples of the Third World since 1945 by the United States, who would like to use tactical nuclear weapons in this kind of war.[44]

More often another kind of argument was used. Thus M. Fernand Dehousse believed that a considerable sacrifice was being asked of non-nuclear States: what was to be given to them in exchange?[45] Others emphasised that the Treaty sanctioned discrimination in law for the first time.[46] According to India, imbalance in the world could only be eliminated "by abolishing the special status of superiority that goes with the power and prestige these States enjoy through the possession of nuclear weapons."[47] The Federal Republic of Germany affirmed the principle of the equality "of the members of the community of peoples" and felt that "a non-proliferation Treaty cannot be allowed to sanction, by institutions and perhaps so on *ad infinitum*, this real lack of equality to the detriment of non-nuclear Powers".[48] Switzerland also remarked that "the Treaty will establish a lasting legal discrimination between States, according to whether or not they possess nuclear weapons."[49]

But reality must be faced, such as it is. If it is not possible to eliminate immediately, at one stroke, all causes of war, there is no reason not to take advantage of a possibility which arises in a limited field thanks to the agreement of the most immediately interested powers. Also – and we shall have occasion to return to this important point – the Non-Proliferation Treaty can only be envisaged and conceived as a step towards disarmament. Looking immediately ahead, "We have nothing to gain and everything to lose if at the end of this century, instead of five nuclear powers, we have fifteen or twenty."[50]

---

[44] A/C.1/PV.1566.
[45] F. Dehousse, "La non-prolifération des armes nucléaires", *Chronique de Politique étrangère*, November 1967, pp. 621–37.
[46] E. Young, *Bulletin of Atomic Scientists*, November 1967, pp. 37–38.
[47] ENDC/PV.370.
[48] A/C.1/963, p. 5.
[49] ENDC/204, p.3.
[50] A/C.1/PV.1567 (El Salvador).

The argument alleging legal discrimination is not relevant either. Many treaties and particularly the Partial Test Ban reflect an inequality between the Parties in the provisions concerning the entry into force of the Treaty as well as the adoption and entry into force of amendments. There is need to recall that several articles in the UN Charter reflect in law the inequality in fact between members. This is legally recognised in particular in the field of international economic collaboration. It manifests itself in the decline of the most-favoured nation clause, in the tendency towards the establishment of non-reciprocal preferences, which are claimed by developing countries. A certain degree of discrimination, as the Netherlands delegate remarked, is an inevitable element in a non-proliferation Treaty and "the different status of the two categories ought therefore to be accepted from the start as being the lesser evil under the actual circumstances".[51] It is only a question of making the adoption of the Treaty speed up the disarmament process.

In any case it is important to beware of the thesis that any measure which benefits one group of States is necessarily harmful to another. The Non-Proliferation Treaty is not a commercial agreement incorporating reciprocal concessions, but the expression of the common interest of international society, which in consequence will benefit from greater security[52] and which if it succeeds in organising itself as it should, will be able to use this to make new progress.

This is perhaps the point to return to France's attitude. She would perhaps have been able by taking part in the drafting of the Treaty instead of remaining loftily apart, to exercise a salutary influence upon the final draft. She would have been allowed to set realistic and reasonable conditions for her adhesion without demanding total nuclear disarmament. Her adhesion would have been sufficiently important to extract from the Super-Powers some extra concessions which would have been valuable for the whole world in the view of those – and they are the majority – who refuse "all or nothing at all".

In this aspect we would not hesitate to go further. The favourable development of the international situation depends on the undermining of nuclear status. To this end, it is a good thing to create a state of mind which refuses to consider normal the possession of nuclear weapons.[53] Already it looks, as far as Britain and France are concerned, as if the fact of being nuclear fails to give them an influence superior to that which

---

[51] A/C.1/PV.1561.
[52] Cf. B. T. Field, *Bulletin of Atomic Scientists*, November 1967, p. 38; *Hearings 1966*, p. 23; ENDC/PV.362 (United States).
[53] Cf. H. Kahn, op. cit.

arises out of their objective, political and economic situation (and ideological situation in the case of de Gaulle's France). It remains true that, in
the absence of an immediate agreement between the Super-Powers upon
total nuclear disarmament, immense progress could be made in the direction indicated by Britain's and France's renunciation of their nuclear
armament. Mr George Ball has shown recently in an extremely convincing
way that the British deterrent force tends to be constantly overtaken on the
technical level, and that it constitutes neither a military nor a political
trump for Britain.[54] If she were freed from this force, the United Kingdom
would without any doubt play a more considerable role in Europe, in the
same way as by becoming nuclear she only strengthened her links with the
United States.[55] Moreover, Mr Kenneth Younger had estimated at the
time that Britain ought to give up the bomb if everyone except the two
Super-Powers did the same.[56] Mr Denis Healey, former Labour Defence
Minister took a stand in 1964 against "the so-called independent so-
called deterrent".[57] The electoral programme of the Labour Party envisaged, at least implicity, the solution advised by Mr Ball, but pressed by
questions from Labour M.P.s Mr Mulley, Minister of State for Foreign
Affairs, told the Commons on 8 July 1968: "We do not think it would
make any significant contribution to progress on disarmament and the
strengthening of world peace by unilaterally abandoning our nuclear
weapons at this time".[58] This position does not seem rational to us and we
hope that it is not definitive.

IV. WEST GERMANY AND NUCLEAR WEAPONS

The lengthy discussions which preceded the drawing up of the Non-
Proliferation Treaty were mainly devoted to the position of West
Germany. The Soviet Union's great fear is the gaining of nuclear
status by this country. It is interesting to note that during these negotiations the Russians got the Americans to discuss internal arrangements
within NATO while they avoided on their side bringing out into the

---

[54] G. Ball, *The Discipline of Power*, pp. 216–19. It has been possible to observe
that paradoxically Britain was taken more seriously when she was militarily less
powerful than she is today. R. N. Rosecrance, *Defense of the Realm* (Columbia
University Press, 1968), p. 292.

[55] R. N. Rosecrance, op. cit., pp. 286–93.

[56] K. Younger, *Britain's Role in a Changing World* (Fabian Tract, 327, July 1960),
pp. 15–16.

[57] D. Healey, *A Labour Britain and the World* (Fabian Tract, 352, January 1964),
pp. 13–14.

[58] *The Times*, 9 July 1968. See also for a defence of Britain's nuclear armament,
M. Wright, *Disarm and Verify* (London, Chatto and Windus, 1964), pp. 154–56.

open the problems which arise out of the existence of the Warsaw Pact.[59]

A brief historical flashback seems necessary at this point about the creation of the M.L.F. (Multilateral NATO force).[60] This idea was launched in 1960 by the United States with a view to satisfying the ego of their former enemy. Originally the force was to consist of three American nuclear-propelled submarines, Britain's Bomber Command, and West German, Belgian, French, Italian, Dutch and Turkish fighter bombers. Placed under the direct command of SHAPE-SACEUR, it was integrated in theory, but in practice would have been under American control. This force, at first multinational, was supposed to become multilateral, each unit containing elements of different nationalities. Later on the plans were modified and envisaged the creation of a fleet of submarines armed with Polaris missiles. The M.L.F would have been financed and controlled collectively by all members of NATO willing to take part. This control would have been exercised by the Control Council of the M.L.F. in which the United States on the one hand, and all the other participants together, on the other hand, would have had a right to veto. Later President Kennedy, probably to quieten Soviet fears, drew up a plan under which the submarines would have been replaced by twenty-five surface vessels. The American veto continued in existence but nothing further was heard of the other one. In 1965, the British government presented a new project called the A.N.F.[61] made up of British and American naval elements and a much smaller number of surface vessels whose crews and command would have been supplied by the other participating countries. Yet from this moment onwards, the Americans kept on insisting on the need for NATO to develop conventional forces. Then, following a proposal of Mr McNamara in November 1965 and December 1966, the NATO Council created two permanent bodies for nuclear planning; a nuclear defence committee to look after general policy and a seven-member nuclear planning group, reporting to the first committee.[62]

Why was it felt necessary to create the M.L.F. and what would have been the consequences? It was clear that militarily speaking, the plan proposed no concrete or advantageous solutions and only raised complications. The idea seems to have originated from a group of intellectuals and officials who succeeded in "selling" it to Congress. For them, it was a way of pacifying West Germany's nuclear ambitions, which they considered

[59] Cf. *Hearings 1966*, p. 5.
[60] For a good résumé see: M. Halperin, *Contemporary Military Strategy* (Boston and Toronto, Little, Brown, 1967), pp. 112–121; J. Moch, *Revue Socialiste*, April 1966, pp. 289–312.
[61] Atlantic Nuclear Force.
[62] *La documentation française, N.E.D.*, No. 3384 to 3387; *Hearings 1966*, pp. 82–83.

inevitable, taking into account Britain's nuclear status, and that which France hoped to attain. The M.L.F. was also conceived as a way of carrying out West Germany's nuclear education while preventing her from becoming an outright nuclear Power. American officials stressed many times that the creation of the M.L.F. inside NATO was not an act of proliferation – rather the contrary.[63] In addition, it was thought that the Force would consolidate European unity, react against French intransigence and be an "organic experiment in co-operation".[64]

But the effects of the plan were quite different from those expected by its authors,[65] and Soviet fears were perhaps not completely unjustified. The idea of the M.L.F. resulted in the creation in Germany of a much greater desire to achieve nuclear status. So the creation of the Force could be considered the simple beginning of a process whose completion could be a serious danger for the whole world. Vice-President Johnson said in Brussels on 8 November 1963 that the possibility of European control of the M.L.F. could not be excluded, which would have involved the removal of the American veto. For West Germany, the creation of the Force would therefore have meant a first step toward an ever-growing nuclear role.[66] The M.L.F. and the A.N.F. would have been a new naval nuclear force, and would thus literally have constituted an act of proliferation. Also, each member country of the M.L.F. would in practice have had a right of veto over all future decisions to be taken in the disarmament field. The existence of mixed units, psychologically and politically unintegrated, would have created new risks over the use of nuclear weapons.

The M.L.F. plan was also equivalent to recognising that nuclear status was the criterion for equality within the Alliance and the condition for influence and effective participation. The attitude towards West Germany was ambiguous. Under the agreement of 23 October 1954, she had renounced atomic weapons, within certain limits. The supporters of the M.L.F. admitted that West Germany was so anxious to get hold of these weapons that she was ready to reject the agreement, so they pro-

---

[63] *Hearings 1963*, p. 40.
[64] G. Ball, op. cit., pp. 206 et. seq.
[65] H. A. Kissinger, *The Troubled Partnership* (New York, McGraw-Hill, 1965), pp. 127–160; Kissinger, *Atlantic Community Quarterly*, Fall, 1966, pp. 430–49; F. W. Mulley, ibid., pp. 450–64; H. Margolis, *Bulletin of Atomic Scientists*, November 1964, pp. 28–30; J. Newhouse, ibid., September 1964, pp. 13–18; J. Silard, ibid., pp. 18–20; W. Young, ibid., November 1964, pp. 19–21; B. T. Feld, ibid., December 1964, pp. 1–6; J. Silard, ibid., September 1966, pp. 15–20.
[66] J. L. Richardson, *Germany and the Atlantic Alliance* (Cambridge, Mass., Harvard University Press, 1965), p. 70.

posed another one to her with the avowed aim of restraining her am-tions.[67]

Let us now examine the Treaty in the light of the considerations that have been described. The Soviet draft Treaty laid down that "nuclear States undertake not to transfer such weapons in any form – directly or indirectly, through third States or groups of States – to the ownership or control of States or groups of States not possessing nuclear weapons and not to accord to such States or groups of States the right to participate in the ownership, control or use of nuclear weapons". This text even excluded West German participation in a consultative committee of NATO on nuclear planning strategy. According to the American proposal, nuclear States undertook "not to transfer any nuclear weapons into the national control of any non-nuclear State, either directly, or indirectly through a military alliance, and . . . not to take any other action which would cause an increase in the total number of States and other organisations having independent power to use nuclear weapons". The qualifying adjective "national" referring to control and the adverb "indirectly", explained by the immediately following clause, ought to be underlined in the text. As for the second sentence, it would have allowed (and Lord Chalfont expressed anxiety about this[68]) the creation of a new "organisation having independent power to use nuclear weapons" if one of the States having such power, i.e. France or Britain, waived it in favour of the new organisation within which it would be merged.

The American amendments of 21 March 1966 try to remedy this fault. Nuclear States undertake: "not to transfer nuclear weapons into the national control of any non-nuclear weapon State, or into the control of any association of non-nuclear-weapon States . . . not to take any other action which would cause an increase in the total number of States and Associations of States having control of nuclear weapons". The term "control" was defined as "the right to or capability of firing nuclear weapons without the additional agreement of a State possessing nuclear weapons". The forbidden acts were not to be committed either directly or indirectly and the latter term was defined in much more detail in the text of August 1965.[69]

Taking into account the corresponding obligations taken on by non-nuclear States, it was clear that the new proposal aimed at preventing the

---

[67] This argument is developed in a lively manner by Kissinger, op. cit., pp. 142–43.
[68] Lord Chalfont in Buchan (ed.), op. cit., pp. 123–42.
[69] ". . . or indirectly through third States or associations of States, or through units of the armed forces or military personnel of any State, even if such units or personnel are under the command of a military alliance."

formation of all Associations of States other than those of which nuclear States were members, with a right of veto.

The Soviet-American proposal was much less precise. Nuclear States undertook "not to transfer to any recipient whatsoever nuclear weapons or other nuclear explosive devices or control over such weapons or explosive devices directly, or indirectly" (Article I). The corresponding under-taking of non-nuclear States figures in Article II. It will be noticed that the word "control" is no longer qualified by the adjective "national" and its meaning is no longer defined. It must therefore be understood in the widest sense. The term "indirectly" is not explained either. We have seen that according to Switzerland, it "concerns the supply of arms, explosives or technical assistance for military purposes carried out through a State whether Third Party or not to the Treaty". The phrase could be added "or through an Association of States". In any case the way the wording evolved is clear: it is no longer a question of not transferring nuclear weapons to the national control of a non-nuclear State or to that of an Association of non-nuclear States, but of not transferring these arms or their control to anyone at all. It could be concluded from this that the text of the pro-posal allows the creation neither of a European deterrent force (even with the participation of a nuclear State, and even dependent on the veto of such a State) nor of an organisation like the M.L.F. That was the interpre-tation of Articles I and II of the Treaty given by a French deputy belonging to the majority party.[70]

The background to the negotiations thus clearly shows that the two Super-Powers agreed together to bury the M.L.F. Mr Dean Rusk said on 10 July before the Senate Foreign Relations Committee that the Treaty banned all transfers of nuclear weapons to anyone at all, including a multilateral body.[71]

But what is the position over what is called the European option? On this point the Treaty seems rather ambiguous, as indeed is American policy. The United States, it appears, had in the past told the Germans privately that they would not be hostile to a European force, while re-assuring the United Kingdom and the Soviet Union to the contrary.[72] As for the Treaty, it has been interpreted by some members of the Com-mittee of 18 as excluding the European option. Such was not the opinion of Mr Dean Rusk, according to whom the Treaty only covered what was

---

[70] *Parlement Européen, Débats*, XI, 67, No. 95, 18 October 1967. Also: Dehousse, op. cit.; A. Spinelli, *Atlantic Community Quarterly*, Summer 1967, pp. 223–33; A/C.1/PV.1556 (USSR); Albonetti, *Survival*, July 1967, pp. 223–26.

[71] *Hearings 1968*, pp. 5–6.

[72] W. B. Bader, *The US and the Spread of Nuclear Weapons* (New York, Pegasus, 1968), pp. 45, 48, 59–62.

forbidden and not what was allowed. "It does not deal with the problem of European unity, and would not bar succession by a new federated European State to the nuclear status of one of its former components." But such a State would have to exercise, if not all functions of government, at least all those which formerly belonged to its members in the fields of foreign policy and defence.[73] It may be asked whether such a situation would seem more attractive to the Soviet Union than the creation of the M.L.F. Happily the risks of a European Nuclear Force being created of the sort defined by Mr Rusk are non-existent on the political level.

At first, the Soviet Union was against West Germany taking part in discussions and decisions within NATO about the use of nuclear weapons. Later, she accepted the new nuclear planning organisation[74] at the same time as the United States abandoned the M.L.F. It seems therefore that the Treaty stabilised the situation such as it was after the previously quoted decisions of the NATO Council in December 1965 and December 1966.

At this point in our analysis it may be necessary to recall briefly that the Treaty caused serious troubles in West Germany.[75] To be specific, it may be recalled that West Germany under the Paris Treaty of 23 October 1954 made certain undertakings about atomic weapons. It was one thing to make promises to the six countries Party to this agreement, it was another to take on obligations towards all and sundry, including particularly the Soviet Union and the Eastern bloc. Also, the Non-Proliferation Treaty goes well beyond the Paris Agreements of 1954. In accordance with these Agreements, West Germany promised not to manufacture any atomic weapons on her territory. Her six partners, it should be noticed, could release her from this undertaking at any time. Besides, the Paris Agreements allowed West Germany to manufacture atomic weapons on another State's territory, and to receive on her own, or someone else's behalf, atomic weapons made elsewhere. So by signing the Non-Proliferation Treaty, West Germany accepted new and important limitations on her freedom of action.

The West German attitude to the Treaty has always been ambiguous. In her memorandum on the Treaty, submitted to the United Nations, the Federal Republic asked for disarmament measures, *détente*, security guarantees, equality of treatment and so on.[76] But the true reasons for

---

[73] *Hearings 1968*, pp. 5–6, 51–52, also 85–86.
[74] *Hearings 1966*, p. 42.
[75] An incomplete and biased account, but one not without interest, can be found in *La documentation du ministère des affaires étrangères de la République Democratique Allemande, Attaques massives contre le traité sur la non-prolifération des armes nucléaires*, 1967.
[76] A/C.1/963, 9 May 1968.

West German opposition were more complex. According to one very penetrating analysis of the situation[77] West Germany wants to keep open the options (a) of taking part in the nuclear strategy planning of NATO; (b) of taking part in an allied nuclear Force (inside which the American veto would operate); (c) of joining a European force as a full member; (d) of using her waiver of nuclear weapons as a bargaining counter in her negotiations with Moscow on German unification.

But if the different German political groups are far from being in agreement on the Treaty, such people as Herr Franz Josef Strauss, Herr Zimmermann, Herr Barzel, and Herr Walter Hallstein see the Treaty as an obstacle to the self-defence of Europe.[78] At one time Herr Barzel, the leader of the Christian Democrat Parliamentary group, went on a propaganda tour abroad to oppose the Treaty, including notably to New Delhi.[79] Other leaders made it known that West Germany might sign the Treaty in exchange for concessions by the Russians. And this brings us back to the position defended by Herr Schroeder in July 1965, that West Germany would not give up the idea of acquiring nuclear weapons as long as Russia would not agree to German reunification.

The invasion of Czechoslovakia hardened German policy still further. Bonn tried again to establish a common front of non-nuclear States opposed to the Treaty, and to make her signature conditional upon the United States giving a unilateral security guarantee of unlimited duration.[80] The American Senate is not keen on this sort of solution. We shall refer to this again later.

This attitude did not help to encourage *détente*. Soviet policy in its more excessive aspects can be explained by fear of Germany, who has not always acted in the best way to improve relations with the Soviet Union. A refusal to adhere to the Treaty would only have heightened tension. Moreover, looking at past history, it would have been politically and morally difficult for West Germany to adopt a negative position before world public opinion.

M. Dehousse has said he is not sure that if the Federal Republic got hold of atomic weapons in any form that this would definitely compromise peaceful reunification. It would bring *détente* to a sudden halt, but there would have to be *détente* and of this M. Dehousse is doubtful.[81] But none

[77] T. Sommer in A. Buchan (ed.), *A World of Nuclear Powers?* (Englewood Cliffs, Prentice Hall, 1966), pp. 39–54.
[78] See for example, *The Economist*, 9 March 1968; *Le Monde*, 6 March 1968; 10 March 1968; 16 March 1968.
[79] *Hindustan Times*, 9 April 1968.
[80] Cf. *New York Times*, 8 July 1968 and *The Times*, 28 August 1968.
[81] Dehousse, op. cit.

would subscribe to this point of view among those who have followed the development of the international situation over the past ten years with any sense of detachment, or who do not demand the establishment of an immediate paradise on earth. The latter would think twice before inviting the risk that M. Dehousse apparently regards without any fear at all.

Be that as it may, during the long debate which preceded the signature of the Treaty by West Germany on 28 November 1969, no politician actually spoke in favour of rejecting it. The debate was over the right moment for signature, this moment not having yet arrived – by a long way – as far as the Christian Democrats were concerned. Herr Strauss for his part wanted to wait until after the opening of negotiations on the proposal for a European Federation.

Russian statements made in August 1968 about a right of intervention in Germany under Articles 53 and 107 of the UN Charter, provided a new excuse for not signing, a refusal formally stated by Herr Brandt on 1 September 1968.[82] Yet this position could not be maintained as it failed to take into account world public opinion, for it was equivalent to isolating Bonn at the same time from her allies and the Eastern bloc. As Herr Brandt recalled: "even France who refuses to sign this Treaty has advised the Federal Republic not to leave the impression that she is trying to get hold of nuclear weapons".[83] Signature was undeniably a condition of the political "opening" to the East.

A curious phase of negotiations then took place between the USSR, the United States and Federal Germany, who tried to get the maximum number of queries answered and general reassurances. This exceptional procedure, during which Washington seems to have taken on the role of mediator,[84] ought to be noted: it consisted of secret three-sided negotiations to define certain provisions of a multilateral Treaty already signed by many States. This proves once again the importance of the German problem in the context of the Treaty. According to Herr Scheel, West Germany "obtained all the explanations required about all questions asked: peaceful development of atomic energy, control, control costs, the European option; with the exception of one question only, that of Russia's claim of the right to intervene, based on the United Nations Charter."[85]

[82] *Le Monde*, 3 September 1968.
[83] *Le Monde*, 1 February 1969.
[84] *Hearings 1969*, p. 341.
[85] *Le Monde*, 29 November 1969. On his side Herr Brandt said: "We have obtained from the USSR written assurances about the peaceful development of our nuclear industry. As for the rest, let us have confidence in our allies and do not let us imagine that the whole world is plotting against Germany". *Le Monde*, 14 November 1969.

The passage on the European option is all the more interesting as the West German Foreign Minister said this on 28 November 1969, that is to say after the statement Mr Gromyko had made on 24 November according to which the Treaty banned the transfer of atomic weapons or their control to any State, group of States, or Alliance. It looks therefore as if this statement is not in conflict with the American position (which is that of the Brandt government) on the European option. There may be regret that so much obscurity surrounds this Treaty but it remains true that it would have been impossible to get public agreement on a text that was much more detailed and precise. Let us also note that during the months which preceded the German signature, the United States must doubtless have put some friendly pressure on Bonn.[86] They did not, however, agree to give West Germany security guarantees going beyond those laid down within the NATO framework.[87]

When it signed the Treaty, the Bonn government published a long statement. The main point was that it will only ratify the Treaty after the conclusion of an agreement between the IAEA and Euratom, about the control measures mentioned in Article III of the Treaty. This agreement would be that control would only be exercised at certain strategic points; each Party would determine what constitutes the "equipment or material" which would fall under the export conditions laid down in paragraph 2 of Article III: and the control costs would be borne in such a way that unfair charges were not made to non-nuclear countries. Some of these demands appear exorbitant; it remains to be seen whether they will be accepted during the coming negotiations which themselves are likely to be influenced by the general development of the international situation.

[86] *Hearings 1969*, pp. 307, 327; *The Times*, 11 November 1969.
[87] *Hearings 1969*, p. 401.

5. POLICING THE BAN

IT was not until 18 January 1968 that the text of Article III about safe-guards was made public for the first time by the Super-Powers. Although it was frequently complained about, it was not discussed in much detail and Romania alone proposed an amendment to it, which was however not accepted. Even before the Article was submitted, Sweden took the initiative of tabling a proposal which went much further. Before going into how the text was drawn up it might be a good idea to summarise the philosophy lying behind it.

The safeguards in question were not aimed at detecting all possible violations of the undertakings given by the parties, but applied to certain nuclear materials used in civil industry "with a view to preventing diversion of nuclear energy from peaceful uses to nuclear weapons or other nuclear explosive devices." The aim of the supervision was not to find out if a nuclear weapon existed on the territory of a non-nuclear State Party to the Treaty, nor whether a nuclear State adhering to the Treaty was proceeding or had proceeded to transfer a nuclear weapon or its control in violation of the Treaty provisions. It was limited to a check on peaceful uses to ensure that they were not diverted from their intended use and that they served no military purpose. This is worth emphasising. The Americans, who on other occasions, have demanded the setting up of an elaborate, watertight control system, agreed in this case that an incomplete and imperfect system was satisfactory. Doubtless the two Super-Powers' means of detection have improved considerably, and in certain cases, these means will be sufficient to observe a Treaty violation, such as the existence of nuclear weapons on the territory of a nuclear State adhering to the Treaty. But as Secretary of State Rogers recognised, "you couldn't give an absolute assurance that if there were clandestine attempts or clandestine efforts to violate the Treaty that they could all be discovered". And he added that a "certain amount of good faith" was necessary from the Parties to the Treaty, which because of its control provisions will have "inhibiting qualities".[1] So according to the Americans, a reasonably effective system, having real, but not absolute power of dissuasion, is enough.

[1] *Hearings 1969*, pp. 335, 362.

I. THE DRAFTING OF ARTICLE III

Agreement over the supervisory provisions turned out to be a delicate matter, not so much because of a difference of views between the two Super-Powers, as because of difficulties raised by certain non-nuclear members of Euratom and by its Commission.[1a]

The Soviet proposal of 24 September 1965 contained nothing about control measures. The USSR, as is well known, refuses to submit to any form of inspection. However, her attitude has changed as far as safeguards to be applied to other States are concerned. When the statute of the IAEA was drawn up, the Soviet Union and the developing countries tried to limit the control powers of the Agency, as it was essential, they said, that the international organisation and the industrialised countries should not inhibit the technological development of weaker countries.[2] But since 1963, the Soviet Union wants the Agency's guarantees[3] fully implemented, and this change following on the heels of the Moscow Treaty is most likely explained by a desire to put an end to proliferation. The Soviet Union, as we have seen, has adopted a control system in its bilateral Treaties, that is less inflexible than those enforced by the United States, but which is no less strict in practice.[4]

The United States, for their part, have adopted since 1954, that is to say, since the beginning of the "Atoms for Peace" Programme, precise and detailed control measures, first of all within bilateral Treaties. From 1956 onwards, these agreements admitted the possibility of replacing bilateral control in the future by that of the International Atomic Energy Agency (IAEA).

American aid in the field of peaceful uses was sometimes visualised as a means of ensuring non-proliferation. Mr Seaborg, President of the American Atomic Energy Commission, explained that the United States supplied enriched uranium to other countries to try and stop them constructing their own radio-isotope separation plants, the building of which could not be economically justified under these conditions. If, in spite of American aid, or its offer, a country were to build such a plant, it would demonstrate thereby that it had aims outside the economic sphere.[5]

[1a] Many contacts and consultations took place about this between the United States on one hand and West Germany and the Euratom Commission on the other. See, for example, *Parlement Européen, Débats*, XI 67, No. 95, 18 October 1967, p. 52.

[2] Cf. G. Fischer, *L'Energie atomique et les Etats-Unis* (Paris, 1957), pp. 338–45.

[3] A. S. Lall, *Negotiating Disarmament* (Centre for International Studies, Cornell University, Ithaca, 1964), pp. 65–67; A. Finkelstein, *Les Activités de contrôle de l'AIEA* (Institut de Droit Comparé, Paris, 1965).

[4] See Chapter 2, note 7.

[5] *Hearings 1966*, p. 62.

From 1963 onwards, the United States transferred to the IAEA responsibility for exercising controls imposed under bilateral agreements.[6] Also they unilaterally put under the control of the Agency certain civil nuclear installations thus giving the international body the chance of obtaining new and valuable experience.[7]

A French author has expressed the opinion that this substitution of control by the Agency for bilateral control was carried out for political reasons.[8] The wisdom of the American aid programme in the sphere of peaceful uses of atomic energy may be open to question. But once this programme was in existence, it seems wrong not to recognise that controls were imposed in the interests of peace, and that international control offered maximum safeguards while still soothing national susceptibilities. For our part, we believe that in the interests of peace and real co-operation, not only should supervisory measures but also aid be under greater international control, so as to make small States less dependent upon large ones.

Yet the American draft Treaty of 17 August 1965 included a very short provision about control. Article III of the draft was put in these terms: "each of the States Party to this Treaty undertakes to co-operate in facilitating the application of International Atomic Energy Agency or equivalent international safeguards to all peaceful nuclear activities". It was this position that was again defended in 1966 by one of the American delegates.[9] The United States draft thus foresaw a system which would be applied to all parties yet without affecting the military activities of nuclear States. In addition, supervision had to be exercised by means of guarantees which were not necessarily those of the Agency.

It seems it was Senator Pastore who proposed to the Senate on 18 January 1966 the formula which was finally adopted in Article III, namely: non-nuclear States accept the safeguards of the IAEA for all their atomic activities and the Parties to the Treaty undertake not to transfer any material or nuclear equipment meant for peaceful uses except under the control of the Agency or in accordance with similar safeguards.[10]

---

[6] R. N. Douglas, *Australian Outlook*, August 1967, pp. 179–197; *Hearings 1968*, p. 99; *Hearings 1969*, pp. 487–488.
[7] See for example J. Simsarian, *American Journal of International Law*, 1966, pp. 502–10.
[8] Goldschmidt, *Les rivalités atomiques 1939–66* (Paris, Fayard, 1967), p. 287.
[9] A. Fisher, *Department of State Bulletin*, 22 August 1966, pp. 281–283.
[10] *Hearings 1966*, pp. 147–48.

II. STATES SUBJECT TO CONTROL

1. Inequality of the Parties

Supervision is exercised over non-nuclear States Party to the Treaty, as well as over those not Party to it, in so far as the latter receive certain equipment and material from States adhering to the Treaty.

In accordance with Article III(1) only non-nuclear States Party to the Treaty are subject to safeguard provisions. These are applied also to all source material and fissile products "in all peaceful nuclear activities within the territory of a non-nuclear State Party, under its jurisdiction or carried out under its control anywhere". It looks as if this text is aimed at activities not only of the State but also of persons, companies, public or private undertakings or organisations which belong to it and are under its jurisdiction or control, whether these activities take place upon national territory or upon that of any other State, even not Party to the Treaty. The latter would evidently have to give its consent to the application of the safeguards, failing which such activities would have to cease. Thus was settled one of the causes for concern taken up by the UAR in an amendment already examined in the preceding chapter.

During the discussions in Geneva, it became apparent that non-nuclear States feared that control measures might become a means of commercial discrimination, so as to perpetuate the technological supremacy of the nuclear States. Of course the ideal solution for soothing the exaggerated fears of certain countries would be the application of a standard system of safeguards to all States. But things being what they are, economic and social inequality being the hallmark of the international community just as much as of individual societies, some discrimination is inevitable, especially in a field where power imbalance is so evident.

As Mrs Myrdal showed so clearly, speaking for Sweden, an acceptable control system has two criteria: first it must help towards disarmament, secondly it must not stand in the way of economic development.[11]

According to the Swiss government's *aide-mémoire*, "in order to maintain equality of competition between States, it would be desirable for control measures to extend also to civil nuclear installations" of nuclear States.[12] As for Sweden, she put forward a more subtle proposal based upon the general application—within a fixed period—of a single universally applicable safeguards system—that of the IAEA. Non-nuclear States would undertake to submit all their nuclear activities to the control of the Agency. Nuclear States, while agreeing in principle to co-operate in the progressive application of the Agency's safeguards to their *peaceful*

[11] ENDC/PV. 300.   [12] ENDC/204.

nuclear activities, would remain free to determine when to do so, if ever . . . On the other hand, each State Party to the Treaty would have to put under the control of the IAEA all transfers of raw materials, special fissile materials, or equipment or products specially made or prepared for the transformation, use, or manufacture of special fissile materials. When a State making a transfer and the recipient State were both Parties to the Treaty, there would be no problem; controls would have to be imposed on both territories. If only the receiving State was a Party, there would be no difficulty either; as soon as the material, equipment or products arrived within the Territory, they would be subject to supervision which would then be extended to all phases of use. When the State carrying out the transfer was the only Party to the Treaty, the problem would be solved by the undertaking suggested by the Swedes that each State Party would make no transfer without putting it under the Agency's safeguards system.[13]

As can be seen, the Swedish system had considerable advantages over one where only nuclear activities of non-nuclear States would be subject to control. The Swedish proposal would have made possible the supervision of transfers made by a State Party to any other State, Party or not, nuclear or non-nuclear.[14] As conceived by its authors, a ban was implied on imports by nuclear States of fissile materials reserved for military use. It would have been therefore an extremely limited disarmament measure which would have reduced the discriminatory character of the Treaty.[15] In any case, the Swedish proposal was more realistic than the 1965 American plan which would have imposed controls on all peaceful nuclear activities of all Parties.

However, the discriminatory character of the Treaty was diminished by the unilateral commitment of the United States, made by President Johnson on 2 December 1967, under which, when the safeguards system comes into force, "the United States will allow the IAEA to apply its safeguards to all nuclear activities of the United States, with the single exception of those directly affecting her national security".[16] The British government gave a similar undertaking on 4 December 1967.[17] The Soviet Union, in contrast, has remained completely silent on this point up till now.

The Swedish representative, while approving of these undertakings

---

[13] ENDC/195; See also Mrs Myrdal's statement on 31 August 1967.
[14] As the Swedish delegate remarked, to apply safeguards only to nuclear activities of non-nuclear States as well as to transfers of materials made to these States' territories, would be a retrograde step as, at present, bilateral controls apply also to transfers from certain nuclear States to another nuclear State. ENDC/PV. 300.
[15] ENDC/PV. 363.   [16] ENDC/206.   [17] ENDC/207.

wondered if they went far enough, because of their unilateral, voluntary character.[18] The American delegate tried to reassure Mrs Myrdal by giving her some detailed information.[19]

The provisions analysed up till now tend to show up discrimination between nuclear States on the one hand, and non-nuclear States on the other. But according to paragraph 2 of Article III *each* Party to the Treaty undertakes not to provide for peaceful purposes,[20] to any non-nuclear State, Party to the Treaty or not, source or special fissionable material or equipment or material especially designed or prepared for the processing, use, or production of special fissionable material, unless the source or special fissionable material is subject to the safeguards required by Article III, paragraph 1. This represents an incomplete and watered down version of one of the ideas in the Swedish plan. Among other differences, there is this: if under paragraph 2 all Parties make the same commitment, this only applies to supplies for a non-nuclear State.

So, under this head, as under some others, the rules drawn up by the Parties do not apply only within the Treaty law they have created, but also to relations between Parties on the one hand and non-member States on the other. There emerges here again, but in a more precise form, *mutatis mutandis* the same norm stated in Article 2 (6) of the UN Charter.

It has been observed that under paragraphs 1 and 2 of Article III, controls or safeguards only apply to supplies to non-nuclear States. This discrimination has been particularly criticised, since at the present time, in accordance with certain bilateral agreements, controls are being exercised over supplies made for peaceful purposes by a nuclear State to another nuclear State.

[18] ENDC/PV. 363.
[19] According to the American delegate, the agreement that his country will make with the Agency "will give details of the activities to which the IAEA will apply its safeguards. They are expected to include the use of nuclear fuel in all power reactors supplying public service undertakings in the United States, as well as the production and chemical reprocessing of nuclear fuel supplied for these reactors. Today, more than eighty reactors of this type, giving a total power of more than 56,000 megawatts, are already in operation or under construction, or on order, or construction plans have been announced. This list is also expected to include nuclear fuel for test reactors, research reactors and university reactors, as well as "critical" plant of which there are about one hundred in the United States as well as the manufacture and chemical reprocessing of these fuels. This offer at the same time as a similar offer made by the United Kingdom on 4 December ought to dissipate any idea of discrimination over safeguards". ENDC/PV. 368. The total number of American installations (facilities) put under supervision since the conclusion of the agreement with the IAEA is about two hundred. *Hearings 1969*, p. 332.
[20] It will be recalled that supply for military purposes is forbidden.

2. State practice

The scope of the discrimination established by the Treaty is likely to be very limited in practice. The United States have stated there is nothing to prevent a nuclear State from demanding the application of international safeguards to deliveries made for peaceful purposes to another nuclear State.[21] Italy has let it be known that she will submit to international safeguards all nuclear supplies to any State whatever, nuclear or not, Party to the Treaty or not.[22] Mrs Myrdal, for her part, observed that the present policy of suppliers was fortunately favourable to the aims pursued by Sweden. She hoped that suppliers would remain in contact and observe a moral standard in applying the Agency's safeguard to their deliveries.[23]

On this point it would suffice to have an agreement between the United States, the United Kingdom, Canada and West Germany for reactors and between the United States, Canada, South Africa and Sweden for uranium.[24]

France, as is well known, refuses international controls, which she has never applied in her international dealings with Spain[25] or Israel.[26] She has signed several contracts for the purchase of uranium, particularly with Niger and the Central African Republic. Negotiations with Canada have dragged on for a long time, as the latter is only willing to deliver under the IAEA safeguards.[27] However, in Autumn 1968, Canada agreed to supply France with plutonium. Fissile materials were supplied under an agreement of 9 October 1959 between the Canadian government and Euratom. As far as controls are concerned, the exchange of letters provides that the procedure laid down in Chapter VII of the Euratom Treaty would be applied.[27a] South Africa stated in 1966 and confirmed in 1968 that she would carry out uranium sales in such a way as not to increase the number of nuclear States, and she renewed her "total support" for the idea of non-proliferation.[28] These statements do not seem to refer to deliveries to nuclear States. In 1964, South Africa signed a secret contract[28a] with France which evidently contains no Agency safeguards. It may be

---

[21] ENDC/PV. 368

[22] A/PV. 1672.

[23] ENDC/PV. 363.

[24] L. Beaton, *Foreign Affairs*, July 1967, pp. 662–69.

[25] Goldschmidt, op. cit., p. 288.

[26] ibid., 296. However, American missions do visit the Israeli reactor.

[27] Goldschmidt, op. cit., pp. 278-79, 288. Such safeguards also apply to a contract for delivery to Britain signed in 1966.

[27a] *Communautés européennes*, *Le Conseil*, Doc. 1594/68. (ASS. 902) of 23 October 1968.

[28] A/C. 1/PV. 1571 and 1579.

[28a] *Le Monde*, 19 July 1968.

recalled that France has stated that she will act as if bound by the Treaty. From the time of entry into force of the Treaty, therefore, she ought not to deliver to any non-nuclear State, equipment and material mentioned in Article III (2) of the Treaty except if this equipment and material is under the safeguards established by the same Article. In the meantime, the correct procedure to follow would be to include in the delivery contract a clause under which the safeguards required in Article III of the Non-Proliferation Treaty would apply from the entry into force of this Treaty. On this it is worth quoting the *Agreement between the United Kingdom, Germany and the Netherlands on collaboration in the development and exploitation of the Gas Centrifuge Process for producing enriched uranium,* of 4 March 1970. This agreement provides for the application "of the procedures resulting from any additional obligations in relation to safeguards binding upon any of the Contracting Parties pursuant to an agreement or agreements concluded with the International Atomic Energy Agency".[29]

As far as the United States are concerned, they tend to make international guarantees applicable over as wide a field as possible. The bilateral Franco-American agreement of 1956, concerning the peaceful use of atomic energy expired on 20 November 1966. At the request of the United States government, responsibility for the supply and control of fissile material of American origin was transferred to Euratom under a double agreement, United States-Euratom and Euratom-France.[30]

Also, the Joint Nuclear Energy Committee of the United States Congress continues to insist that the Agency safeguards apply to American nuclear aid in the civil field, even when this aid is given to countries like Britain and India, particularly unwilling to comply with these safeguards.[31]

3. Conclusion of agreements with the IAEA

The safeguards required by Article III have to be defined by agreements that non-nuclear States, Party to the Treaty, are to conclude with the Agency. Negotiation of these agreements has to commence within 180 days from the entry into force of the Treaty. Under Article IX (3), the Treaty will enter into force after its ratification by Britain, the United States and the Soviet Union and by forty other signatory States. For States depositing their instruments of ratification after the 180-day period, negotiations with the Agency shall commence not later than the date of

[29] Cmnd. 4315, Art. VII.
[30] Commissariat à l'Energie atomique, *Rapport annuel*, 1966, p. 196.
[31] *Hearings 1966*, pp. 160, 173. The actual reference was to the delivery of enriched uranium to Britain and aid given to India for the construction of a chemical treatment factory.

such deposit. It is clear, therefore, that the latter States can, if they so wish, commence negotiations with the Agency before ratifying the Treaty. In any case the agreements must enter into force for each Party not later than eighteen months after the start of negotiations.

Thus, non-nuclear States agreed to draft an agreement within a fixed period. The Non-Proliferation Treaty is quite exceptional as it does not just recommend negotiations, but obliges agreements to be made. In fact the non-nuclear Parties committed themselves with full knowledge of what they were doing; they were in their great majority members of the Agency whose safeguards system was familiar to them. There may be some problems over the agreement to be concluded with the five members of Euratom and we shall return to this point. But it must be realised that the Parties to the safeguards agreements were not on an equal footing. The Agency, on the basis of its own safeguards system, would establish a basic form of agreement which, logically, would only be subject to minor variation, given the principle of equality of all non-nuclear States Party to the Non-Proliferation Treaty. These States could moreover be relied upon to defend this principle. Politically, morally and psychologically, one or several Parties would find it very difficult to refuse to conclude agreements to which a great number of others had already consented.

What happens if a State does not conclude the required agreement within the time specified? The Treaty does not foresee this possibility. Two aspects of the problem ought to be envisaged. Firstly, the preparatory work and the text of Article III show that the application of safeguards under the agreements concluded with the Agency is an essential corollary, a fundamental condition of the commitment to remain non-nuclear. Secondly, the principle of equality between all non-nuclear States Party to the Treaty forms one of the main legal and political devices of the Treaty. So it is clear that a non-nuclear State refusing to conclude the Agreement with the Agency would not be able to continue to remain a Party to the Treaty without making a nonsense of the whole system. It is no less obvious that in practice such a state would take upon itself, politically and morally, extremely grave responsibilities.

However, certain countries that distrust the safeguards system will tend to put off the moment of their ratification and to wait for others to conclude their Agreement. When these late-comers have deposited their instruments of ratification there may be in future two sorts of Parties to the Treaty: one already under Agency controls after the conclusion of an agreement; another still outside the safeguards system because of the timetable. It is also worth noticing that some signatories made statements attaching conditions to their ratification. Thus the Japanese government, in its statement of 3 February 1970 says it will take into account in its decision to ratify the Treaty, the following main points: the safeguards agreement with the IAEA must not put Japan in an unfavourable position in relation to agreements concluded by other States either individually or collectively (this is doubtless a reference to Euratom); these safeguards ought to apply only to certain strategic points of the nuclear cycle (this demand has already been made by West Germany and by the Conference of non-nuclear States); no inequitable burden should be imposed upon non-nuclear States because of the safeguards; and concrete measures ought to be taken to translate into reality the provisions of Articles IV and V of the Treaty.

Another problem has been raised by the Swedish representative.[32] According to paragraph 2 of Article III no nuclear material or equipment may be supplied to a non-nuclear State without the application of IAEA safeguards. It might be deduced that during the interim period, before the conclusion of agreements with the Agency, these States would find themselves deprived of all nuclear assistance. On this point, the United States delegate gave every possible reassurance by explaining "that the safeguards required under the terms of the present Article" (Art. III (2)) are not demanded immediately upon the entry into force of the Treaty but only at latest at the end of the transition period. During this period, the United States will continue supplying under appropriate safeguards which later on will have to be adapted to conform with the agreements concluded with the IAEA. And the United States representative expressed the hope that other States would follow the same policy.[33]

It is worth noting at this point that safeguards are applied also to non-nuclear States not adhering to the Treaty, to the extent that such States receive certain equipment and material from a State Party to the Treaty. Under these conditions, it is evident that a non-nuclear State not Party to the Treaty will have to conclude a safeguard agreement with the Agency which will of course resemble other agreements as to methods and procedures. However, in this case the safeguards will not cover all peaceful nuclear activities but only materials delivered or produced with the help of equipment supplied by the State Party to the Treaty.

III. INSTITUTIONS AND SAFEGUARDS

The safeguards system is aimed at reducing international tension, increasing confidence, encouraging the development of peaceful collaboration,

[32] ENDC/PV. 363.   [33] ENDC/PV. 368.

the transfer of information, material and equipment in complete security and without hesitation. It is evident that those who support greater control measures *ratione personae* ought to be in favour of the exclusive application of the Agency's safeguards. The system is standard, universal, apolitical, non-discriminatory and democratic, as it is administered by those who have agreed to accept it.[34] If a large number of non-nuclear States agreed to accept Agency control over all their nuclear activities, there might be some reasonable hope of extending control to the peaceful nuclear activities of nuclear States. The universal system does seem that most easily acceptable to the great majority of States, as it is both the most economical system and the one which inspires most confidence.[35]

1. The Treaty and the role of the Agency

How are the safeguards required in Article III defined? "Each non-nuclear weapon State Party to the Treaty undertakes to accept safeguards, as set forth in an agreement to be negotiated and concluded with the International Atomic Energy Agency in accordance with the Statute of the IAEA and the Agency's safeguards system" (paragraph 1). This wording may reflect a concession by the Russians: it is not the application of the Agency's safeguards by the Agency which is automatically required, even at a later date, but safeguards to be defined in an agreement concluded with the Agency. However, these safeguards must be in accordance with the Statute and safeguards system of the IAEA. The same idea in a more restrictive, precise form already existed in the 1959 agreement between the United States and Euratom, to which we shall refer later. The Treaty in any case requires the agreements to be concluded to be in accordance with the Agency's safeguards system. But, as the American delegate observed, the present safeguards system of the Agency is not incorporated in the Treaty, and in order to modify this system it will not be necessary to revise the Treaty.[36] Moreover the preamble to the Treaty includes a paragraph stressing the efforts needed in research and development to "further the application, within the framework of the Agency's safeguards system, of the principle of safeguarding effectively the flow of source and special fissionable materials by use of instruments and other techniques at certain strategic points". For its part, the Agency's present safeguards system (paragraph 8) enacts that "the principles and methods laid down

---

[34] Cf. Seaborg in W. Young (ed.), *Existing Mechanisms of Arms Control* (Oxford, Pergamon Press, 1966), pp. 11–22.

[35] H. D. Smyth, "Nuclear Power and Proliferation", *Department of State Bulletin*, 3 January 1966, pp. 28–36.

[36] ENDC/PV. 357.

in the present document shall be revised from time to time in the light of new experience acquired by the Agency and of technological progress".[37] It is a simple question, therefore, of finding a sufficiently flexible method of rapidly and effectively modifying agreements concluded by the Agency with Parties to the Treaty. On this, the American delegate has indicated that any modification made to the Agency's safeguards system by the Board of Governors after the negotiation of safeguards agreements can only be made by the IAEA with the consent of the Parties to such an agreement, "a consent that must either be given in accordance with a general procedure agreed in advance, or by means of modifications made at a later date to agreements concluded with the Agency".[38]

The operation of the safeguards system laid down by the Treaty will not fail to create financial problems. It appears, however, that the cost of control and in particular of inspection is quite small, and that it can be calculated at less than 1 per cent of the cost price of energy produced in nuclear power stations.[39] Under the Statute (Art. XIV B–1, C and D), the costs of the Agency's safeguards system are regarded as administrative expenses, and form part of the ordinary budget. Their amount is arrived at after deduction of sums recoverable under agreements concerning the application of safeguards made between the Agency and Parties transferring responsibility for control to it under bilateral or multilateral Treaties previously concluded by them. Up to now, this deduction has not been made and the cost of safeguards applied by the Agency following the transfer of bilateral controls has been divided in the ordinary budget, among all the members. This is in line with the Anglo-Saxon argument which has been criticised by the Soviet Union as well as by France. For them, Parties to the Treaties whose safeguards systems are transferred to

---

[37] INFCIRC/66/Rev. 1.   [38] ENDC/PV. 368.

[39] H. D. Smyth, op. cit. Certain sets of figures were quoted to the Foreign Relations Committee of the American Senate, according to which the cost of control would be considerable and the number of people to be employed very high. *Hearings 1968*, pp. 277–88. The American Atomic Energy Commission found these figures completely wrong. It calculated alternatives based on the forecasts of electricity to be produced by nuclear power stations. The total cost of control was put at $29 million for 1971, $93 million for 1985 and $143 million for 1990. These figures would correspond respectively to 3, 0.4 and 0.4 per cent respectively of the total value of nuclear electricity produced and 0.16, 0.02, and 0.02 million per kWh of nuclear electricity. The number of people employed for control purposes would be, according to the Commission, 775 in 1971, 1,766 in 1985 and 2,374 in 1990. *Hearings 1968*, pp. 153–55. As an American Congressman has aptly stated, the cost of control is insignificant in relation to the sums devoted to armaments. ibid. p. 150. In 1975, if all American peaceful installations are put under controls, the total cost would be $10 million per annum. *Hearings 1969*, p. 502.

the Agency ought to pay the expenses resulting from that transfer.[40]

The powers given to the Agency by the Non-Proliferation Treaty and the Treaty on the denuclearisation of Latin America were not envisaged under the Statute. Most likely, in order to finance these new activities, the Agency will have to establish a separate budget[41] which will be subscribed to not by all members, but by the Parties to the above-mentioned Treaties. It must also be expected that the non-nuclear countries will insist on the nuclear States taking on an important part of these financial burdens. The Agency, whose staff will necessarily have to become more numerous, will have to establish a method of finance which can then be applied through agreements to be concluded with Parties to the Non-Proliferation Treaty. For its part, the Swiss government felt that "control costs ought to be met by the control organisation so as to prevent the peaceful export of nuclear material by non-possessor States being commercially discriminated against, to the benefit of possessor States not observing safeguards, or of non-possessor States outside the Treaty."

We have observed that many States have considered this problem very important and that some, such as West Germany and Japan, have stated that their ratification was contingent on its satisfactory solution. It appears there is a shift of attitude towards the American position and that West Germany has obtained concessions on this point from the Soviet Union to this effect.[41a]

As far as institutions are concerned, it has been proposed that the Parties to the Treaty should have the right to be fairly represented within the organs of the IAEA, and even that a Special Committee should be created, within the Agency framework, whose members would be non-nuclear States adhering to the Treaty and which would be entrusted by the Board of Governors with all inspection questions.[42]

It has been said the Agency is not technically equipped to take on such extensive control operations and that it ought therefore to devote itself entirely to the development of industrial technology, and to hand over the control function to an espionage service, to the CIA.[43] But the peaceful development of nuclear energy and supervision are inseparable ideas. The Agency's activities in the control field, even if modest, are constantly on the increase. According to the author whose criticism has just been

---

[40] Cf. Finkelstein, op. cit.; IAEA, CG (XI)/OR. 114 (France); CG (XI)/COM. 1/ OR. 76 (Yugoslavia).
[41] CG (XI)/OR. 113 (Belgium).
[41a] *Hearings 1969*, p. 311; *The Times*, 29 November 1969.
[42] A/C1/PV. 1569 (Spain).
[43] S. Rosen, "Proliferation Treaty Controls and the IAEA", *Journal of Conflict Resolution*, June 1967, pp. 168–75.

quoted, in 1964 the American Atomic Energy Commission inspected 121 installations in 14 countries, whilst in 1963–64 the Agency inspected only 23 installations in 7 countries. However, on 30 September 1967, the Board of the Agency approved 38 safeguards agreements applicable to 65 reactors in 29 countries. In August–September 1967, the Agency's inspection team inspected for the first time a large chemical treatment factory which the United States voluntarily submitted to supervision.[44] It is evident that with the entry into force of the Non-Proliferation Treaty, the Agency's activities will become wider and its staff of inspectors will have to increase.[45]

An extremely important and delicate problem arises over the application of safeguards. These must apparently be based upon the relevant articles in the Agency Statute as well as upon the actual system approved by the Board of Governors in 1965.[46]

A large number of countries have expressed anxiety about possible discrimination over the content of different agreements concluded with the Agency.[47] This anxiety is especially acute over the Euratom problem, which will be dealt with later. Generally speaking, reference must be made to the interpretation of the Co-Chairman. According to the American representative, "safeguards agreements made under the Non-Proliferation Treaty will incorporate, for reference purposes, relevant elements from documents relating to the Agency's safeguards system".[48] This point of view was reaffirmed by the Soviet delegate, according to whom Article III of the Treaty, the IAEA Statute and this Agency's document on Safeguards will all ensure "an indispensable degree of uniformity in applying controls in different countries." This will also follow from the fact that agreements concluded with the Agency will have to be approved by its Board of Governors, a body that is already sufficiently representative, and in case of need, may be referred to the general Conference of the IAEA.[49]

---

[44] IAEA, INFCIRC/103, 30 October 1967.
[45] Cf. IAEA, GC/XI/OR 112–16. According to American officials the Agency is and will be capable of carrying out effectively the functions entrusted to it by the Treaty.
[46] It figures in the document INFCIRC/66/Rev. 1.
[47] ENDC/PV. 367 (U.A.R.) and 370 (India); A/C. 1/PV. 1565 (Ceylon and Japan) and 1567 (Yugoslavia).
[48] ENDC/PV. 368.
[49] ENDC/PV. 377. The Board of Governors is in fact a slightly aristocratic body, whose composition was criticised by the smaller States when the Statute was drawn up. Cf. Fischer, L'énergie atomique et les Etats Unis, pp. 317–22, 346. The competent American authorities intend to give the Agency all possible technical help. Hearings 1969, p. 499.

2. The problem of Euratom

According to Article III (paragraph 4): "non-nuclear weapon States Party to the Treaty shall conclude agreements with the International Atomic Energy Agency to meet the requirements of this Article either individually, or together with other States . . . "

These five last words obviously refer to the five members of Euratom. But by whom will the safeguards agreement be concluded? The Treaty does not mention Euratom, only States. Yet according to the United States delegate's interpretation, the provision in the draft quoted above enables the Agency to conclude an agreement with another international organisation whose functions are similar to those of the Agency and of which the interested Parties are members.[50] The UAR opposed this interpretation, pointing out that Article III (4) does not mention organisations.[51]

It may be asked whether Articles 101 and 102 of the Euratom Treaty could not be applied in this case. Article 101 provided that while acting within its powers "the Community may contract with a third State, an international organisation, or a subject of a third State by concluding an agreement or convention". Article 102 refers to the same agreements or conventions to which, besides the Community, one or several member States are Party. But the agreement mentioned in Article III (4) of the Non-Proliferation Treaty only concerns five member States at best and remains *res inter alios acta* for France, which remains outside.

But there is no reason for France to want to hold up agreement between Euratom and the Agency, an agreement covering only five countries.[52] Yet during a debate which took place in the European parliament on 18 October 1967, M. de La Malène, no doubt reflecting the official French position, thought the five member States of Euratom ought to adopt a common position, but that each should conclude its own bilateral agreement with the Agency. It is true that according to Article 103 of the Euratom Treaty, member States are bound to inform the Commission "about plans for agreements or conventions with third States, international organisations, or subjects of third States, in so far as these agreements or conventions come within the scope of the present Treaty". The Commission has certain powers to oppose the conclusion of an agreement frustrating the application of the Treaty.

---

[50] ENDC/PV. 357. The American negotiators have revealed they "negotiated quite hard" on this point in order to get a form of words which would make a Euratom-IAEA agreement possible. *Hearings 1969*, pp. 353–54.
[51] ENDC/PV. 367.
[52] Cf. *Hearings 1968*, p. 106.

This text has often been quoted to prove the difficulty encountered by the five members of Euratom in concluding the agreement with the Agency required by the Non-Proliferation Treaty.[53] It would appear that there is nothing to prevent the Commission negotiating with the Agency on behalf of the Five, or concurrently with them as the Netherlands representative proposed.[54] After all, the Commission has already negotiated, as was recalled, with the United States, about the drafting of Article III of the Non-Proliferation Treaty. Yet it seems as if the agreement with the Agency ought to be concluded by the five members of Euratom, either individually or collectively.

What would this agreement include? General opinion among the five member States of Euratom is that the Agency ought simply to verify the safeguards applied by and within the Community. In an extreme form, this argument has been put by the West German Deputy Herr Furler, according to whom Euratom ought to take priority over the Non-Proliferation Treaty. He asked, what does verification mean? "If it means a formal confirmation of the proper functioning of Euratom and its safeguards, there is something to discuss. But if this verification, under the Non-Proliferation Treaty, because it is omnipresent, effectively nullifies Euratom's own control system, and is really a second control to be considered as final, the situation is of course completely different".[55]

The intentions of those who drafted the Non-Proliferation Treaty are not clear. We have seen that in spite of fears expressed in some quarters about possible discrimination in favour of the five member States of Euratom, the Soviet Union has stated that the safeguards agreements concluded with the Agency will be governed by the principle of uniformity. On the other hand, the United Kingdom representative has said that the agreements will take into account the fact that some States are members of a regional organisation with its own safeguards system.[56] The United States representative also leaned in this direction.[57]

It is worth taking a look back at American policy. Under an agreement

[53] Dehousse, *Chronique de politique étrangère*, November 1967, pp. 621–37; *Parlement Européen, Debats*, XI, 67, No. 95, 18 October 1967, pp. 54–56 (M. Scelba).

[54] A/C.1/PV. 1561.

[55] *Parle, Europ., Débats*, XI, 67, No. 95, 18 October 1967, p. 60.

[56] ENDC/PV. 358.

[57] This is the relevant passage in his statement. "In order to avoid any unnecessary overlapping, the IAEA should make appropriate use of existing documents and safeguards, if, under such mutually accepted agreements, the IAEA can be sure that no nuclear material is being diverted for the manufacture of nuclear weapons or other nuclear devices or nuclear explosives". ENDC/PV. 357.

concluded on 9 November 1958,[58] the United States entrusted to Euratom control over the peaceful use of American aid to the Community. The Parties recognised that this control was principally based upon Article XII of the Agency Statute. For the purposes of the creation and application of its own control system Euratom stated it was "ready to proceed to consultations and exchanges of experience with the IAEA with a view to establishing a reasonably compatible system to that of the Agency." It was also planned to ask the Agency for technical assistance in the fields of control, public health and security "recognising the Agency's importance". The Parties also reaffirm "their common interest in promoting the peaceful use of atomic energy through the medium of the IAEA".[59]

It has been noticed that the United States-Euratom agreement was received unfavourably by American supporters of the Agency's universalist policy.[60] And yet as has just been shown, the point of view of the latter has not been ignored. What is more, during the examination of the Agreement by the Joint Atomic Energy Committee of Congress, Mr Douglas Dillon, who played a prominent role in the negotiations, stated: "In case of the establishment of an international inspection system by the Agency, Euratom and the United States will consult about the Agency taking over safeguards and control over fissile materials used in the fulfilment of the programme" (of the Euratom-United States agreement). In addition, when agreement is reached with the Soviet Union over international control of fissile materials, Euratom intends to integrate itself within this agreement. It will be able to do so easily since its control system will have been developed in accordance with the Agency rules.[61] In 1966, an influential member of the Joint Committee said he thought Euratom ought to become a member of the Agency.[62]

The foregoing shows, therefore, that American policy has not made a final definitive choice between the Agency and Euratom. Yet some fervent supporters of "Little Europe" have claimed to have detected in Article III of the Non-Proliferation Treaty a neglectful attitude on the part of the United States towards Euratom.[63]

Other criticism has been directed towards the effects of the Treaty

---

[58] La doc. fr., *N.E.D.*, No. 2505, 3 February 1959; Fischer, *Annuaire français de droit international*, 1958, pp. 540–55.

[59] Cf. Art. 3-E, 12-A, 12-D, 13 Annexe B *in fine*.

[60] Goldschmidt, op. cit., p. 267.

[61] *Proposed Euratom Agreements, Hearings before the Joint Committee on Atomic Energy*, Part 1, July 1958, pp. 84–85.

[62] *Hearings 1966*, pp. 159–60.

[63] Dehousse, op. cit.; C. Gasteyger, *Agenor*, 1967, No. 2, pp. 3–6; Spinelli, *The Atlantic Community Quarterly*, Summer 1967, pp. 223–33.

upon Euratom. During the debate on 18 October 1967 in the European Parliament, Signor Martino insisted on the fact that control by the Agency over the members of Euratom would be discriminatory.

The whole Euratom system, so it is said, is based on non-discrimination, which would be challenged by the Non-Proliferation Treaty. According to M. Brunhes, a Belgian Liberal Deputy, "it is certain that from the moment this Treaty begins with two different Articles, the first addressed to nuclear States, the second to non-nuclear States, then we have discrimination within our six countries, which is precisely what Euratom has always tried to avoid". Euratom members adhering to the Non-Proliferation Treaty would have to submit to a new control system in addition to and on top of the one already applicable within the six-member Euratom community. The commercial and industrial discrimination which would follow from adhesion to the Non-Proliferation Treaty is also stressed: we shall return to this point.

Now Euratom itself has not succeeded in eliminating discrimination. Within the community, control is exercised only over peaceful nuclear activities. Of the six, only France is a nuclear State and only West Germany has, under the Paris Treaty of 23 October 1954, given up the right to manufacture nuclear weapons. The French government has stated that the creation of Euratom cannot vary the obligations taken on by West Germany.[64] Protests against discrimination could be damning. As far back as 1956, Herr Strauss remarked about Euratom: "if some countries keep the right to manufacture weapons, to the exclusion of others, control will be illusory or unfair".[65]

Let us recall that the 1954 Paris Treaty which set up WEU, established as a counter-weight to the obligations assumed by West Germany, a system of balances between the contracting Parties and an Arms Control Agency that has never really come into operation. The 1957 Convention authorising this Agency to carry out inspections is not in force. Control depends upon the will of member States. Contrary to expectations, neither the West German undertaking not to manufacture nuclear weapons, nor French atomic armament, have been supervised.[66] So this limited regional body has shown its powerlessness as well as a tendency towards discrimination.

[64] Fischer, *Annuaire français de droit international*, 1956, p. 702.
[65] *L'Information*, 27 July 1956. Such attitudes have caused some to observe: "it is hardly surprising that it is now widely suspected that the real German aim is to keep open a nuclear option that the (Non-Proliferation) treaty would close". *The Economist*, 30 December 1967, p. 1276.
[66] R. Fletcher in W. Young (ed.), *Existing Mechanisms of Arms Control* (Oxford, Pergamon Press, 1966), pp. 1–9; A. Imbert, *L'Union de L'Europe occidentale* (Paris, Librairie Générale de Droit et de Jurisprudence), 1968, pp. 62–77.

Whatever the cause, the general protest inside Euratom against international control was all the less understandable because, as a Dutch Deputy pointed out, Euratom's main purpose was not control, but research, which was supposed to be carried out in collaboration with Great Britain. Looking at the problem in this way, nothing in the Non-Proliferation Treaty can restrict the role that the Community is called upon to play.[67]

At present, it must be admitted, Euratom is sick, and France finds in the Community more hurdles to cross than fields for action. The Supply Agency, one of Euratom's key organisations, has proved an embarrassment in a situation where there is no longer a lack of funds. Differences in technological development among the Six in their economic and industrial policy, in their concept of relations with other nations, have prevented the creation of a real community of interests.[68]

It appears, therefore, that to a great extent, the argument used by Euratom supporters against the Agency and its control is only a pretext, an ulterior motive. In the European Parliament debate on 18 October 1967, quoted previously, M. de La Malène after having recalled that Articles I and II of the draft Treaty threatened the M.L.F., the structure of the military organisation of NATO, and the European atomic force, said: "Europe must not provide a sort of alibi for this Non-Proliferation Treaty. The questions raised by the Non-Proliferation Treaty in Articles I and II are of course fundamental, key issues; as for problems relating to control and to compatibility of this Treaty with the nuclear Common Market over industrial non-discrimination, although these are very important questions relating to European progress, they are only relatively secondary matters. These secondary questions, therefore, ought not to take precedence over fundamental questions and obscure them".

In accordance with Article III of the Treaty, the Agency must have a real role to play[69] and it would not be possible for a State to adhere to the

[67] *Parle. Europ.*, *Débats*, XI, 67, No. 95, 18 October 1967, pp. 60–62 (Burger).
[68] Goldschmidt, op. cit., pp. 281–83.
[69] Here is the American Co-Chairman's interpretative statement about this: "1. All non-nuclear weapon States must have such safeguards as inspire confidence by all Parties in their efficacy. Consequently, the safeguards established under an agreement negotiated and concluded with the IAEA, in conformity with the IAEA Statute and the Agency's safeguard system, must allow the IAEA to fulfil its responsibility – which is to supply reassurances that no diversion has taken place.
"2. By carrying out their duties under Article III, non-nuclear weapon parties may negotiate separate safeguard agreements with the IAEA or with other parties, and, more particularly, an agreement laying down such duties may be made between the IAEA and another international organisation whose

Treaty with the reservation that it would only conform to Euratom's control.[70] Perhaps the United States-Euratom agreement of 1958 could provide the basis for a solution to the problem of the adjustment of Euratom's controls to those of the Agency.

It had been understood by the five non-nuclear members of Euratom that negotiations between the European Communities Commission and the IAEA would only begin when everyone had signed, a stage that has now been reached. Also each of the five made a statement when signing making ratification conditional upon the conclusion of an agreement corresponding to Article III of the Treaty between Euratom and the IAEA. As far back as 1967 the five countries concerned imposed several conditions upon the future Treaty, namely: controls would be exercised only over the use of nuclear material, not over installations as such; adhesion to the Treaty ought to be conditional upon the conclusion of satisfactory agreements between Euratom and the Agency; these agreements ought to provide not for direct control by the Agency, but verification of Euratom Control methods; until the conclusion of this agreement, the supply of nuclear material to Euratom ought to be guaranteed; and no clause should provide for the automatic application of the Agency's safeguards (if the agreement could not be concluded between Euratom and the Agency within a fixed period) or threaten Euratom's exclusive jurisdiction over the inspection system.[71]

This is the moment to quote an official State Department statement: "if a non-nuclear weapon country, including a non-nuclear member of Euratom, does not sign the NPT, the Treaty would not prevent the transfer of nuclear material or equipment to that country if the nuclear material or that used or produced in such equipment, were made subject to the safeguards required by Article III. If a non-nuclear weapon country, whether signatory or not, does not conclude a safeguards agreement with the IAEA, we would of course, feel obliged to review the situation in the light of the existing circumstances."[71a]

---

work is connected with that of the IAEA and whose membership includes the interested parties.

"3. In order to avoid any unnecessary overlapping, the IAEA ought to use in an appropriate way existing data and safeguards, on condition that under such mutually acceptable agreements the IAEA may ensure that no nuclear materials are diverted for the manufacture of nuclear weapons or other explosive nuclear devices." ENDC/PV. 357.

[70] *Hearings 1968*, pp. 106–7.
[71] *Hearings 1969*, pp. 308, 310, 468–69.
[71a] *Hearings 1969*, p. 489.

An interesting precedent was created by the agreement dated 4 March 1970 between the United Kingdom, W. Germany and the Netherlands on collaboration in the development and exploitation of the Gas Centrifuge Process for producing enriched uranium. This is a document which binds two non-nuclear States, both members of Euratom, and a nuclear State that is not a member. The safeguards provided for are those of Euratom, certain control methods established by the United Kingdom government, and those which might result from an agreement, or agreements concluded by one of the Parties with the IAEA.[71b]

IV. THE SCOPE OF SAFEGUARDS

1. Arms Control

Article III (1) lays down that the only purpose of safeguards is the "verification of the fulfilment of obligations assumed (by a non-nuclear Party) under this Treaty with a view to preventing diversion of nuclear energy from peaceful uses to nuclear weapons or other nuclear explosive devices".

This text raises one problem among others, that had already been raised by the United States in relation to the Treaty for the denuclearisation of Latin America. The IAEA, like Euratom, applies safeguards aimed at detecting diversions of nuclear material from peaceful to military use. A different sort of safeguard would be that sanctioned by Article III under which non-nuclear States Party to the Treaty undertake to refuse to accept nuclear weapons or other explosive nuclear devices. New methods ought to be applied to determine if nuclear weapons have been brought into the Territory of a State bound by the Treaty;[72] but it does not look as if the authors of the Treaty thought of this, or felt the risk to be sufficiently serious. After the adoption of the Treaty, the American negotiators explained that Article III applied to declared installations and factories and it was not aimed at detecting anything clandestine.[73]

However, Romania had proposed an amendment to Article III under which there would have been special control over military applications, as distinct from the Agency's control. The Romanian amendment provided for the establishment, through the offices of the Security Council, of controls "which would be such as to ensure that non-nuclear weapon States, Parties to the Treaty, on whose territory there are foreign military

---

[71b] See note 27(b) of this chapter.
[72] See the text of the note dated 29 August 1966 from the United States Ambassador in Mexico, A. G. Robles, *The Denuclearisation of Latin America* (Carnegie Endowment for International Peace, 1967), p. 152.
[73] *Hearings 1968*, p. 52. See also note 1 of this chapter.

bases will not gain access, in any form whatsoever to nuclear weapons by means of these bases".[74] This proposal was in fact a restatement of a problem that the Soviet Union had stressed at the beginning of negotiations when she was trying to prevent West Germany having access to nuclear weapons. At that time the Americans and the Russians clashed, the former defending non-proliferation, the latter opposing access to nuclear weapons.[75] It is interesting to observe that the Romanians returned to this question at a period when the Soviet Union had already been losing interest in it for some time.

2. General Machinery

Without going into detail, it would be useful to make some general observations about the Agency's safeguards system. It works in the same way as the Euratom system: both derive from American control practice exercised through bilateral Treaties.[76] The system includes the examination of plans of all nuclear installations or processing factories.[77] In certain cases, if the Board of Governors expressly decides, the Agency may ask a State to stop building or using a nuclear installation to which safeguards apply.[78] It is worth remarking that on this point the American Atomic Energy Commission has greater powers in its own sphere of jurisdiction; it can demand the modification of the plans in question.[79] In accordance with an accounting plan approved by the Agency, the State under safeguards must keep accounts including inventories of nuclear materials and summaries of operations at installations. The Agency examines these accounts. Under a system drawn up jointly with the Agency, the State has to supply regular reports and special reports. The Agency can ask for extra information. It carries out regular inspections and special inspections.

The IAEA safeguards apply also to materials used and also produced within the framework of the programme placed under safeguards. Under certain conditions, the Agency approves procedures used for the chemical treatment of radioactive elements. Finally, it can demand the storage under its control, of special fissile materials recovered or obtained as by-products, in excess of the immediate needs of the State.

[74] ENDC/223/Rev. 1 and END/PV. 376.
[75] *Hearings 1966*, pp. 42–43.   [76] Rosen, op. cit.
[77] INFCIRC/66/Rev. 1, para. 30–32. See also P. C. Szasz, "The Law of IAEA Safeguards", *Revue belge de droit international*, 1967, pp. 196–240; M. Willrich, "Safeguarding Atoms for Peace", *American Journal of International Law*, 1966, pp. 34–54. See also Art. 12 of the IAEA Statute.
[78] INFCIRC/66/Rev. 1, para. 11.
[79] *Nuclear Industry*, February 1968, pp. 33, 42.

The fact that the Agency, in contrast to what happens in theory in Euratom, does not own the materials it controls, does not change much in practice. Control norms are set, in the case of the Agency, by its Statute, by the rules adopted by the Board of Governors, and by agreements concluded with each of the interested States. Within Euratom there are no agreements and the control system is operated through the Rome Treaty and the decisions of the appropriate bodies.

On the other hand, the field covered by controls differs according to organisations. The European Nuclear Energy Agency only controls common undertakings, and member countries' installations using fissile materials produced in such undertakings.[80] Euratom control covers everything, its only limit being the territory of member States. However, materials and installations used for defence remain outside its scope as well as materials in military establishments.[81] The IAEA exercises its control over: (a) products, installations and services supplied by the Agency; (b) at the request of Parties, products, installations and services supplied under a bilateral or multilateral agreement; (c) at the request of a State, such or such nuclear activity of that State.[82] Besides, as we shall see later, the Treaty on the Denuclearisation of Latin America gives the Agency the task of disarmament supervisor. Poland, Czechoslovakia, Hungary, Bulgaria and the German Democratic Republic suggested, with the same end in view, that they place all their installations under Agency control if West Germany did the same. This she has refused to do up to now.[83]

It would be possible, by going into detail, to establish other differences between the Euratom control system and the Agency's.[84] Here are some. Euratom deals directly with individuals and companies (Art. 78 of the Euratom Treaty) whilst the Agency only deals with governments. Inspectors' rights are wider in the Agency system (Art. XII, A, 6 and B) than in Euratom's (Art. 82). It seems that the Agency's inspectors may, in certain cases, make snap inspections which is not the case for Euratom's inspectors. Euratom has a system of sanctions which does not exist within the Agency. Lastly, Euratom's control is only effective within the frontiers of the Community (Art. 77 and 79), whilst that of the Agency is exercised also over transfers outside the territory of States subject to safeguards. (INFCIRC/66/Rev.1). It is, therefore, clear that the Euratom system

[80] Huet, *Annuaire français de droit international*, 1958, p. 516.
[81] J. van Helmont, in Young (ed.), op. cit., pp. 23–36.
[82] Cf. Art. 3 of the Agency Statute and J. E. Hall, in Young (ed.), op. cit., pp. 49–65.
[83] GC(X)/OR. 103, 104; GC(XI)/OR. 112, 113, 114, 116.
[84] A detailed picture of these differences has been drawn up by the American Atomic Energy Commission. *Hearings 1968*, pp. 266–76.

CARL A. RUDISILL LIBRARY
LENOIR RHYNE COLLEGE

would have to be modified to a certain extent to be compatible with the Agency's system.

Under the Non-Proliferation Treaty, the Agency is to have extensive control over the nuclear activities of non-nuclear weapon States Party to the Treaty.[85] Control will be less extensive over non-nuclear States not adhering to the Treaty; in this case it will cover source materials or fissile products that such a State obtains from a Party to the Treaty, or materials and products, treated or used or manufactured with equipment or from materials transferred to it by a State Party.

Let us notice also that the Treaty imposes no safeguards upon the provision of technical assistance and know-how.

3. Controversial Problems

The extent of the safeguards system has aroused much criticism in Geneva as well as at the UN General Assembly. Industrial espionage has been mentioned, commercial discrimination, and impediments to the proper running of undertakings. A Swiss *aide-mémoire* shows this preoccupation, but in a very attenuated form: "Safeguards ought to be limited to the flow of source and special fissile materials, as moreover paragraph 5 of the preamble specifies. They ought not to supersede their aim, which is to prevent these products being used for the manufacture of weapons. In consequence of this, a precise definition is needed of what may be put under control, in conformity with the rules of the IAEA of December 1965."

It is evident that such a precise definition cannot be included in a Non-Proliferation Treaty. The Romanians for their part proposed amendments which would in essence have safeguarded only the quantity and quality

---

[85] According to Art. III (1), safeguards will apply to all source or special fissionable material "whether it is being produced, processed or used in any principal nuclear facility or is outside any such facility". According to the IAEA, a principal nuclear facility means "a reactor, a factory for processing nuclear materials exposed to radiation in a reactor, a factory for separating isotopes from a nuclear material, a factory for processing or manufacturing nuclear materials (except mines and ore-extraction factories) or a facility or factory of any other type which could be designated as such from time to time by the Board, including adjacent storage facilities". INFCIRC/66/Rev. 1, para. 78. The text of Art. III (1) of the NPT states that safeguards apply to source material and fissile products, wherever they are situated. It will be noticed that these expressions are nowhere defined by the Treaty. They ought to be, on the basis of the definitions given in the IAEA Statute since Art. III refers to it constantly. *Hearings 1968*, pp. 64–66. Thus the expression "source material" refers basically to uranium containing the same isotope mixture as found in nature, to uranium whose U-235 content is below normal, and to Thorium. See the definition in Art. XX of the IAEA Statute.

of source and fissile materials capable of enabling the production of nuclear weapons or other explosive nuclear devices.[86]

In addition South Africa was concerned about controls which might be exercised over uranium mines and ore-processing factories.[87]

In order to weigh up these criticisms, it is necessary to observe that Article III (3) says that the required safeguards must satisfy the provisions of Article IV which is intended to promote international co-operation in the field of peaceful uses. Article XII of the Agency Statute states several times that safeguards are intended to prevent materials, products and installations from being used for military purposes. The safeguards system was "developed so as to avoid hindering the economic and techno-logical advance of States."[88]

As far as the problem raised by South Africa is concerned, the following interpretation seems correct to the author. In accordance with IAEA practice, safeguards do not apply to mines, ore-processing factories and uranium ore. Safeguards begin to be applied at the stage of refined concentrates produced by ore-processing factories. Nuclear materials containing uranium ore or unrefined ore concentrates are subject to safe-guards when they are exported by one Party to the Treaty to any other non-nuclear State, but only for the purpose of controlling the use of materials derived from these ores or concentrates. The provisions of Article III (2) also apply to equipment supplied by one Party to a non-nuclear State even using uranium coming exclusively from domestic sources.[89]

Moreover, the rules of the Agency's safeguards are sufficiently flexible and enable certain materials to be exempted from safeguards altogether

[86] ENDC/223/Rev. 1.
[87] A/C1/1571 and 1579.
[88] INFCIRC/66/Rev. 1, para. 9.
[89] A/C. 1/PV. 1573 (Canada); PV. 1577 (United States): *Hearings 1968*, p. 115. An interesting discussion took place at the Board of Governors of the IAEA meeting on 13 June 1968, on the occasion of the examination of the text of the agreement between the IAEA and Mexico about the application of safeguards in the framework of the Treaty forbidding nuclear weapons in Latin America. According to Art. I (i) of this agreement, "by nuclear materials are meant any source or special fissile material defined in Art. XX of the Statute, with the exception of source materials in the form of ores". Although it was understood that this agreement could not serve as a precedent, and although the Mexican delegate specified that the text was in accordance with the common practice of the Agency whose jurisdiction did not extend to unexcavated uranium ore and whose safeguards did not apply to unrefined ores or concentrates, some delegates expressed anxiety about a text which put ores into the same category as source materials in the sense of Art. XX of the Statute. However, the text remained unaltered at the request of both the Soviet and American representatives. GOV/OR. 403.

because of their small quantity or unconcentrated state.[90] Safeguards can be suspended when it is a question of research and development.[91] Inspectors sent to a State are chosen in consultation with it. "The number, length, and severity of actual inspections are reduced to the necessary minimum . . . "[92] The actual frequency of inspections of a reactor takes into account the nature and quantity of nuclear material produced by or used in the reactor.[93] Ordinary inspections are carried out with one week's notice and special inspections with twenty-four hours notice. The Agency has an instant right of access to certain important facilities. In such cases, it can, to the extent this is necessary for the proper application of safeguards, dispense with notice. But the details of how they are to be applied are fixed by the safeguard agreement.[94] So the system is indeed flexible; as we have seen, the principles are set out in the Agency Statute, developed and defined in the rules adopted by the Board of Governors, and applied in fact through safeguards agreements.

Criticism of inspection arrangements often appears irrelevant. Mr Goldschmidt, for example, protests at the possibility of an inspection being carried out by subjects of East European countries which refuse to accept controls.[95] Now all non-nuclear Eastern States will be Party to the Treaty. In addition a State may refuse to accept an inspector sent by the Agency. According to a German expert, controls do not entail a risk of industrial espionage; West Germany would simply have her inspection carried out by a Norwegian.[96] Only countries with advanced nuclear technology could really take advantage of information obtained by their

[90] INFCIRC/66/Rev. 1, para. 21–22. When the Agency Statute was drawn up, it was officially admitted that source materials would be subject to less strict control than fissile materials. IAEA/CS/OR38. See also Art. XI F-4(b).

[91] ibid., para. 24, 57, 59, 60.

[92] ibid., para. 47. It is not without interest to quote here a comment of the US Atomic Energy Commission: "The variety of nationalities represented among the IAEA's inspectors permit the Director-General to designate inspectors for a particular State, which (sic) will not be unacceptable, while avoiding a situation where a State accepts only inspectors of friendly nationalities". *Hearings 1969*, p. 505.

[93] INFCIRC/66/Rev. 1, para. 58.

[94] ibid., para. 50 and 57 and Szasz, op. cit.

[95] Goldschmidt, op. cit., p. 289. Years ago, in the French Parliament, supporters of Euratom expressed anxiety about the Agency's international control "which might be carried out by Egyptian or Chinese delegates". Fischer, *Annuaire français du droit international*, 1956, pp. 704–705. This is pure racial discrimination, although no one dared to say so.

[96] H. Mandel, *Der Spiegel*, 8 April 1968, p. 29. The American reactor Yankee is inspected by a Japanese, a Swede, and a Yugoslav. Simsarian, op. cit. Espionage has no need of inspections, as was shown by a recent espionage case in which East Germany was alleged to have obtained secrets of the Gas Centrifuge process. *The Observer*, 8 March 1970.

citizens working as inspectors, and these countries are not very numerous.

Also, according to Herr von Weizsäcker, it is impossible to accept controls over the super-regenerative reactor as the Americans would learn all the secrets.[97] Another German expert who also asks for international controls to be restricted, feels that his country ought to obtain a guarantee from the United States over deliveries of nuclear fuel.[98] West Germany, whose atomic industry basically depends on the United States, ought to be reassured by the previously quoted American statement accepting Agency supervision of peaceful nuclear installations.

The giving away of secrets by the Agency is really all the more difficult in that States are only bound to give very fragmentary information about plans for nuclear installations. The obligation is still less strict over construction materials.[99] It has been said that inspectors will not in practice have access to any information that is commercially useful.[100]

In any case the Agency takes all necessary steps to protect commercial and industrial secrets. No secrets of this kind, and no other confidential information of which members of the staff might have knowledge through the application of safeguards may be revealed, except to the Director-General and officials authorised by him.[101] These arrangements might perhaps be improved by stipulating that inspectors, after leaving the service of the Agency, may not accept a post in nuclear industry for a fixed period after their departure and that the Agency would be financially responsible if a member of its staff revealed commercial or industrial information he had obtained through the application of safeguards.

In any case, as Sir John Cockroft showed before his death, industrial or commercial secrets only exist at the "research and development" stage, not at that of power-producing reactors.[102] Now it is at this first stage that controls, if not non-existent, are, to say the least, weak. Even in other cases they are hardly an encumbrance. The Agency's safeguards system, applied to the Bradwell (UK) and Yankee (USA) reactors have caused no more difficulty for the smooth running of these installations than inspections under the Factories Act.[103]

Also, we know that control methods are not inflexible. As they become

[97] *Survival*, May 1967, pp. 146–49.
[98] ibid., pp. 144–46.
[99] *Nuclear Industry*, November 1967, pp. 15–17.
[100] *Hearings 1968*, p. 100; *Hearings 1969*, p. 504.
[101] Let us note that the American Atomic Energy Commission makes public the accounting for materials of undertakings it controls. *Nuclear Industry*, February 1968, pp. 33, 42.
[102] *Survival*, November 1967, pp. 349–51.
[103] ibid., *Hearings 1969*, p. 503.

perfected and more sophisticated, they will become less all-embracing and will be concentrated above all at the fuel extraction and treatment stage.[104]

It appears that the Safeguards system does give a reasonable degree of security. Great Britain put the treatment factory at Windscale under safeguards, and experience has shown that without causing any interruption to work, using very flexible methods, the margin of error using the system was equal to 2 per cent of the plant's production.

Several ways of getting round safeguards have been envisaged. A country could always manufacture the envelope and detonator of the bomb and insert fissile materials taken from a reactor at the last moment. But it is questionable whether one solution suggested, that is to say the internationalisation of isotope separation plants and plutonium factories, or the buying in by the Agency of all surplus fissile materials would be practical or useful.[105] Another proposal was for the drawing up of an international list of scientific and technical staff from all countries. Any interruption in freedom of movement, identification, or freedom of expression and communication of these persons would be considered cause for suspicion.[106] The same author also proposed that international organisations, through radio and television, should call on citizens in each country to denounce violations of disarmament agreements.[107]

A study of such proposals is by no means useless even when they appear Utopian. But it is as well to notice that a control system, in order to work properly, needs a minimum of confidence, and that it can rarely guarantee absolute security.[108] As a great Indian expert, H. J. Bhabha, said, minor violations do not count: after all no police force can prevent a madman from committing a murder.[109]

What steps are envisaged then in case of violation of the ban? Article X (1) of the Non-Proliferation Treaty gives all Parties, in certain conditions, the right to withdraw by giving notice in advance to other Parties and to the Security Council. Besides, International Law in general allows a Party to take certain steps as a consequence of the violation of the Treaty

---

[104] ibid.; B. T. Feld, *Bulletin of Atomic Scientists*, December 1964, pp. 3–6; M. Kalstein, ibid., pp. 18–19; Smyth, *Department of State Bulletin*, 3 January 1966, pp. 28–36.

[105] L. Beaton, *Foreign Affairs*, July 1967, pp. 662–69; G. H. Quester, *Bulletin of Atomic Scientists*, November 1967, pp. 35–37.

[106] K. Deutsch, in Q. Wright (ed.), *Preventing World War III* (New York, Simon and Schuster, 1962), p. 68.

[107] *Journal of Conflict Resolution*, September 1963, pp. 360–69.

[108] R. A. Falk and R. J. Barnet, *Security in Disarmament* (Princeton University Press, 1965), pp. 15–49.

[109] *Disarmament and Arms Control*, Autumn 1964, pp. 434–40.

by another Party. We shall consider this matter in another chapter.

It suffices to note here that the Treaty contains no sanctions.[110] However, the IAEA has its own system under Article XII of its Statute, whose relevant provisions could be incorporated in each safeguards agreement concluded under the Non-Proliferation Treaty. The Director of the Agency brings to the knowledge of the Board of Governors violations observed by the inspection staff. The Board is immediately bound to inform the UN General Assembly and the Security Council of the violation. This measure was doubtless planned to put immediate pressure upon the violating State. The simultaneous jurisdiction of the Assembly and the Council enables the following possibilities to be envisaged, if the violation is considered an act falling under Chapters VI and VII of the Charter: (a) the Security Council could declare its competence to deal with the matter and in this case the provisions of Article 12 (1) of the Charter would be applied; (b) the Security Council, for one reason or another would wash its hands of the matter in which case the Assembly would recover its jurisdiction; (c) the Security Council would not reach any decision and in this case the provisions of Resolution 377 (v) could be put into operation. Let us note that the Security Council is not limited to using the specific powers granted to it by Chapters VI, VII, VIII and XII of the Charter, but that Article 24 confers implicit, general powers of exercising its responsibilities.

The Board of Governors may also bring the violation to the notice of all members of the Agency, call upon the State at fault to stop its violation, and may reduce or withdraw aid granted by the Agency or by a member and demand the return of materials or products supplied.[111] Let us mention once more that agreements concluded by the Agency envisage the obligatory jurisdiction of an arbitration Tribunal in case of dispute,[112] a provision that could be repeated in agreements concluded under Article III of the Non-Proliferation Treaty.

[110] *Hearings 1968*, p. 52.
[111] Euratom is also enabled to put a guilty undertaking under the administration of a person or group of people appointed jointly by the Commission and the interested State (Art. 83 of the Euratom Treaty). The Agency has no comparable powers.
[112] See for example Art. VII of the Safeguards Transfer Agreement United States–South Africa-Agency, 26 July 1967, INFCIRC/98.

6. PEACEFUL USES OF NUCLEAR ENERGY

THIS problem has been the subject of long debates which have been devoted mainly to the use of nuclear explosives in civil engineering.

I. PEACEFUL COLLABORATION IN GENERAL

The drawing up of the Treaty was marked by the growing revolt of small- and medium-sized Powers who demanded, sometimes a little too insistently, the application of the principle of the equality of States. They forgot that this was a field where equality in the abstract had no place and where, as the Canadian delegate remarked, "a Non-Proliferation Treaty, in its very essence must be discriminatory to a certain degree."[1] But this wisdom was hardly shared by the majority of States, who thought it was the right moment to get rewards and promises for the future from nuclear States. According to Signor Fanfani, accession to the Treaty ought to be encouraged by giving non-nuclear States "an appreciable moral and material reward for giving up nuclear weapons."[2] For his part, the Romanian delegate repeated the statement made by Mr Nicolae Ceausescu on 24 July 1967: "The non-dissemination of nuclear weapons must lead to the end of the division of the world into nuclear and non-nuclear countries, to a strengthening of equality between States and to a real lessening of the danger of war."[3]

So the non-nuclear countries asked for compensation which might benefit them directly, particularly in the form of increased collaboration in the field of peaceful uses of atomic energy.

However, the problem is not well stated in this form. For it is not the giving up of atomic weapons which is an obstacle to progress in nuclear industry. On this, the Canadian representative once more quoted the example of his country whose scientific and technological capacity has in no way been affected by the absence of a nuclear weapons industry.[4] It is underdevelopment that prevents atomic industry starting up in the countries of the Third World. These countries have tried to use the drafting of the Non-Proliferation Treaty as a means of putting pressure on developed countries to get more substantial aid from them. Too often

[1] ENDC/PV. 319.
[3] ENDC/PV. 320

[2] ENDC/PV. 318.
[4] A/C. 1/PV. 1573.

they are obsessed by the mirage of advanced technology and neglect more traditional and well-tried methods. Now it is well known that nuclear energy, even in developed countries, has only recently become competitive with energy from traditional sources. Also, as has been recalled, only large units are economically and financially viable, which makes them of less interest to backward countries. Besides, nuclear installations require numerous technicians and specialists, continual safety and security measures, storage facilities, etc., all matters which create more problems in developing than in industrialised countries.

It is none the less true, however, that the communication and diffusion of modern technology are becoming more and more tangible factors in contemporary international life. This evolution is reflected in the changes the text of the Treaty underwent during its drafting. The American and Russian drafts of 1965 and 1966, contained no provisions about the peaceful use of nuclear energy. The preamble and Article IV of the draft of 24 August 1967 stipulate the inalienable right of all Parties to develop the research, production and use of atomic energy for peaceful uses without discrimination and in conformity with Articles I and II. The signatory States also have the right to participate in the fullest possible exchange of information in this field.

Several non-nuclear States tried to strengthen these provisions by introducing a legal obligation. According to one amendment by Nigeria, each Party would undertake to co-operate, directly or through the IAEA, in good faith and to the extent of its technological and/or material resources, with any other State or group of States Party to the Treaty, in the development and progress of nuclear technology as well as in the broadest possible exchange of scientific and technical information about the peaceful uses of nuclear energy.[5] The Mexican delegation had also tabled an amendment of the same kind, creating a similar obligation for Parties able to take it on, in accordance with their means. As the Mexican delegate showed, the obligation would have had real legal force "although it would be an imperfect generalised obligation whose meaning would depend in practice in the end upon the will of the nuclear weapon Powers. What matters at the present moment is to gain recognition of the principle of this obligation. The expression 'in accordance with their means' refers not only to financial and technical possibilities but also to legal capacity, given the fact that much of this information is protected by patents which are private property."[6]

In any case, legally speaking, this was an attempt to gain recognition of

[5] ENDC/202.   [6] ENDC/PV. 331.

a new principle according to which economic, technological or social power brings with it the duty, in international society, to use it for the benefit of the weakest who are prepared to respect certain norms (by accession to the Non-Proliferation Treaty). This principle was incorporated in more precise form in Article IV of the draft of 18 January 1968. This is the new addition which owes its origin to the Mexican amendment: "Parties to the Treaty in a position to do so shall also co-operate in contributing alone or together with other States or international organisations, to the further development of the application of nuclear energy for peaceful purposes especially in the territories of non-nuclear weapon States Party to the Treaty."

But this form of words still far from satisfied the developing countries. Nigeria expressed the opinion of some of them by claiming that Article IV only confirmed an evident right already in existence, when it proclaimed the right to participate in an exchange of information. Nigeria asked for a dialogue not a monologue, and said that what ought to be asked of the Treaty "was not the listing once more of each of the sovereign rights of States but the definite promise that States banned by the Treaty from carrying on certain activities" would obtain advantages that would not make the sacrifice to which they had consented too burdensome.[7] As can be seen this delegate has a point of view that has been criticised here. Yet, in accordance with the amendment he had tabled,[8] the Co-Chairmen did agree to modify Article IV (2) which now says the Parties "undertake to facilitate" the exchange of products and information. The new wording introduces an idea of obligation but its scope remains somewhat vague. Mexico unsuccessfully proposed a formula under which all Parties to the Treaty would have had a right of access to scientific and technological information.[9]

The first sentence in Article IV (2) when it mentions exchange of information also applies to information about peaceful applications of nuclear explosions. That at least is the interpretation given by the American Co-Chairman.[10]

On behalf of Italy, Signor Fanfani had proposed the conclusion of an agreement, perhaps outside the Treaty, under which (a) nuclear Powers would from time to time transfer to non-nuclear States, for peaceful purposes, a quantity, to be determined, of fissile materials produced by them; (b) these materials would be sold at a reduced price, part of which would be paid to the United Nations Development Fund; (c) the transfer of materials would be controlled, in accordance with the Non-Proliferation

[7] ENDC/PV. 371.   [8] ENDC/220/Rev. 1.
[9] A/C. 1/PV. 1569.   [10] ENDC/PV. 378.

Treaty.[11] This system would reduce the amount of fissile material available for military use in nuclear States. On the other hand, the system proposed under (b) would satisfy certain demands of non-nuclear States, for the Non-Proliferation agreement to accelerate progress in developing countries towards harnessing atomic energy for peaceful purposes and to facilitate the transfer to these countries of resources made available by disarmament measures. One of the Brazilian amendments tried to incorporate this principle into the Treaty in the form of a legal undertaking by the nuclear States.[12]

Italy later tabled another amendment in these terms: "Nothing in the present Treaty may be interpreted as threatening the inalienable right of all Parties to the supply of source and special fissile materials or equipment intended to be used in connection with source and special fissile materials for peaceful purposes".[13] The Italian delegate wanted in this way to get appropriate guarantees of equal access to source materials and fissile products, without any hindrance due to discrimination or monopoly. Italy, which has no uranium deposits, felt that Article IV "represents a rough attempt to codify a new Rights of Man . . . To the right to technological information, which may be considered a spiritual victory of our time, must be added the right to nuclear supplies whose material complement this is".[14] The Italian amendment was not accepted and the American Co-Chairman said that in his opinion the second paragraph of Article IV corresponded to the meaning of this amendment, which is far from being evident.[15]

According to the Soviet delegate, Article IV means "that States which have arrived at the highest stage of development in the use of atomic energy for peaceful purposes, and in first place, nuclear weapon Powers, will contribute to the development of peaceful atomic activities of countries without nuclear weapons.[16]

Two questions may be asked about this. Firstly, Article IV at the end,

[11] ENDC/205, and ENDC/PV. 318.   [12] ENDC/201/Rev. 1.
[13] ENDC/18/Corr. 1.   [14] ENDC/PV. 367.
[15] ENDC/PV. 378, also 367, 371 and 379.
[16] ENDC/PV. 366. The comments of the American Atomic Energy Commission are extremely prudent. "We will not, however, interpret Article IV as meaning that the US will be compelled to embark on any costly new programs or as obliging the US to meet all requests and demands. Neither do we construe Article IV as overriding the provisions of the US Atomic Energy Act, nor will it remove the discretion we have in determining the nature of our co-operative relationships with other countries, on a case by case basis. The words 'fullest possible exchange' in Article IV clearly imply that the Parties will be expected to co-operate only to the extent that they are able to do so and that reciprocity may well be a factor in determining what is possible in certain circumstances." *Hearings 1969*, p. 498.

puts "developing regions of the world" in a privileged position. Does the mention in this passage of regions instead of countries mean that the Co-Chairmen have finally understood that development, and in particular the development of nuclear industry, cannot take place within the frontiers of backward countries but only on the scale of large enough groups? One can only ask the question in the hope of an affirmative reply.

Secondly, is the benefit of the provisions of Article IV reserved only for Parties to the Treaty? It does not seem likely, as is proved by the use of the term "alone" in the second sentence in paragraph 2. Several delegates insisted strongly on this interpretation; in their opinion, as far as the advantages provided in Article IV were concerned, there ought to be no discrimination, in comparison with States Party to the Treaty, against non-acceding countries, on the one condition that the latter should conform to Article III and submit to the control procedure laid down in this Article.[17] What States do in practice, will perhaps not correspond entirely with this way of thinking. It is interesting to remember that when the Agency Statute was being drawn up, India had unsuccessfully proposed that IAEA assistance be limited to States which did not manufacture nuclear weapons.[18]

Government officials and the American Atomic Energy Commission have said the Treaty in no way prevented acceding States from co-operation in the field of peaceful uses with non-member States on condition that the latter observe the obligations imposed on them under Article III (2) of the Treaty. However, "we also believe that it may be possible for us to provide some special advantages in terms of our co-operation to those non-nuclear weapon nations that adhere to the Treaty".[18a] The Soviet Union for its part, defined "the conditions under which uranium belonging to States Party to the Non-Proliferation Treaty may be enriched in the USSR." (To the extent necessary for nuclear power stations producing electricity.)[18b]

In any case, if greater international co-operation is desired in the nuclear field, the role of the IAEA ought to be reinforced. Nigeria had proposed that each Party address to the Agency an annual report on the nature, extent and result of its co-operation with other Parties in the peaceful use of nuclear energy. The American Co-Chairman thought that Article IV implied exactly this,[19] a doubtful proposition. It seems to us it would be better to go further. The IAEA ought to appoint a permanent committee of

[17] ENDC/PV. 373 (Sweden); A/C. 1/PV. 1561 (Netherlands).
[18] Fischer, *Indian Yearbook of International Affairs*, 1957, p. 124.
[18a] *Hearings 1969*, pp. 498, 362–63, 372, 425.
[18b] GC (XIII)/OR. 129, para. 63.
[19] ENDC/202; ENDC/PV. 371 and 378,

independent experts on long term contract who would be forbidden at the end of their contract, or if it were cancelled, to take up employment in private nuclear industry. These experts would have free access to information about the peaceful use of atomic energy and would publish a report each year which by using all available information would enable all aspects of international collaboration to be made public, as well as the means used, possible tendencies towards discrimination, monopoly, or unfair competition. The Committee would present concrete proposals at the end of its annual report.

In the meantime, in accordance with a resolution of the Conference of Non-Nuclear States, repeated by Resolution 2456A (XXIII) of the General Assembly, the Secretary-General of the United Nations nominated a group of experts whose report was published in July 1969. These experts showed the advantages of the development of nuclear energy. They insisted on the difficulties relating to finance and investments, deplored the difficult financial situation of the IAEA, hoped that international credit organisations, particularly the IBRD would reconsider their attitudes over criteria and conditions for financing large nuclear installations, taking into account "not only the immediate profits which will flow from the first projects but also the long term contributions that such projects can bring to developing countries."[19a]

II. NUCLEAR EXPLOSIONS

The problem of nuclear explosions was one that raised the keenest controversies. Article V which deals with the matter, underwent numerous modifications, even during the General Assembly debate.

What is the problem? We are once again faced with a specialised technology, which unlike power reactors is still at a completely experimental stage. Nuclear explosive devices may be used in excavation and digging (canals, tunnels, etc.) as well as in the extraction of raw materials (gas, petroleum, and mineral ores).

A recent study shows that for excavation and digging and in particular digging a new Panama Canal, the use of nuclear devices involves risks and unknown factors without giving positive advantages of economic viability.[20]

As far as the development of natural resources is concerned the United States has communicated a first report on their "Gasbuggy" project. The aim of this was to obtain information on the use of nuclear explosives for the extraction of natural gas. The first results, although encouraging, are

[19a] A/7568, para. 258–62.
[20] D. R. Inglis and C. L. Sander, *Bulletin of Atomic Scientists*, December 1967, pp. 46–53.

far from being conclusive and the final results will only be available later.[21]

1. Previous history and drafting of the Treaty

The problem of nuclear explosions had already arisen in the past. Originally, and in 1949 in particular, the Russians refused to consider nuclear explosions carried out for civil engineering purposes as being in the same category as nuclear weapons.[22] In December 1958, during the Test Ban negotiations, the Soviet Union insisted that if the future Treaty were to allow peaceful tests, she could carry out as many by herself as the two Western Powers together. (This would have given her an effective right of veto over the West's peaceful tests.) In addition Moscow asked that each of the nuclear States should carry out a complete examination of the internal and external components of the device used by the other State during tests. This demand seemed unacceptable to the West.[23]

One of the two American drafts of 27 August 1962, the one which generally speaking was the model for the Moscow Treaty, allowed peaceful explosions under certain conditions, and with the unanimous agreement of the three original Parties. However, the Moscow Treaty bans, in the three forbidden areas, "any nuclear weapon test explosion or any other nuclear explosion". These last four words refer to peaceful explosions. The reason is simple: it is not possible to distinguish them, by present detection methods, from nuclear weapons.[24] Some American Senators expressed anxiety about the obstacles thus put in the way of scientific research and technical applications. It was explained to them that in the immediate future, peaceful explosions had no practical useful purpose.[25] American

---

[21] ENDC/213, 25 January 1968. In his speech of 25 July 1968, the American Co-Chairman insisted on the fact that even in his own country the new technology was only in its infancy and that very many problems remained to be solved, particularly over the manufacture of nuclear explosives with industrial applications, as well as the relationship existing between the shape of the crater or the chimney and the nature of the terrain where the explosion takes place. ENDC/PV. 384. The report of a group of United Nations experts contains the following passage: "The group believes these techniques will develop thanks to the pursuit of research and tests, but that developing countries will not necessarily gain an immediate advantage from these technical innovations. There is hope none the less that completely underground explosions and earth-moving explosions will have practical applications at the end of the seventies." A/7568 dated 24 July 1969, para. 229.

[22] J. L. Nogee, *Soviet Policy towards International Control of Atomic Energy* (University of Notre Dame Press, Indiana, 1961), p. 257.

[23] H. K. Jacobson and E. Stein, *Diplomatists, Scientists and Politicians* (Ann Arbor, University of Michigan Press, 1965), p. 156.

[24] *Hearings 1963*, p. 822.

[25] The Moscow Treaty, we know, conditionally allows underground tests and in this field the Americans have developed the Plowshare programme, aimed precisely at the development of the use of nuclear explosives in civil engineering.

leaders, and particularly President Kennedy, in his letter of 10 September 1963, expressed their intention to do their best, at the appropriate time, to negotiate a new agreement, within the Treaty, to allow explosions of this kind. It seems that at the time of the Moscow negotiations, the Russians were not hostile to the principle of such a revision at some time in the future.[26]

Let us recall that the Moscow Treaty allows underground explosions and tests on condition that they do not entail the presence of radioactive fallout outside the territorial limits of the State under whose jurisdiction or control such an explosion is carried out. The term "underground explosion" is not defined by the Treaty. It appears that it might be possible to reconcile explosions intended to extract natural resources with the Moscow Treaty, while certain explosions for excavating or tunnelling, particularly those which would be necessary for a new canal in Central America would not be compatible with the Treaty.[27]

We now come to the drafting of the actual Treaty. The draft of 24 August 1967 contained no Article about peaceful nuclear explosions and limited itself to observing in the eighth paragraph of the preamble that peaceful applications of nuclear explosions ought, by means of appropriate international procedures, to be accessible to non-nuclear States Party to the Treaty, on a non-discriminatory basis and by means of a payment, as small as possible, from which would be excluded expenses for research and development. Also, as we know, Articles I and II ban the transfer of explosive nuclear devices or their control, as well as the manufacture or acquisition of these devices.[28]

The first strong attack against these provisions was begun by Brazil which proposed the suppression in Articles I and II of the expression "or other explosive nuclear devices". The Parties would thus have been able, according to the Brazilian argument, to manufacture devices of this kind and use them without international control. The Brazilian delegate

[26] *Hearings 1963*, pp. 26, 210, s. 693; *Congressional Record*, 11 September 1963, p. 15915; *Hearings 1966*, p. 24. It appears that the provision of the Moscow Treaty that amendments could be carried by a simple majority instead of the two-thirds majority originally provided for, was adopted to allow the easy modification of the Treaty on this specific point. Cf. W. B. Bader, *The U.S. and the Spread of Nuclear Weapons* (New York, Pegasus, 1968), pp. 53–54.

[27] Cf. Bader, op. cit., p. 125; *Hearings 1968*, pp. 105, 116, 126–27; M. Mueller, *Science*, 10 January 1969. On the escape of radioactivity following the Plowshare excavation tests see *SIPRI Yearbook on World Armaments and Disarmament, 1968/9*, pp. 252–54.

[28] The United States representative explained that it is only the manufacture and acquisition of the explosive device itself that is forbidden, but that research and development concerning its use for civil engineering are allowed. A/C1/PV. 1568.

said it was impossible to give up the physical means of shortening the road to progress: "no government would feel it had the power to impose such restrictions on future generations."[29] On this point, the two Co-Chairmen were very strict; Articles I and II could not be changed, given that there was no basic difference between an explosive nuclear device and a nuclear weapon. Let us remember however that according to certain countries' interpretation, when technological progress allows a distinction to be made between nuclear weapons and nuclear explosive devices, the ban affecting the latter will have no purpose.[30] It may be asked whether this interpretation is correct. Who would decide whether such a difference existed? It appears, strictly speaking, that the Treaty ought to be amended on this point at the appropriate time.

Less demanding than Brazil, Switzerland asked for the provision in the preamble to the draft of 24 August 1967 to be changed into an article of the Treaty which "might envisage the creation of a special body where non-nuclear weapon States would be represented, whose task it would be to determine the conditions under which nuclear explosions for peaceful purposes might take place".[31] The Canadian representative proposed a similar idea. His proposal was that: (a) each non-nuclear State Party to the Treaty, which wanted to carry out a civil engineering project by means of nuclear explosives should transmit a request to this effect to the IAEA which would examine the technical and economic conditions of the undertaking; (b) if the project were accepted, the nuclear Powers would supply, through the Agency, the equipment and necessary technical assistance; (c) the operation would be placed under an international system of inspection and safeguards; (d) the nuclear devices used would remain under the care and control of the supplying States.[32] Both the Canadian and Swedish[33] delegates thought the problem ought to be the subject of a special Treaty so as to speed up the adoption of the Non-Proliferation Treaty. This argument was accepted by Mexico, which however recommended the inclusion in the latter instrument of an Article under which nuclear States would supply the means and necessary facilities, through the appropriate international bodies, to put at the disposal of non-nuclear weapon States the advantages arising from the peaceful application of nuclear explosions.[34] Nigeria went further, since she proposed an Article under which nuclear States would put at the

[29] ENDC/201; ENDC/PV. 302, 310, 327.
[30] A/C. 1/PV. 1569 (Mexico and Japan). See also Chapter 4.I.3.
[31] ENDC/204.
[32] ENDC/PV. 329.
[33] ENDC/PV. 302.
[34] ENDC/196; ENDC/PV. 331.

disposal of other States, all scientific and technical information on the peaceful applications of nuclear explosions and would offer to experts of non-nuclear States facilities for collaborating with their own experts doing research into explosive nuclear devices.[35] We have seen that according to the American Co-Chairman, the exchange of information mentioned in Article IV would satisfy Nigeria's request. The same Co-Chairman has also stated his agreement to the proposal about collaboration between experts.[36]

The draft of 18 January 1968 took into account observations made by non-nuclear States. Paragraph 8 of the preamble became Article V. But it was no longer a declaration of intent. "Each Party to this Treaty undertakes to co-operate to ensure that potential benefits from any peaceful applications of nuclear explosions will be made available . . ." In addition, it is laid down that non-nuclear weapon States may obtain these benefits "on a bilateral basis or through an appropriate international body with adequate representation of non-nuclear weapon States." But the new wording was still far from satisfactory to non-nuclear States, and it underwent a final modification during the debate which took place in the General Assembly. The definitive version of Article V stipulates a formal undertaking and thus is more binding than previous versions.

2. The Monopoly of Nuclear States

Let us examine some of the problems that it raises. Several countries have cited Article V as being a sign of "the oligopoly of science and technology"[37] an instrument making non-nuclear States dependent on the Big Three in the technological field for the next twenty-five years.[38] However, Canada for example said it was not ready at the moment to risk investments in nuclear explosion projects as long as their profitability in comparison with traditional methods had not been proved.[39] The British delegate thought it unlikely that his country could, from an economic point of view, develop the technology of peaceful explosions in the near future.[40]

In addition it was pointed out that for non-nuclear States Article V represented an excellent bargain. The new technology will be put at their disposal at the lowest possible price, and without them being obliged to make the necessary investments for research, development and perfection. It is as well not to forget that the technology of nuclear explosions is only a sort of by-product of military manufactures. The American delegate has

[35] ENDC/202; ENDC/PV. 327.
[36] ENDC/PV. 330.
[37] A/C. 1/PV. 1560 (Brazil).
[38] ENDC/PV. 370 (India).
[39] ENDC/PV. 368.
[40] ENDC/PV. 358. See also note 21 to this chapter.

said that the ten-year research programme on nuclear explosions, of which Gasbuggy was the last test, cost 100 million dollars (5 million of which were for Gasbuggy). This figure does not take into account sums invested in the weapons programme since 1945.[41] Let us also note that explosions can have the effect of upsetting the ecological balance in the sea, in the air and on the ground.[41a]

Such arguments have not convinced everybody. Economic and technological independence is one of the major objectives of developing countries and of many others.[42] It is evident that this objective is not to be taken literally; it reflects the desire to change the nature of the relationships existing between countries of unequal strength. Looked at in this way financial arguments do not appear decisive; one may recall the many historical examples of States having developed their national industry for political reasons and without taking into account short-term economic considerations. This argument, which is not wrong in general terms, seems generally unacceptable in the technological field of nuclear explosives, if the economic difficulties and the situation in the majority of non-nuclear States are taken into account.

Article V means in practice that the two Super-Powers will put at the disposal of non-nuclear weapon States explosive nuclear devices which will remain under the care and control of the supplying State.[43] As the Swedish delegate observed, this is a discriminatory measure because if the explosive nuclear device is a by-product of the disarmament effort, its research and development may in its turn serve military purposes.[44] So Mrs Myrdal asked for balance to be restored by the creation of international machinery to authorise and supervise explosions to be carried out by both nuclear and non-nuclear States.

[41] ENDC/PV. 358.
[41a] See for example Mueller, *Science*, 10 January 1969.
[42] However, developing countries have at the same time a certain interest in seeing that the new technology is not used in the main by the industrialised countries. It has been shown for example, that if, thanks to this technology, it is possible in the three Western States of the United States to extract petroleum from veins embedded in layers of clay, the United States, on the basis of their present level of consumption, will have enough petroleum to last 500 years. Bader, op. cit., p. 124. This would strike a heavy blow at the oil exports of the developing countries.
[43] ENDC/PV. 369 (United States). A draft law was put before Congress in July 1968 to allow the American Atomic Energy Commission to carry out the duties assumed by the United States under Art. V. This draft lays down the conditions under which these duties may be fulfilled. The draft covers a transition period during which regulations are expected to be drawn up about responsibility and indemnity over security, health and protection. ENDC/PV. 384 (United States).
[44] See on the whole discussion ENDC/202, 204, 216; ENDC/PV. 358, 364, 367, 369, 373.

Three questions are raised here. In the first place who benefits from Article V? It is enough to compare the wording of this Article with that of Article IV to see that Article V puts more emphasis upon co-operation with non-nuclear States Party to the Treaty. To be logical, one ought to conclude that the advantages proposed in Article V are limited to these States to the exclusion of States not Party to the Treaty. However official American opinion, while stressing that Article V presents a bonus to non-nuclear member States, makes it understood that this does not prevent collaboration with non-Party States.[45] This position seems to be in line neither with the spirit nor the letter of the Treaty.

What exactly is the scope of Article V? Here again it seems best to refer to the opinion of American officials. According to them, Article V only covers commercial applications – when such applications become feasible – and not research and development, a phase that has not yet been completed. The Treaty therefore puts no obligation on the United States to undertake tests in foreign countries or operations relating to research and development. The problem arose over participation by the American Atomic Energy Commission together with the Australian government (which at the time had not yet signed the Treaty) in research into the possibility of building a port on the West Coast of Australia by means of a nuclear explosion. This undertaking illustrates the pressure and effect of private interests. Some years ago, important iron ore deposits were discovered in Western Australia. They are exploited by a large American Company, the Sentinel Mining Company, and its Australian associates, which are absolutely convinced of the need to construct a port not too far away from the mines to ship away the ore.[46]

What is the meaning of the expression "on a non-discriminatory basis"? According to American officials it applies to the financial conditions of the peaceful explosion service. In other words, the cost of the service will be the same, whatever the State which benefits. No distinction is thus made between a developed or rich country and a developing, or poor country. The expression also means, in the author's opinion, that the service may not be withheld for reasons relating to the kind of State requesting the service, i.e. to its political attitude. The supplying country will have a certain measure of freedom in classifying the projects submitted, particularly over whether the project is feasible, commercially applicable and appropriate.[47]

---

[45] *Hearings 1969*, pp. 362–63, 373. Some States, such as Brazil, India and Pakistan, keep insisting that the IAEA nuclear explosion facilities should be available to all member States, irrespective of whether they have acceded to the Non-Proliferation Treaty.

[46] ibid., pp. 315–16, 327–30.   [47] ibid., pp. 320, 373.

3. International Procedure

The text we are examining states that the benefits which may arise from any peaceful applications of nuclear explosions will be made available in accordance with the present Treaty "under appropriate international surveillance and through appropriate international procedures". This form of words helps to safeguard first of all the provisions in Articles I and II banning the transfer of explosive nuclear devices or their control, as well as their manufacture or acquisition or even assistance received in such manufacture or acquisition. Let us repeat that neither the explosive device nor its control may be transferred by nuclear States to any recipient whatsoever, not even to an international organisation. It is as well to make the same distinction here as for nuclear weapons and to avoid confusing access to these devices with their ownership, care and control.[48]

These devices may only be used under international surveillance and in accordance with international procedures. But here again we are up against double discrimination. The international machinery only applies to the service supplied by a nuclear State Party to the Treaty to a non-nuclear State, also Party. So services supplied by a nuclear State Party to the Treaty to any other nuclear State escape from these provisions as well as explosions made on its own territory by a nuclear State Party to the Treaty. This discrimination was seriously criticised by the Swedish delegate.

What is the purpose of surveillance and appropriate international procedures? It is a question of ensuring that services rendered are only in the field of peaceful uses, and that they do not violate Articles I and II. According to an official note of the American Atomic Energy Commission, the main purpose of international observation is to reassure other Parties that the explosive device used remains under the care and control of the nuclear State providing the services and that the explosion is carried out in accordance with the aims previously indicated.[49] In addition, the expression "international procedures" covers the possibility of the conclusion in the future of a Treaty banning underground tests. According to the American Co-Chairman, if, through such a Treaty "international approval were necessary to carry out a nuclear explosion for peaceful purposes, this approval would constitute an 'appropriate international procedure' which would be applicable to the services provided on a bilateral basis or through an appropriate international organisation".

[48] The international surveillance mentioned in Art. V cannot give international observers the right of access to the plans and internal workings of explosive nuclear devices. ENDC/PV. 384 (United States), *Hearings 1968*, p. 113.
[49] *Hearings 1968*, p. 113.

These provisions far from satisfied Mrs Myrdal, who demanded that an international body should authorise *all projects* involving the use of nuclear explosives, including those conceived and developed by a nuclear State. But even within the framework of Article V, it seems to the author that the term "international procedure" ought to refer to yet another possibility, namely the granting of international authorisation after examination of the project and after confirmation that there is no risk of violating Articles I and II of the Treaty, nor of the rules laid down by the Moscow Treaty.

As a general rule, it is provided that the benefits from a nuclear explosion will be made available by special international agreement or agreements through an international body with adequate representation of non-nuclear States. A special international agreement in this context appears to mean the basic instrument which defines the functions and powers of the international body.[50] As for special international agreements, these are the agreements between this body and the States carrying out a planned nuclear explosion.[51]

Must the appropriate international body mentioned in Article V be a new institution? Some developing countries are tempted by such a solution. The predilection of these countries is well know for the establishment of new international organisations where they are what they consider to be adequately represented and where activities and policies favourable to them are pursued. We have shown that particularly in the field of economic co-operation, this policy has not been unjustified.[52]

The same could not be said for the body mentioned in Article V. Here we are still in a relatively unexplored field, dealing with a technology still in its infancy. The creation of a new body might lead to a waste of technicians and senior staff who are still scarce.[53] Also, some countries, particularly the United States, reject the creation of a new international organisation and emphasise the experience and competence of the IAEA which, they say, ought to carry out the duties mentioned in Article V regarding the establishment of procedures governing the provision of services in the field of peaceful nuclear explosions.[54] But what would be the legal means of

[50] According to Mexico, the proposed international body ought to be approved by the General Assembly. A/C. 1/PV. 1569. On the other hand, according to the United States, consultations over the special international agreement may begin even before the entry into force of the Treaty. A/C. 1/PV. 1577.

[51] A/C. 1/PV. 1580 (Mexico).

[52] G. Fischer, "UNCTAD and its Place in the United Nations System", *Annuaire français de droit international*, 1966, pp. 234–45.

[53] See in this connection Mrs Myrdal's statement, ENDC/PV. 383.

[54] See President Johnson's message, ENDC/228 and the statement by the American delegate. ENDC/PV. 384.

reaching this goal? One way might be to conclude in each case, an *ad hoc* agreement between the IAEA, the country providing the services and the recipient State.

This method would be rather unsafe and would lack a solid, permanent basis. The amendment of the IAEA Statute might also be considered, or again, the conclusion of a general agreement between the latter and the three depositary governments acting in the name of all Parties to the Non-Proliferation Treaty, and with a mandate from them. Another possibility might also be envisaged: the General Assembly might draft a text and the UN might conclude a general agreement with the IAEA on the basis of this. It is, however, very doubtful whether the two Super-Powers would accept such a method, so contrary to their general practice and the spirit in which the Geneva Committee works. For their part, some developing countries might not be so enthusiastic about the role to be played by the IAEA. This organisation, which dates back to 1957, is already old-fashioned and does not reserve the same place for developing countries as other more recently created institutions. However, taking into account the existing problems in this field, and the relative strength of those involved, it is unlikely that they will be able to achieve the creation of a new organisation. Let us also notice that the majority of member States of the UN feel that responsibility for this international service ought to be given to the IAEA.[55]

4. Bilateral agreements and the role of the private sector

The last sentence in Article V enables States so desiring to obtain the same advantages through bilateral agreements. This provision has aroused bitter and frequent criticism. Bilateral relations are often the source of secret bidding, suspicion and blackmail. In particular, in the field with which we are dealing, bilaterals breed mistrust. However, the American Co-Chairman has said that in the case of the bilateral option, as in that of the international option, the explosive device will remain under the care and control of the supplying State and that the same international surveillance will operate in both cases.

It still remains true however that in a context where the principle of non-discrimination applies in theory, bilateral relations are anomalous. Doubtless the American Co-Chairman has stated that as soon as new techniques have been perfected, there will be no shortages and all demands will be satisfied. Besides, the international or bilateral option will depend on the non-nuclear State wanting to benefit from the advantages of Article

[55] Resolutions 2456C (XXIII) and 2605B (XXIV); also documents A/7678 and addenda.

V.[56] The Soviet Co-Chairman also insisted on the fact that the choice between the two options is free and that no nuclear Power will be able to use Article V to bring pressure to bear or for bargaining purposes.[57]

However, the problems do appear a little more complex. The benefits of Article V are available on a non-discriminatory basis. The cost of the explosive devices supplied must be as low as possible and exclude expenses for research and development. The American delegate explained that in any case, the price of the device will not be more than that quoted to American national users. And he added that, according to his country's legislation, private companies or individuals are not allowed to manufacture or acquire such devices.[58]

But the American law of 1954 legislates for the progressive transfer of nuclear fuel to private ownership and enables the Atomic Energy Commission to provide certain services to foreign users.[59] Other legislative measures may be taken in the future. In any case the Non-Proliferation Treaty shows how important it is in the United States as elsewhere, to safeguard the role of the public authorities in the nuclear field. What ought to be stressed above all is, in the United States, the ever closer relationship between certain large private companies and official research and development work in the field of nuclear explosions. Thus the Gasbuggy test was carried out jointly by the Atomic Energy Commission, the Bureau of Mines, and the El Paso Natural Gas Co., which contributed $1,925,000 to the cost of the operation (which was $4,700,000). Other projects are

[56] Mr Dean Rusk was a little more cynical. His speech reflects the division of the world. In his opinion, the bilateral option means that the United States will make arrangements with certain countries and the USSR with others. It is possible that both nuclear States would help a determined country. *Hearings 1968*, p. 33.

[57] A/C. 1/PV. 1571.

[58] The President of the American Atomic Energy Commission had to reassure Senators who were worried about what they considered a softening in the American attitude. Here is an extract from Mr Seaborg's statement: "All costs of furnishing the explosion service, including, among other things, the full cost of all materials, the fabrication of the explosive devices, and the firing of them, would be borne by the foreign user and not the Atomic Energy Commission. Appropriate overhead costs would be also included. We would also be reimbursed if we undertook work relating to a particular adaptation of a nuclear device or of our operations for the benefit of a specific user. This overall approach is consistent with the pricing policy which the Commission follows in connection with other materials and services that it provides domestically and abroad." *Hearings 1969*, pp. 312, 314. This statement certainly devalues the specially favourable character to the beneficiaries of the provisions of Art. V.

[59] 68 Stat. 919. The President of the American Atomic Energy Commission has said that the Commission did not exclude the possibility of undertaking work abroad jointly with foreign contractors, and thus applying outside the United States the methods it already uses inside the country. *Hearings 1968*, p. 104.

being carried on with the collaboration of the Continental Oil Co., Austral Oil Co., Kennecott Copper Co., Holmes and Narver, and the Lockheed Missile and Space Co.[60]

All nuclear industrial development in the United States demonstrates the fact that a few large companies, thanks to contracts concluded and relations established with the Atomic Energy Commission, have been able to benefit from the technical and economic results of the enormous investments made by the government since 1945. The same phenomenon can be observed in the field of the use of nuclear explosives. In January 1968 the Nobel Paso Geonuclear Company was set up, to include the El Paso Company, the French Nobel Bozel Company and the Belgian Pouderies Réunies. The aim of this company was to market know-how and research into the use of explosive nuclear devices all over the world, except in the United States. This entry of big business into the field of nuclear civil engineering foreshadows a battle for profits hardly compatible with the principle stated in Article V of the Treaty. Besides, these private interests may exercise strong pressure against the conclusion of a total Test Ban Treaty.[61]

It is curious that in fact the USSR has not denounced the capitalism and greed of private companies, which she did not fail to do during the debate on the commercial exploitation of telecommunication satellites.[62] In the latter case it was a question of an American monopoly, whilst in the nuclear explosion field a certain amount of competition may be expected between the two Super-Powers.

5. The role of the international body

Much will depend upon the attitude of the non-nuclear States, upon their solidarity and mutual understanding. If they show themselves capable of taking up a common position, if they come out strongly in favour of an international body that really works, and if they avoid the bilateral option, then they may overcome their relative weakness.

The international body ought to have among its powers that of granting individual permission for each nuclear explosion carried out under Article V, after examining the project, the plans and any information it deems necessary. This body should have complete freedom to appoint committees of *ad hoc* experts or permanent committees whose members would have

---

[60] *Nuclear News*, March 1968, pp. 37–43; A.E.C., "Authorizing Legislation for Fiscal Year 1968", *Hearings before the Joint Committee on Atomic Energy*, Part 3, February–March 1967, pp. 1798–1801.

[61] Inglis and Sander, *Bulletin of Atomic Scientists*, December 1967, pp. 46–53.

[62] Cf. F. Batailler, *Annuaire français de droit international*, 1965, pp. 145–73.

the right and the duty enshrined in an international agreement, to communicate and publish available information whatever the internal regulations in force in the particular country concerned.[63]

In addition, the body mentioned in Article V might create a truly common undertaking modelled upon that which has been studied and sometimes applied in a European framework.[64] Such an undertaking might possibly take the form of an international public authority run only under the auspices of governments or public institutions. The Board of administration would be appointed by participating governments or public institutions. Finance would come out of public funds; private capital would only be able to participate through a bond issue with an eventual possibility of profiting from the advantages resulting from the research and profitability of the undertaking. This formula is necessary in a field where the object of the undertaking is of general interest and there is no real problem of profitability.

Such an undertaking ought to have the same right of effective access to know-how and patents held by public bodies in nuclear States as any other individual or company, national or foreign. It even ought to get specially favourable treatment in order to reduce the extent of the advantages enjoyed by the big American companies which have already been associated for some time in the execution of different phases of their country's nuclear programme. The right of competent national and international authorities (Euratom under certain conditions) to use an atomic energy patent without the owner of the patent being able to refuse, ought to favour this sort of international undertaking.[65] The common undertaking would have to employ first rate technicians under long-term contract incorporating a clause which would forbid them from taking employment in private

---

[63] According to the Swedish delegate, the international organisation to be created should have three functions: (a) examine the project and decide if it is economically and technically sound, and if it is worth making an exception for under the the total test ban that the Swedish delegate hoped to see adopted soon; (b) observe and inspect the project as it develops and determine whether it violates the provisions of Treaties in force; (c) contribute to the financing of civil engineering works, prospecting and development (we know that Art. V only mentions the price of the nuclear explosive device). The functions mentioned under (a) and (b) would be entrusted by international agreement to the IAEA, whilst those under (c) would be exercised by the United Nations Development Programme. A/C. 1/PV. 1564. This last idea appears extremely interesting and fruitful to the author. As for Australia, she fiercely resisted all attempts to give an international body the power to pronounce on the technical and economic aspects of projects. A/C. 1/PV. 1570.

[64] See for example P. Huet, *Annuaire français de droit international*, 1958, pp. 512–35; P. Strohl, ibid., 1961, pp. 569–91.

[65] Cf. Fischer, *L'énergie atomique et les Etats-Unis*, pp. 150 et seqq.; G. Finnis in *Il diritto della energia nucleare* (Milano, Giuffre, 1961), pp. 393–410.

industry for a fixed period following the end or cancellation of the contract.

These few suggestions are made here for information only. They might, in conjunction with other measures, contribute to the solution of the problem aptly defined by M. François Perroux as the antithesis of large firms and small nations. The problem arises particularly acutely in the field we are interested in, because of the overlapping, to a greater extent than in other sectors, of public and private interests.[66]

[66] The Board of Governors of the IAEA adopted a much narrower viewpoint in a report which was approved by the General Conference on 29 September 1969. The Agency said it was ready to exercise or to cause to be exercised the appropriate international surveillance mentioned in Art. V, the aim of this surveillance being mainly "to take appropriate measures at international level with a view to guaranteeing that nuclear devices used for peaceful explosion services remain under the care and control of the nuclear weapon State providing the services and that explosions are not carried out for other than declared purposes". CG (XIII)/410, para. 7. The Agency could also, according to the report, encourage the exchange of information; provide services such as economic studies, security studies, technical assistance, studies on the possibility of completing a project (bearing upon technology, health and security problems, protection against radioactivity, economic problems and costs); act as go-between between the supplying and receiving States; conclude co-operation agreements with a view to allowing national and international scientific organisations to benefit from the results of the use of nuclear explosions for peaceful purposes. ibid., para. 10. See also A/7678 and A/7678/Add. 2.

7. FINAL CLAUSES

IN a Treaty of such complexity and affecting so many vital interests, the final clauses have a significance that goes far beyond simple legal jargon. We shall examine here successively entry into force and accession, duration, amendment, Treaty revision, and finally conditions for withdrawal.

I. ENTRY INTO FORCE AND ACCESSION

Under a provision to be found in many other Treaties, as soon as it was signed by the three original Parties (United States, Britain and the Soviet Union) the Moscow Treaty was opened to signature to all other States, but it was not to enter into force until it had been ratified by the original Parties (Article III). After 5 August 1963 there was an avalanche of signatures, a sort of international referendum, which did not fail to put moral pressure on the US Congress where the Treaty had its opponents as well as its supporters. It will in any case be noticed that the qualification laid down by the Treaty is really a minimal one: three ratifications are sufficient for it to enter into force. This was all the more understandable as at the time only the three original Parties were capable of carrying out nuclear weapons tests; by acceding to the Treaty, they alone were giving up activities which they had already been pursuing and which they alone for the immediate future were able to pursue.

Similar considerations explain the provision of Article XIV of the Treaty of 27 January 1967[1] under which entry into force is subject to the deposit of five ratifications including those of the three nuclear States.

The Soviet draft Treaty of 24 September 1965 limited itself to declaring that the entry into force of the Treaty would take place as soon as it had been ratified by the nuclear signatory States (that is to say the three nuclear States). On the other hand the American draft of 17 August 1965 provided that the Treaty would enter into force as soon as the ratification instruments of a certain (unspecified) number of governments, including those of the three nuclear States, had been deposited. It appeared that under the Non-Proliferation Treaty, a large number of governments were giving up an option that they might have exercised and that these

[1] On the Principles Governing the Activities of States in the Exploration and Use of Outer Space.

governments had a right to demand that a considerable number of members of the international community should accede to the Treaty before it came into force. The joint draft of 24 August 1967 had more or less the same wording as the previously quoted American draft.

On this point, Switzerland observed that the Treaty could achieve its purpose only if it became universal. The Swiss said they could only accede to the Treaty if all Powers capable of having nuclear weapons as well as all the important industrial countries acceded to it. This double condition was justified respectively on the grounds of security considerations and anxiety about the competitive power of the atomic industry of signatory States.[2] The draft of 18 January 1968 replied to these arguments with an important modification: the Treaty would enter into force after ratification by all nuclear signatory States and by 40 other signatory States. This provision was kept in the final text.

The purely quantitative aspect of this criterion was challenged on several occasions.[3] Some countries asked for the entry into force of the Treaty to be conditional upon the accession of quasi-nuclear States.[4] The Swedish representative thought "the importance of the Treaty will depend above all on its signature and ratification by certain key countries".[5] In the opinion of the Spanish government, at least 12 of the ratifying countries ought to be States with power reactors in operation or under construction, or with uranium deposits in their territory capable of being economically exploited. Spain also asked for the figure of 40 countries to be replaced by 60.[6]

The American Co-Chairman rejected these requests. He explained that the number 40 had been chosen in order to avoid delay, and he recalled that the Moscow Treaty had received 30 ratifications, 9 months after signature, 60, 16 months after and 80, 30 months after. According to the American Co-Chairman the introduction of qualitative norms was hardly possible as it would give a power of veto over the entry into force to all countries fulfilling such norms. The United States delegate also rejected the possibility sought by Sweden of ratifying on condition that another State or States specified by name would also ratify. Of course all countries would be able to take into account the attitude of other States by deciding when to deposit their instrument of ratification.[7]

In any case it is worth noticing, together with Mr Dean Rusk and certain

[2] ENDC/204.
[3] An extreme example was that of Uganda who demanded the signature and ratification of all nuclear States. A/C. 1/PV. 1566.
[4] ENDC/PV. 363 (Brazil); A/C. 1/PV. 1566 and 1580 (Pakistan).
[5] A/C. 1/PV. 1579.
[6] ENDC/219 and A/C. 1/PV. 1569.
[7] ENDC/PV. 368 and 369.

American Congressmen, that even if the Treaty is not ratified by all States, it represents great progress all the same and that the situation it brings about is much better than that which existed before.[8]

Article IX (1) enables all States to sign the Treaty or to accede to it. This provision also exists in Article III of the Moscow Treaty and Article XIV of the Treaty on the Principles governing the Activities of States in Outer Space. It reflects the opinion of certain countries according to which all States have the right to accede to multilateral Conventions. This principle, as is well known, is insufficiently respected in Conventions of this kind concluded under the auspices of the United Nations.[9]

The instruments of ratification and accession will be deposited with the governments of the United States, the United Kingdom and the Soviet Union, designated as depositary governments. This formula, the same as that used in the Moscow Treaty and in the Treaty on Outer Space, raises some delicate legal problems; what for example will be the legal relationship between States which have not all deposited their instruments of ratification with the same governments?[10]

In order to understand the meaning of the formula about depositaries, it is worth returning to the Moscow Treaty and to remember the excellent, concise comment contained in the Swiss Federal Council's message: "This provision introduces something new into diplomatic practice: the possibility, created for political reasons, of signing in one, two or three places and depositing the instruments of ratification there. It is sufficient, however, in order to be validly bound, to have signed in the presence of one only of the depositary Powers."[11]

The reason for the existence of this provision is perfectly clear: it allows

---

[8] *Hearings 1968*, pp. 18, 32, 150, 162. As has already been shown, a certain friendly pressure has been brought to bear by Washington on reluctant States. Perhaps this can also be inferred from the statement made by Dr Seaborg, President of the American Atomic Energy Commission, when he told the Senate Foreign Relations Committee that he had high hopes that Israel would accede to the Treaty. *Hearings 1969*, p. 321. Let us add that among countries having the capacity to reach nuclear status sooner or later, the following had not yet signed the Treaty at the moment it entered into force: Argentina, Brazil, India, Israel, Pakistan and South Africa.

[9] Cf. E. Schwelb, *American Journal of International Law*, 1967, pp. 965–66.

[10] Cf. S. Rosenne, *American Journal of International Law*, 1967, pp. 943–44. This legal expedient, adopted for political reasons, has been wittily commented on by an American writer: "This idea offended the purists of international law for apparently no one would really be able to know who the signatories were, but that did not worry practical minds". A. M. Schlesinger, Jr., *A Thousand Days*, 1965.

[11] Message of the Federal Council to the Federal Assembly concerning approval of the Treaty forbidding nuclear weapons tests in the atmosphere, in outer space and in water, 13 September 1963, no. 8831.

a State not recognised by one of the original Parties to be bound by signing and depositing its instrument of ratification with another original Party.

The main problem was the accession of East Germany. During the drafting of the Moscow Treaty, Western drafts spoke of States and authorities, then insisted on the necessity of screening accessions to the Treaty. The Soviet Union on the other hand wanted the unconditional accession of all States.[12] Some contend, completely wrongly, that the American concession on this point opened the door to the recognition of East Germany.[13] But really the formula agreed upon in the Moscow Treaty and repeated in later instruments was invented by the United States and Britain precisely to avoid the recognition of East Germany. It is evident that this expedient was, legally speaking, quite useless. In accordance with a generally agreed principle "refusal to recognise has never resulted in preventing a State or government whose existence is effective, from acceding to an open international Convention of universal character."[14] The Swiss Federal Council's message of 13 September 1963 raises and clearly answers the problem in international law: "the German Federal Republic has publicly as well as through diplomatic channels expressed its anxiety over the consequences that the Moscow Treaty might have upon the status of the German Democratic Republic. According to the general principles of customary law, the participation of an unrecognised State at an international conference or its signature of a multilateral agreement (or its accession to such an agreement) involves no explicit or tacit recognition. There are many precedents for this. Switzerland has always held fast to this principle for its observance alone allows universal agreements to be concluded, leaving aside political differences. For this reason Switzerland has no particular statement to make in the present circumstances."

Moreover, the legal opinion of the State Department dated 12 August 1963[15] recognised and admitted the validity of the principle recalled in the Swiss Federal Council's message. It observed that the United States was Party to eleven multilateral agreements to which East Germany belonged. In some cases, they answered notification by the depositary government of the accession of the GDR to the effect that, not recognising the so-called GDR, they attached no importance to its accession. However, in the case of the 1949 Geneva Conventions on the Protection of War

[12] H. K. Jacobson and G. Stein, *Diplomats, Scientists and Politicians* (Ann Arbor, Univ. of Michigan Press, 1966), pp. 328–39.
[13] Bader, op. cit., pp. 52–53.
[14] R. Pinto, "Le statut international de RDA", *Journal du droit international*, 1959, no. 2, 126.
[15] *Hearings 1963*, pp. 15–17.

Victims, the American government informed the depositary government that it did not recognise the "GDR" but that taking into account the nature and aim of the Conventions, it acknowledged the acceptance by the "government of the GDR" of the provisions of the Conventions and of the declared intention of this government to apply them . . .

The provision of the Moscow Treaty concerning the three depositaries was inspired by political motives. The legal opinion of the State Department recognised this when it indicated that the original parties understood "that no depositary is bound to accept a signature or communication from a regime that it does not recognise. Thus, contacts between the United States as depositary and unrecognised regimes will be reduced to the strictest minimum and remain below the level that the general principles of international law prescribe for a depositary". The United States, by adopting the text of Article III, wanted to reassure the German Federal Republic, which is opposed to any act by the Western Powers which might imply a change of attitude towards the GDR. Pressure was applied by the Bonn government as soon as it seemed that agreement was in sight. The Western draft of 27 August 1962 only mentions a single depositary government.

Be that as it may, the government of the GDR did sign in Moscow. In notes of 16 August, the British and American governments refused to accept notification by the Soviet Union of the accession of the GDR. The Soviet Union replied on 23 August, recalling the nature and aim of the Treaty, declaring the two German States equal "from the international point of view", and also that the claim of the German Federal Republic to represent the whole of Germany went "against the universally recognised norms of international law".[16] The Soviet Union, in its turn, in a note dated 4 September 1963 addressed to Washington protested against the accession of Formosa; the United States answered that this accession was fully valid since it emanated from a legitimate authority.[17]

These were political, rather than legal attitudes. In fact the Soviet Union, as well as the two original Western Parties all had an interest in seeing the greatest possible number of States accede to the Treaty. Whence arose the contradictions in the Western position. On 12 August, Mr Dean Rusk argued that the GDR would assume unilateral obligations by signing the Treaty, an act that the United States considered void.[18] According to the Foreign Office, in spite of the signature of the Treaty by

---

[16] Cf. USSR, Bulletin published by the Soviet Information Bureau, 26 August 1963, p. 4.
[17] *Le Monde*, 4 October 1963; Déclaration du gouvernement soviétique, 21 September 1963, Collection études soviétiques, p. 16.
[18] *Hearings 1963*, p. 34.

the GDR, no Treaty link existed between the latter and Great Britain. The British government would object if the East German authorities, who promised to respect the provisions of the Treaty, tried to exercise the rights and privileges belonging to Parties to this instrument.[19] It is evident that such an attitude was not compatible with the nature and aims of the Treaty, which, in so far as possible, was to extend the agreement to every country in the world; nor was it compatible with the system resulting from a multilateral convention, which implied a certain balance of rights and duties and the equality of all Parties, unless there was an indication to the contrary in the text. Of course the United States and United Kingdom representatives were not wrong when they stated, in reference to Article IX of the Non-Proliferation Treaty, that it did not imply recognition by other States nor did it change the status of an unrecognised regime or entity which might accede to the Treaty. But the attitude of those delegates who spoke about a regime or entity "claiming to accede to the Treaty" and who could state that their governments would oppose the participation of such a regime or entity in the conferences provided for in Article VIII, cannot but be deplored.[20] It even seems, according to these statements, that the United States and the United Kingdom would refuse to take into consideration the accession of certain countries when it is a question of reaching the quorum of forty required for the entry in force of the Treaty.

II. DURATION, AMENDMENT AND REVISION

The Moscow Treaty was concluded for an indefinite period. The same was also the case for the 1967 Treaty on Outer Space. Similarly according to the draft of 24 August 1967, the Non-Proliferation Treaty was to last for an indefinite period. According to an Italian amendment, it ought to be for a fixed period, to be determined, and then automatically renewed by all Parties not giving six months notice of withdrawal.[21] The aim of

[19] Foreign Office News Department communiqué, 15 August 1963; see also the similar views expressed by Mr Rusk, *Hearings 1963*, p. 18. The British government also declared it refused to accept the Soviet notification of the signature of the Treaty by East Germany, as it did not recognise this zone as a State or entity possessing national sovereignty, nor the local authorities as a government. *House of Commons*, 13 November 1963, col. 1.

[20] A/PV. 1672.

[21] ENDC/200. Later, Italy tabled a new amendment in these terms: the Treaty will last twenty-five years. It will be automatically renewed for periods of time equal to the initial period for those governments which, having reserved the right to give six months' notice at the end of each period of the Treaty, have not communicated their intention to withdraw. ENDC/218/Corr. 1. It seems clear that in general this amendment was less favourable to the permanence of the Treaty than the actual Art. X.

this amendment was to introduce more flexibility. This is what Switzerland also requested, which called attention to the "rapid and unpredictable evolution" characterising nuclear science and its military, political, economic and technical applications. The Swiss therefore recommended a limited duration at the end of which a revision conference would decide upon renewal. As they saw it, non-nuclear States would not agree to such renewal unless nuclear States adopted concrete measures tending towards arms control. The draft of 18 January made a slight concession. Article X (2) provided: "Twenty-five years after the entry into force of the Treaty, a conference shall be convened to decide whether the Treaty shall continue in force indefinitely or its validity shall be extended for an additional fixed period or periods. This decision shall be taken by a majority of Parties to the Treaty". With slight modifications this was the text adopted in Article X (2) of the Treaty.[22] Each State Party may withdraw before twenty-five years have passed, but only under conditions set down in the Treaty, to which we shall return.

As far as amendment procedure is concerned, it is worth recalling the provisions of the Moscow Treaty. Article II of this Treaty says that any Party may propose amendments to the Treaty. If at least one-third of the Parties so demand, the draft amendment must be submitted to a Conference of all Parties, called by the depositary governments. Any amendment approved by a simple majority of Parties, including the three original Parties will be considered adopted. It will enter into force for all Parties when it has been ratified by a majority of them including the three original Parties.

Here again we see the lack of equality among the Parties, the three original signatories having a right of veto. This right represents a guarantee against hasty measures taken by a simple majority of member States. But it is also a fact that new duties could be imposed upon a widespread minority of States. They would then have the possibility of denouncing the Treaty, in conformity with Article IV. As the Swiss Federal Council's message notes, "it could be, it is true, under difficult conditions from a political and psychological point of view".

Mr Dean Rusk stated that the United States will not be forced to sit at the same table as States they have not recognised (here again East Germany is the problem). But it would be possible, according to the

[22] The United Kingdom thought an indefinite period would have been preferable taking into account the clause allowing withdrawal for serious reasons. ENDC/PV. 358. On the other hand twenty-five years seemed too long to Spain which proposed twenty years. ENDC/219. The preparatory work shows that in spite of the ambiguity of the text, Art. X (2) allows the majority of Parties to put an end to the Treaty after twenty-five years.

Secretary of State, for the three original Parties to agree on the text of an amendment and communicate it to the other Parties who would give their views in writing.[23] Such a method would be perfectly compatible with the provisions of Article II. This text, although it provides for the summoning of a conference if a third of the Parties ask for it, then goes on to stipulate that the Treaty may be amended by the majority indicated above, without requiring a conference to be called for this purpose.

Yet the Moscow Treaty used a very advanced technique by which a simple majority of the Parties could change the rules of the Treaty for all Parties. A quite different method was used in the 1967 Treaty on Outer Space, which distinguished between the objective and subjective entry into force of an amendment. It entered into force as soon as it had been accepted by the majority of Parties, but only for those who accepted it. Each Party thus had the possibility of accepting or rejecting the amendment for itself.

To return to our Treaty, the amendment procedure was, according to the draft of 24 August 1967, similar to that laid down in the Moscow Treaty. The amendment entered into force for all Parties as soon as it had been ratified by a majority of Parties, including all nuclear States Party to the Treaty, as well as all other Parties which, on the date the amendment was communicated to them, were members of the Board of Governors of the International Atomic Energy Agency. This gives some idea of the progress made, since in the Moscow Treaty only the three original Parties were entitled to a special mention. However, both Brazil and Romania, giving proof of a fairly outdated idea of Treaty technique, proposed that an amendment ratified under these conditions would only enter into force in relation to the ratifying Parties. The draft of 18 January 1968 as well as the final text of Article VIII (1 and 2) gave them satisfaction. As has been observed, these provisions may have the effect of creating different Treaty rules depending on whether or not Parties have ratified an amendment. This is rather a shocking state of affairs in a Treaty of such importance—all the more since Article VIII already gives a right of veto to the three nuclear States as well as to Parties who are members of the Board of Governors of the IAEA.[24] It is worth remembering that

---

[23] *Hearings 1963*, pp. 18, 34, 968–69. Mr Rusk even hints that the United States would be against the GDR being able to vote on an amendment or take part in the conference foreseen in Art. II. This is a quite exceptional attitude in American diplomatic practice. In 1954 in Geneva, and since then, the United States have not hesitated to sit down at the same table as delegates from Peking. Mr Harriman himself moreover recalled this precedent in bringing up the case of East Germany. See *New York Herald Tribune*, 1 August 1963.

[24] ENDC/PV. 367 (UAR).

the final text of Article VIII was the result of a concession made by the Co-Chairmen to certain member countries of the Committee of 18. As this example shows, pressure by small or medium Powers does not always produce a happy result.

Let us recall once more, on amendment procedure, that it can be carried out either through a conference, or failing this, by simple written consultation carried out by the depositary governments.

The problem of revision was in its turn the subject of long discussions and numerous proposals. The Moscow Treaty, it will be remembered, contains no provisions on this point. An American disarmament proposal in 1959 was that there should be a sort of periodic revision of the operation of the control system every two years.[25]

Within the framework of the Non-Proliferation Treaty, the problem was raised in connection with disarmament measures. The non-nuclear States showed that they were determined to get assurances from nuclear States over concrete disarmament measures. Promises, although still rather vague, figured in the preamble and in Article VI of the Treaty. The non-nuclear States wanted to keep in reserve some means of bringing pressure to bear on nuclear States to honour their disarmament promises.

According to the draft of 24 August, which was not modified on this point by the 18 January version, a conference of Parties was to take place five years after the entry into force of the Treaty in order to examine the way it was being applied, and to ensure that its aims and provisions were in process of being accomplished. Brazil had proposed that this conference should deal mainly with the carrying out of promises made about disarmament. In this way moral pressure would have been put on nuclear States. This idea was suggested by the United Kingdom who thought, however, that it was necessary not to overload the Treaty nor multiply points of difficulty. According to the UK, the above-mentioned conference ought also to make sure that the aims of the preamble were being achieved.[26] Such was also the opinion of the UAR: it was necessary to include disarmament among the problems to be discussed by the conference; in the meantime, the Big Two ought to give the world reason to hope that disarmament measures would be taken before the conference met.[27] Romania, in order to increase the pressure upon nuclear States, asked for such conferences to take place every five years.[28] This proposal was repeated by Italy[29] and Spain.[30]

[25] GEN/DNT/44.
[26] ENDC/203.
[27] ENDC/PV. 333.
[28] ENDC/199.
[29] ENDC/218/Corr. 1.
[30] ENDC/219.

The final text of the Treaty – Article VIII (3) – includes the British amendment as well as a Swedish one,[31] under which, after the first revision conference, other conferences would meet at five yearly intervals if the majority of Parties so desired. So the regularity of conferences is not automatic.

What will be the effect of such a conference? According to the Swedish delegate, if it appears that no progress has been made in the nuclear disarmament field or towards stopping the arms race, Parties will have the right to consider that they are in the presence of an "extraordinary event" in the sense of Article X (1) which defines the right of withdrawal.[32] But how can the revision conference proceed to make declarations of this kind? It would have been useful to fix the majority by which the conference will be called upon to make its decision.[33] As the text of the Treaty does not make it clear, the rule ought to be: a simple majority of Parties attending the conference.

III. DENUNCIATION OR RIGHT OF WITHDRAWAL

Article X (1) gives the right of withdrawal to each Party if "in exercising its national Sovereignty . . . it decides that extraordinary events, related to the subject matter of this Treaty, have jeopardised the supreme interests of its country." Three months' notice of withdrawal must be given to other Parties and to the Security Council. Such notice must explain the nature of the above-mentioned extraordinary events.

The corresponding provision in the 1967 Treaty on Outer Space is still less restrictive, except as to time; it allows withdrawal just by giving one year's notice.[34] On the other hand the Moscow Treaty in its Article IV, includes a similar provision to that of the Non-Proliferation Treaty; the reason for withdrawal is defined in exactly the same way, but no giving of notice to the Security Council is necessary and the Party giving notice of withdrawal is not bound to give the reason for it.[35] I had at the time emphasised the vague and ambiguous character of this Article IV, still

---

[31] ENDC/215.

[32] ENDC/PV. 363. According to Japan, if the revision conference found that the aims and provisions of the Treaty were not being fully achieved, the Parties would be forced to reconsider their position. A/C. 1/PV. 1565.

[33] Nigeria proposed an amendment under which the conclusions of revision conferences would be adopted by a majority of signatory States present. ENDC/220, and PV. 371. But what would signatory, yet non-Party, States have to do at a revision conference?

[34] Art. XVI. V. Also J. E. S. Fawcett, *International Law and the Uses of Outer Space* (Manchester University Press, 1968), pp. 1–16.

[35] Art. IV speaks of "exceptional events" and not of "extraordinary events".

less satisfying than the one which figured in the American draft of 27 August 1962. According to this draft, any Party, if it decided (a) that another party had violated the duties established by the Treaty or (b) that a State not Party had carried out tests; or (c) that nuclear explosions had taken place without it being possible to identify who carried them out; might call for the meeting of a general conference of all Parties. It would then submit the facts to this conference for examination and evaluation. After the end of the conference or at latest at the end of two months from the time of making the request, the Party in question could exercise its right of withdrawal. The draft had therefore listed the events which might justify a denunciation and considered the intervention, in flexible, rudimentary form, of an international body.

Nothing of the kind exists in the Moscow Treaty. The message, already quoted, from the Swiss Federal Council complains about it: "no arbitrating authority is nominated to make an objective and binding judgement on the validity of the reasons for denunciation, and, if necessary, to prevent or at least to make the restarting of tests more difficult. It is undeniable that the Moscow Treaty does not completely satisfy the needs of customary law relative to a contractual Treaty. The duties it lays down appear on examination incomplete and uncertain".

A severe, but correct judgement, legally speaking.[36] Yet it is not sufficient. The problem the three Powers had to resolve was not a legal one. It was to take a step forward in an atmosphere still filled with mistrust, and to turn a momentary balance of power into something permanent upon which depends the survival of each of the two Super-Powers. It is evident that in this field, neither of them could agree, above all, on the occasion of this first agreement, to tie themselves down too severely. Whence arose the ambiguity, the flexibility, the elasticity, and the vague character of the Moscow Treaty and of a Treaty law which was at the same time indisputably important and long lasting.

What were the origins and meaning of Article IV? It seems to have been the United States which proposed the text and that the chiefs of their Armed Forces thought it necessary to enable the government to take the requisite measures without serious difficulty.[37] The Soviet Union was understood to have recommended the elimination of any provision about withdrawal or denunciation. For she thought that a treaty of unlimited

---

[36] See the same opinion in A. Martin, *Legal Aspects of Disarmament* (London, British Institute of International and Comparative Law, 1963), pp. 79–83; B. P. Sinha, *Unilateral Denunciation of Treaty* (The Hague, Nijhoff, 1966), pp. 191–92.

[37] *Hearings 1963*, p. 347.

duration could be denounced at any time.[38] Thus the State Department legal adviser stated that the withdrawal clause figuring in the Moscow Treaty translated the intention of the United States to limit the sovereign rights of the parties, not to make them permanent.[39]

The words "extraordinary events, related to the subject matter of this Treaty" are very equivocal. The American Secretary of State stated it was in conformity with the intention of the Parties and he had no intention of defining the meaning. However, examples have been given of events which might lead the United States to invoke Article IV.[40] Such would be the case if tests were carried out by a non-Party State, especially the People's Republic of China. But at the beginning of July, the head of the American Disarmament Agency said that the test by China of a nuclear device would not modify the balance of power.[41] Among the other causes of withdrawal mentioned were the transfer of nuclear weapons by one Party to another State and a change in the present balance (substantial progress achieved by the Russians in the field of knowledge or technology).

Does Article IV cover the possibility of violation by one Party of obligations laid down by the Treaty? The United States felt that if the Soviet Union were to violate the Treaty, they would withdraw immediately and that in this case the rule about notice would not apply.[42] The State Department tried to prove, in a legal opinion, that doctrine and practice revealed the principle that violation by one Party of its Treaty obligations allowed another Party automatically to release itself from its obligations. This is debatable. But it seems clear that political and psychological factors, the pressure of public opinion, the existence and importance of the Treaty rules to which so many States subscribe, form effective barriers against over-hasty decisions. A relevant example was the Rush-Bagot Treaty of April 1817 on naval disarmament in the Great Lakes, which was violated several times but never denounced.[43] We have seen that in January 1965, the Soviet Union accidently violated the Moscow Treaty. The United States did not denounce it[44] and it has remained in force even after the French and Chinese tests.

[38] ibid., p. 28.
[39] A. S. Fisher, "Arms Control and Disarmament in International Law", *Virginia Law Review*, November 1964, pp. 1200–219.
[40] *Hearings 1963*, pp. 34, 51, 189, 290, 393–94.
[41] *Le Monde*, 7–8 July 1963.
[42] *Hearings 1963*, p. 18; A. S. Fisher, op. cit.
[43] A. Gotlieb, *Disarmament and International Law* (Toronto, Canadian Institute of International Affairs, 1965), pp. 166–67. This Treaty, it will be recalled, binds the United States, Great Britain and Canada.
[44] Cf. ibid., pp. 167–68. Remember that the United States have themselves committed violations of this sort.

To return now to the Non-Proliferation Treaty. The text of Article X (1) remained unchanged after the draft of 24 August 1967. This text provided that the decision to withdraw was a matter for the sovereign appraisal of each Party, but this time it was called upon to justify its attitude. This provision appeared too demanding to some parties. Romania asked for the need to give reasons for withdrawal to be eliminated.[45] Such was also the position of Brazil which also objected to giving notice to the Security Council. According to Brazil, the right of withdrawal ought also to be allowed in cases where a Party felt that events capable of jeopardising its supreme interests might happen.[46] As for Nigeria, while it accepted the principle of notice with an indication of the reason for withdrawal, it felt that this also ought to apply in two extra cases, namely when one Party felt (a) that the aims of the Treaty had been frustrated; (b) that the failure to accede by a State or a group of States compromised the actual or potential balance of power in its area, so threatening its security. Thus widespread efforts were made by non-nuclear States to make the Treaty more flexible, and to get provisions inserted allowing the Parties to be released from their obligations.[47]

The provision in Article X (1) is characteristic of the spirit and life of Treaty relations. The freedom allowed to the Parties to withdraw is at first sight very wide. But in reality, it is a right which could only be exercised in the case of "dramatic events".[48] The countries which, inside and outside the Committee of 18, asked for the limitation of the duration of the Treaty, realised it very well. In fact the exercise of the right to withdraw will be very difficult in the face of public opinion and also that of certain important governments. In addition, the Party deciding to withdraw and which, at the end of three months' notice, would escape the safeguards arranged in Article III would need time before its nuclear force became operational.[49] This would give the other Parties the chance to take appropriate counter-measures.

In any case, the importance attached by the two Co-Chairmen to the text of Article X is shown by the fact that they accepted no amendments to it. This text clearly meant a serious threat to the national interest of a

---

[45] ENDC/190 and 223; ENDC/PV. 362.
[46] ENDC/201/Rev. 2. In the first document (Rev. 1) instead of using "might happen" Brazil used the words "risked happening".
[47] ENDC/202. In a second document Nigeria simplified its amendment, by supporting the text of Brazil's first amendment, referring to events which *risked* happening. ENDC/220.
[48] The phrase is that of the Italian delegate. ENDC/PV. 350.
[49] Cf. D. Vital, "Double Talk or Double Think", *International Affairs*, 1968, pp. 419–33.

country exercising its right to withdraw. It appears that the two Super-Powers intended through the Security Council, to exercise control over the reasons for withdrawal by making this depend upon objective and verifiable facts and not arbitrary hypotheses.[50] Here again, the intentions and agreement of the Co-Chairmen gave real meaning to a provision of the Treaty. Also, during the examination of the Treaty by the Foreign Relations Committee of the United States Senate, possible causes of withdrawal were given. Mr Dean Rusk in particular, indicated that if NATO were to be dissolved, any NATO member might properly have recourse to the provision in Article X (1) in the same way as a State involved in a war.[51]

In any case, since the denunciation would be motivated by national security considerations, it would be of interest to the Security Council which would in this case fulfil the duties defined in Chapters VI and VII of the Charter. The two Co-Chairmen indicated that the role of the Security Council was all the more justifiable since under the relevant General Assembly resolutions proliferation was considered a danger to the security of all States and thus to peace and world security. It was consequently normal to oblige a State wanting to withdraw to reflect on the importance of its act and in order to justify it, to prepare a document setting out its reasons, addressed to the Security Council.[52] The decision to withdraw is of such importance that the Security Council, like the other Parties, has a powerful and legitimate interest to know the reasons. The Council and the Parties must have the possibility of verifying that the State giving notice of withdrawal is not violating the Treaty and is not denouncing it for reasons other than those laid down in Article X (1).[53]

It will be observed that Article X (1) mentions notice to the Security Council, but not to the General Assembly. This provision puts a premium

---

[50] See the statements of the Polish delegate, which here evidently reflect the views of the Soviet Co-Chairman. ENDC/PV. 369.

[51] *Hearings 1968*, pp. 27–28, 93. The development has also been envisaged by the United States of an A.B.M. system that is exclusively defensive and totally effective. In such a case, it is said, Washington might be persuaded to hand over this weapon to non-nuclear States and then invoke Art. X (1). But there is no exclusively defensive weapon. ibid., p. 186. According to a member of Congress, in case of grave events, notice would take effect immediately without it being necessary to wait for the expiry of the three-month period. ibid., p. 157. This view seems wrong to the author. The Bonn Foreign Minister has said that the dissolution of NATO, if it occurred before the expiry of the Non-Proliferation Treaty would lead Germany to invoke the withdrawal clause. *Le Monde*, 14 November 1969.

[52] ENDC/PV. 377 (USSR).

[53] ENDC/PV. 368 (United States).

on the Security Council at the expense of the General Assembly. Even the disarmament plan of the Soviet Union, a country so attached to the prerogatives of the five permanent members of the Council, provided for the Security Council and the General Assembly to be informed in case of violation.[54] Also, according to Article XII–C of the IAEA Statute, any violation of the obligation taken on by a State to use aid provided by the Agency for exclusively peaceful purposes, is brought to the attention of the Board of Governors, who must immediately inform the General Assembly and the Security Council. It is possible, therefore, to find in Article X (1) a reversal of the tendency which had become apparent with the adoption of Resolution 377 (V) of the General Assembly (also called the Acheson or Uniting for Peace Resolution).[55]

Some have criticised the role given to the Security Council, a body including members who will not be or cannot be Parties to the Treaty. This argument does not appear relevant to the author. The practice of the Council shows that it is not limited to using the specific powers given to it under Chapters VI, VII, VIII and XII of the Charter, but that Article 24 of this instrument confers implicit, general powers to exercise its responsibilities. In addition, organs of the United Nations can exercise jurisdiction over non-member States;[56] so it is not easy to see why the role given to the Council under Article X (1) of the Non-Proliferation Treaty should seem excessive.

The problem of violation as distinct from that of withdrawal has been examined in relation to the Moscow Treaty. It also exists in the framework of the Non-Proliferation Treaty. The principles of Article 60 of the Vienna Convention of 23 May 1969 on Treaty Law might perhaps be applied. According to this article, the substantial violation of a multilateral Treaty (that is to say in particular the violation of a provision that is essential for the realisation of the object or aim of the Treaty) by one of the Parties has the effect of permitting: (a) the other Parties, acting in unanimous agreement, to suspend the application of the Treaty or put an end to it; (b) a Party whose rights have been particularly affected to suspend the application of the Treaty in its relations with the State that has carried out the violation; (c) any Party other than the State that has carried out the violation, to use the violation as a reason to suspend, in total or in part, the application of the Treaty as far as it is concerned, if the Treaty is such that a substantial violation of its provisions by one Party radically changes

---

[54] Cf. A. Gotlieb, op. cit., pp. 153–68.
[55] This Resolution, in case of failure by the Security Council, gives the General Assembly powers reserved for it under the Charter.
[56] Art. 2(6) and 35(2).

the position of each Party in regard to the later fulfilment of its duties under the Treaty.

These principles are open to discussion. In the opinion of some, the violation of basic rules, seriously attacking the aims and objectives of the Treaty, ought only to involve its suspension, an emergency measure to be followed up by an investigation by the International Court of Justice.[57]

According to Article 66 and the Annex of the Vienna Convention on Treaty Law, any Party may submit to arbitration differences over the interpretation and application of certain Articles in the Convention, including Article 60.

Be this as it may, the State Department's legal adviser back in 1964 had found that the case envisaged under Article 60 of the Vienna Convention, subsection c, ought to apply to the Moscow Treaty. In his opinion this was a multilateral Convention in which the carrying out of duties by each Party depended on reciprocity by other Parties in carrying out their duties.[58] If you apply this argument to the Non-Proliferation Treaty, the United States would have the right to be freed from its obligations, without giving notice to anyone, if another Party violated its obligations. But it seems to the author that in the context of the latter Treaty, it would be in the interests of the United States to take another attitude. The violation of the Treaty would be an event to be halted, not repeated, above all from the point of view of the nuclear signatory States. This is yet another argument for Security Council intervention.

The examination of the Treaty by the Foreign Relations Committee of the United States Senate appears to support the argument defended here. The new Secretary of State, Mr Rogers, stressed the very grave and exceptional character of the decision mentioned in Article X (1).[59] For his part, General Earle Wheeler, Chief of Staff, seemed to admit that violation of the Treaty by one Party did not allow another to consider itself immediately freed from its obligations, but rather to withdraw under the conditions laid down by the Treaty, whilst in case of war, the Treaty provisions would immediately become void.[60]

But the State Department attitude has even greater nuances. In their opinion, only a general war in which nuclear States took part would put an immediate end to the Treaty. On the other hand, the Treaty would not be affected by a local war in which no nuclear State was involved. This

[57] Q. Wright, *American Journal of International Law*, 1967, pp. 1000–05.
[58] A. S. Fisher, op. cit.
[59] *Hearings 1969*, pp. 367–68.
[60] *Hearings 1968*, p. 78.

interpretation is based principally on the first and second paragraphs of the preamble to the Treaty.[61]

To conclude, let us mention a Swiss proposal for mandatory arbitration of disputes over the interpretation and application of the Treaty. Taking into account the traditional attitude of the USSR as well as the delicate, flimsy compromise represented by the Treaty, which also contains a whole series of vague and ill-defined duties, the Swiss proposal seems singularly unrealistic, and imbued with an abstract, not to say anti-democratic, legal attitude.

[61] *Hearings 1969*, pp. 367, 369, 424.

8. SECURITY GUARANTEES

Security considerations preoccupied non-nuclear States during the whole period the Non-Proliferation Treaty was being drafted. It appeared to many of them that accession to the Treaty was a sacrifice for which compensation had to be obtained in the form of security guarantees from the nuclear States. This view, it is suggested, arose from a wrong analysis of the problem. In fact the Non-Proliferation Treaty contributed to the general security of international society and to the reduction of tension.[1] To talk of compensation in this context seems really nonsensical.

It is a fact, however, that the Treaty is only one element in the organisation of international society which it must assist by enabling better relations to exist between members of this society. It is, therefore, interesting to examine the different ideas and proposals put forward during discussions about international security, the undertakings given by the nuclear States in this field, and finally the attitude adopted towards these undertakings by an important non-nuclear State—India.

I. PROPOSALS SUBMITTED

It is evident that the best solution to the problem lies in general and complete disarmament which is unattainable in the foreseeable future and which was only considered a pre-condition to the Non-Proliferation Treaty by those who wanted to sabotage such a Treaty. Supporters of this argument, calling attention to the equality of States, were mistaking the shadow for the substance. As the American delegate said to his Indian colleague; by making non-proliferation contingent upon disarmament, you are making sure you get neither.[2] It would equally have been possible to imagine all States signing the Treaty renouncing the use of force, in particular to change existing frontiers. This was among proposals made by the White House Committee on Arms Control and Disarmament in December 1965.[3] But this proposal was not supported by any other State.

On the other hand a promise by each nuclear State not to be the first

---

[1] Finland went as far as to state that each nuclear State was being penalised for the fact that it formed a target for other nuclear States. A/C. 1/PV. 1559.
[2] ENDC/PV. 336.
[3] *Bulletin of Atomic Scientists*, February 1966, p. 44.

to use nuclear weapons would be more realistic. Some feel that such a promise would have at least three advantages: (a) the psychological and mental mechanisms and attitudes of the nuclear States, with their fingers twitching on the atomic trigger, would undergo a profound and salutary change; (b) NATO strategy could at last be changed in a logical way and based upon an increase in conventional forces, as Europe has every reason to give up nuclear strategy; (c) the recommended promise would diminish the prestige of nuclear weapons and would itself contribute to the foundation of a non-proliferation policy logically following on from it. But this argument also had its detractors. Such a promise, it was said, might lead to an increase in the number of conventional conflicts and consequently to greater instability. Also, as it would only be a declaration of intent, it would not represent a significant step towards *détente* and would be such as to delay the conclusion of really meaningful agreements.[4] It is worth noting that on 9 May 1966, the Peking government published a solemn declaration according to which, at no time and under no circumstances would China be the first to use nuclear weapons. At the same time China invited other powers to make identical promises. The United States rejected this proposal saying it would only make sense if the promise was subject to some proper form of control. As has been rightly remarked, it is difficult to see what use a control system would be in this case or what it would cover. The idea was then suggested to try and get China to accede to the Moscow Treaty in exchange for an undertaking from Washington in accordance with the Chinese proposal.[5] But nothing came of it.

Objections, resistance and difficulties thus made unlikely the conclusion of a general agreement not to be the first to use nuclear weapons. So a more limited idea was arrived at, recommended both by Switzerland[6] and Romania[7]: nuclear States were to promise, formally and solemnly, never to use nuclear weapons nor threaten to use these weapons against States which did not possess them and which undertook not to manufacture or acquire them. But such a form of words was difficult for the USSR to accept. West Germany, if it signed the Treaty, would become one of the category of States covered by the Romanian amendment. There exist on

---

[4] R. C. Tucker, K. Knorr, R. A. Falk, H. Bull, *Proposal for no first use of Nuclear Weapons, Pros and Cons* (Centre of International Studies, Princeton University, 1963); B. T. Feld, *Bulletin of Atomic Scientists*, May 1967, pp. 47–48.

[5] R. B. Russel, *The United Nations and United States Security Policy* (Washington, Brooking Institution, 1968), p. 112.

[6] ENDC/204.

[7] ENDC/199. Later, Romania hardened her position further, proposing an unconditional, absolute promise not to use nuclear weapons against States not possessing them, nor to threaten these States with the use of nuclear weapons. ENDC/PV. 362.

West German territory American nuclear weapons, and consequently the USSR would hardly have been able to accept the renunciation of the possibility of replying to an American nuclear attack by using her own atomic weapons against West German territory. Also, on 1 February 1966, Mr Kosygin made it known that the Soviet Union was ready to accept an article forbidding "the use of nuclear weapons against non-nuclear countries Party to the Treaty and not having nuclear weapons on their own territory."[8] This was exactly the same form of words which was repeated in an amendment put forward by the UAR.[9]

The Romanian-Swiss proposal represented a sort of basic idea whose implementation was demanded by many States[10] which, to support their case, quoted Resolution 2153 (XXI) of the General Assembly[11] and the additional protocol No. II of the Treaty for the denuclearisation of Latin America.[12] Most of these States would moreover have been happy with the Soviet form of words. But this was unacceptable to certain members of NATO and in particular to West Germany, which did not want either to give up the nuclear arms on her territory, or to be excluded from the security guarantee. Also, according to the Canadian delegate, the undertaking not to use nuclear weapons against non-nuclear States not having these weapons on their territory would have meant the conclusion of an agreement that was difficult to achieve, on the detailed and complicated verification of "denuclearisation".[13]

II. THE UNDERTAKING BY THE THREE NUCLEAR STATES

On 17 June 1968, the three nuclear powers each made a statement in identical terms to the Security Council, offering security guarantees to non-nuclear States acceding to the Treaty.[13a] Each of the three stressed the serious character of aggression using nuclear weapons or the threat of

---

[8] ENDC/167.

[9] ENDC/197.

[10] See in particular A/C1/PV. 1562 (Iran and Kenya); PV. 1560 (Czechoslovakia and Brazil); PV. 1561 (Ethiopia); PV. 1565 (Ceylon); PV. 1579 (Trinidad and Tobago); PV. 1580 (Libya); PV. 1582 (Spain, Algeria, Uganda, Burma, Romania, Yugoslavia).

[11] The General Assembly invites the Geneva Committee to examine urgently the proposal that nuclear weapon powers should guarantee that they will not use or threaten to use nuclear weapons against States not possessing such weapons and not having these weapons on their territory.

[12] Under Art. 3 of this protocol, nuclear States acceding undertake "not to have recourse either to the use of nuclear weapons or to the threat of their use against contracting Parties to the Treaty banning nuclear weapons in Latin America".

[13] A/C. 1/PV. 1573.

[13a] See Annex VI and S/PV. 1430.

such aggression against a non-nuclear State: such an aggression, or such a threat, would constitute "a completely new situation . . . " Each of them announced its intention in such a case, to act immediately through the Security Council, to ensure that the Council should give immediate help to the victim, in accordance with the Charter, and it confirmed the natural right of self-defence, individual or collective, recognised by Article 51 of the Charter in case of armed aggression, until the Council took the necessary steps to maintain peace and international security. It appears that the reference, in this context, to Article 51 of the Charter meant that the Three would come to the help of the victim, under this provision, in a case where such a step was not supported by the required majority or unanimously by the permanent members. But contrary to the other paragraphs of the statement which refer to aggression and the threat of aggression, the one which reaffirmed the right to legitimate defence only mentioned armed aggression (thus copying the text of Article 51). In any case, on 19 June 1968, the Council adopted a resolution welcoming with satisfaction these statements solemnly made before it.[14] We shall quickly comment upon these two texts.

The first problem concerns the actual nature of these unilateral and identical statements. A large number of countries have criticised the form and method of the guarantee offered; in their opinion it would have been infinitely better for the three nuclear States to make the guarantees in the actual body of the Treaty. In that way, the guarantees would have had the character of a legal obligation, and their value, both politically and psychologically, would have been considerably enhanced. In support of this argument, the precedent of the Treaty on the Denuclearisation of Latin America has been cited, whose additional Protocol II was drafted precisely in order to force nuclear States to give the undertakings already described towards countries acceding to the Treaty.[15]

It is true that "a bilateral act (and often a multilateral convention) in the form of a reciprocal exchange of concessions, is its own justification for the protection of each of the two contracting Parties".[16] However, as doctrine and practice show, unilateral declarations do result in valid legal

---

[14] Annex VII.

[15] A/C. 1/PV. 1560 (Brazil), 1562 (Kenya and Ruanda), 1565 (Ceylon), 1567 (Mauritania and Yugoslavia), 1580 (Barbados).

[16] G. Venturini, "La portée et les effets juridiques des attitudes et des actes unilatéraux des Etats", Recueil des Cours de L'Académie de Droit International de La Haye, vol. 112, 1964, pp. 363–468. It is an observation which is hardly true of multilateral conventions which tend more and more to set objective, impersonal norms. A balance of concessions and reciprocity of duties become quite secondary elements, when they do not disappear completely.

obligations, independently of the will of other States. But a unilateral declaration naturally cannot create duties for Third States and its action must be allowed by international legal authorities.[17]

In the case under consideration, we have to decide whether we are dealing with a unilateral declaration. As the last paragraph of the three declarations shows, each is based on the fact that the two others have made a similar declaration.[18] So there is no unilateral declaration, but an agreement among the three nuclear States, put in an unusual form. The validity of an agreement does not of course depend upon the form in which it is concluded. One might even go further and say that it is a real agreement between on the one hand, the three nuclear States, and on the other, the United Nations acting through the Security Council. In fact, the three States in question decided to act in a certain way within the United Nations, and the Security Council approved the declarations made by these States. But one cannot talk of an agreement in the sense of Article 43 of the Charter nor of a mandatory decision taken by the Council in the context of Chapter VII of the Charter which lays down the way the Council is to act in concrete cases of threats to peace, breaking the peace, and acts of aggression.

Moreover, the declarations of the three States create no new duty, in relation to the Charter, and envisage no new eventuality; they simply emphasise some of the acts covered by Chapter VII. In relation to this, it is worth noting the insistence with which American officials as well as Congressmen have stated that the guarantee given by the United States in the Security Council implies no new duty or promise for their country, except perhaps the duty to inform the Security Council if the possibility mentioned in the Resolution were to become a fact.[19]

On the other hand, two of the States giving guarantees indicated that these were necessarily given outside the framework of military alliances and within that of the United Nations, which made it possible to include the guarantees in the actual body of the Treaty. In fact, not only did the interests of countries forming part of an alliance differ from those of non-allied States, but also the situation even within the alliances was far from harmonious. Under these conditions, it was necessary to avoid creating a new security system parallel to the system organised by the Charter which was the only one to offer an appropriate framework for working

---

[17] PCIJ, Series A, Nos. 5 and 7; E. Suy, *Les actes juridiques unilatéraux en droit international public* (Paris, Librairie Générale de Droit et de Jurisprudence, 1962), pp. 25–33.

[18] Before the Foreign Relations Committee of the United States Senate, Mr Dean Rusk vehemently insisted on the fact that the guarantee is not unilateral and that it is limited by the right of veto. *Hearings 1968*, p. 17.

[19] *Hearings 1968*, pp. 9, 17, 34–35, 40–48; *Hearings 1969*, pp. 306, 354–55.

out the guarantees offered by the three nuclear States. The flexibility of means used corresponded to the diversity of the situations.[20]

The vague character of the promises given has also been challenged, and the Security Council Resolution (paragraph 2) welcoming "with satisfaction the *intention* expressed by certain States . . . " has been criticised. These declarations of intent have been contrasted with real legal duties.[21] In fact this attitude is not new. Even in the closest Treaties of alliance the problem of the automatic nature of a promise arises. Each member of the alliance always tries to obtain the most watertight guarantees from its partners, to enjoy absolute certainty of protection in case of need. Now it has been proved in practice that these are demands that can never be entirely satisfied although there are naturally differences in the degree of security obtained, which always remains problematical even within NATO.[22]

Some observers, moreover, feel that, paradoxically, the vague and ambiguous character of the guarantee given in the Security Council by the three nuclear States gives it strength and a certain credibility. Thanks to this guarantee, the non-nuclear States have a hold over the guarantors; the psychological and political conditions created by it would tend to lessen the risk of nuclear aggression. Moreover, a firm guarantee by the Three could be combined with more specific and more precise individual guarantees.[23] West Germany, foreseeing the possibility of the dissolution of NATO after 1970, asked Washington for automatic bilateral guarantees against nuclear attack. American officials refused to give such guarantees.[24] However, in the statement made on the day it signed the Non-Proliferation Treaty, the Bonn government assumed that NATO will continue to guarantee the security of the Federal Republic, and the Resolution 255 of the Security Council as well as the three nuclear States' declarations of intent "will be equally valid without restriction for the German Federal Republic". It appears that the Soviet Union agrees with this interpretation.[24a] So the undertakings made under this Resolution and these declarations apply equally to non-nuclear States on whose territory are nuclear weapons controlled by a nuclear State.

---

[20] ENDC/PV. 368 (United States); A/C. 1/PV. 1558 (United Kingdom). For Mr Dean Rusk, the United States right of veto in the Council constituted a guarantee and a security. *Hearings 1968*, p. 17.

[21] S/PV. 1433 (Brazil).

[22] Cf. M. Sherman, *International Journal*, Autumn 1966, pp. 484–90.

[23] W. B. Bader, *The US and the Spread of Nuclear Weapons* (New York, Pegasus, 1968), pp. 110–14.

[24] *Hearings 1968*, p. 80; *Hearings 1969*, p. 401.

[24a] *Le Monde*, 4 April 1969.

Many other sorts of criticism have been levelled at the guarantee as formulated by the three nuclear States. In practice, so it is said, the veto paralyses the Security Council too often. Has it not up to now proved itself incapable of making Rhodesia respect the basic principles of the United Nations?[25] It has also been asked whether the guarantee did not amount to calling in the doctor after the patient had died.[26]

It has also been emphasised that a guarantee can only really inspire confidence if ties of all kinds between the guarantor and the beneficiary increase in number and strength.[27] Some countries probably have this in mind when they state that the guarantee amounts to creating a protectorate or condominium over non-nuclear States[28] and that the Resolution adopted by the Security Council constitutes an invitation to non-nuclear States to become members of military alliances with nuclear States.[29] One cannot help noticing the rather worrying contradiction between, on the one hand, blame for this type of guarantee, considered too vague and ineffective, and on the other hand criticism that this same guarantee will enable States to establish a hegemony over others. History shows that if nuclear Powers wish to create or consolidate a hegemony, they do not use nuclear weapons to do so.

Different proposals have been made to increase the scope of the guarantee. Some authors believe that the creation of an A.B.M. network in the United States and the Soviet Union would make a counter-attack by these two countries against an aggressor more plausible. But these same authors feel that in order to succeed, a nuclear State like the United States ought to install an A.B.M. network in certain important countries it decides to protect, or around them, perhaps by a naval network.[30] It is not very likely in the present state of affairs that such a proposal would have a chance of being taken into consideration.

Attempts have been made to make the nuclear States' promise more precise. Such was the aim of the Nigerian amendment: "Each nuclear weapon State Party to the present Treaty undertakes, if requested, to come

---

[25] A/C. 1/PV. 1563 (Ghana) and 1572 (Zambia).
[26] A/C. 1/PV. 1574 (Madagascar).
[27] B. M. Russett, "The Calculus of Deterrence", *Journal of Conflict Resolution*, 1963, pp. 97–109. A/C. 1/PV. 1574 (Madagascar).
[28] S/PV. 1433 (Algeria); *International Studies*, October 1967, p. 54. (This review contains an account of discussions at a seminar held in India.)
[29] A/C. 1/PV. 1565 (Ceylon).
[30] Bader, op. cit., pp. 110–14; L. A. Frank, *Orbis*, Spring 1967, pp. 67–79; R. L. Rothstein, *Foreign Affairs*, April 1968, pp. 487–502. Such a tendency also appeared during discussions within and in evidence before the Foreign Relations Committee of the United States Senate during examination of the Treaty. *Hearings 1968*, pp. 159–61, 181–99, 211.

to the help of any non-nuclear weapon State threatened or attacked by nuclear weapons".[31] This idea of a guarantee of help given automatically at the request of a threatened or attacked non-nuclear State was taken up again by the delegate from Pakistan.[32] We have seen that an automatic mechanism of this kind was hardly conceivable in the present condition of international society. It would, moreover, have involved nuclear States in innumerable conflicts and would have favoured States that began to panic too easily at the threat of aggression or who were too prone to call acts of legitimate defence, aggression or the threat of aggression.

The security guarantee raises many other problems. Does it not doubly harm the security system established under the Charter? The basic United Nations instrument forbids recourse to the threat or use of force, whatever the means used, conventional or nuclear. The guarantee only applies to an aggression involving the use of nuclear weapons or the threat of such an aggression. That would be a sort of limitation of the field of action defined by the Charter. We do not believe it is necessary to attach much importance to this argument. What the three nuclear States have actually done, is to declare that their vital national interests demand that there should be no aggression or threat of aggression by means of nuclear weapons.[33] Moreover, the preamble to the Treaty, whose importance is emphasised again in Article VIII (3) (about conferences to review the operation of the Treaty), recalls in its last paragraph that States must, in accordance with the Charter, refrain from the threat or use of force.

The objection that under the Charter, it is the duty of each member of the United Nations to come to the help of another member who is the victim of an armed attack, seems more serious. It is inconceivable that a distinction should be made whether or not the victim had or had not acceded to the Non-Proliferation Treaty. The security guarantees, it has been stated, neither can nor ought to be a reward given to those who have acceded to the Treaty. Put as they are, these guarantees are clearly discriminatory. Now "when the Security Council is called upon to take a decision, in accordance with Article 39 of the Charter, it does not begin to enquire whether a particular State has or has not signed a particular Treaty".[34] But the delegates supporting this argument did not fail to recall the failures and impotence of the United Nations. Legal and moral rules

[31] ENDC/202.
[32] S/PV. 1433.
[33] A/C. 1/PV. 1568 (United States).
[34] S/PV. 1433 (India and Algeria); see also the statements by the Indian delegate. A/C. 1/PV. 1567.

are, sad to say, still far from reigning supreme in international affairs and it would hardly be realistic to hope that the Great Powers will abide by them in the immediate future. The security guarantees we are discussing simply mean that it is in the interest of the three nuclear States that the largest possible number of States should accede to the Non-Proliferation Treaty and that they are prepared in exchange to make some effort for the benefit of these countries.

Does not the Big Three agreement do harm in another way, by prejudic-ing the rules of the Charter which give special responsibilities – and special rights – to the five permanent members of the Security Council? It does not seem to the author that such an argument is valid. After all, the Security Council Resolution on guarantees was carried by 10 votes with 5 abstentions, including France, who did not therefore oppose it. Unity of the five permanent members has only been very rarely achieved; the important fact was agreement on a specific point by some of them, who had always clashed in the past. It even seems to the author that we are witnessing a return to the spirit of the Charter, a rebirth of the Security Council. Doubtless what was envisaged was the possibility of the Security Council not being able to function properly in applying its basic governing rules, but the Big Three declaration shows much more respect for the Charter than did the General Assembly, when in 1950 it passed Resolution 377 (V) called the Uniting for Peace. Of course, the last para-graph of the Big Three declaration might give the impression that the guarantee would not be valid against any one of them. But even if that were true, we should still follow the logic of the security system established under the Charter and based upon the agreement of the five permanent members of the Council. The concentration of power that has taken place since 1945 makes agreement between the two Super-Powers vital: no system of collective or partial security can prevail against either one of them.

It is worrying to observe that, in practice, the guarantee is basically aimed against China, the only country to have stated it would never be the first to use nuclear weapons. China ought to take her rightful place in the United Nations.

The use may be regretted in Resolution 255 and in the declarations of intent of the term "aggression" which has never received a generally accepted definition. It would have been better to have used an expression such as "any attack or threat of attack". But it is questionable if this change would have brought about the desired clarification. Whether you use the word "aggression" or "attack", it must in the end be interpreted in relation to the expression "legitimate defence". The real problem to be solved was the following: can a nuclear reply to a non-nuclear attack be considered a legitimate act of self-defence? But a solution to this problem presupposed a solution to many others over which the nuclear Powers had disagreed for a long time, and particularly the most difficult problem: how to define "aggression" and "legitimate defence". If a solution to these problems had been awaited, the Security Council Resolution and the declarations of intent would never have seen the light of day. Instead of launching interminable negotiations, the Big Three were content to use once again the vocabulary of the Charter. In addition the analysis first made here puts in some doubt, in the author's opinion, the argument used by Canada at the Conference of non-nuclear States. According to this argument, the undertaking made by the Three under Resolution 235 was equivalent to a promise that a nuclear State would not use or would not threaten to use its nuclear weapons against non-nuclear States Party to the Treaty.[34a]

The question now arises of knowing how the guarantee would be honoured. It seems to follow from the context that if the possibility envisaged took place, the guarantors would use nuclear weapons. Let us recall on this point that even within NATO the automatic use of nuclear weapons in case of aggression is far from being the actual state of affairs.

Also, for peace-keeping purposes, the guarantees given on 17 June 1968 might justify the Big Three keeping their nuclear forces, putting them at the disposal of international security by process of "functional division", a concept dear to Georges Scelle. Now, as has been noted, the Non-Proliferation Treaty does not allow the transfer of nuclear weapons to an international force constituted under Articles 43 et seqq. of the UN Charter.[35] In the past, the Soviet Union was against the idea of a possible peace-keeping force being supplied with nuclear weapons, but she did in 1963 agree to the idea of stage by stage disarmament and the retention of a minimum dissuasion force by nuclear States, until the Third Disarmament Stage was reached.[36] It is not perhaps impossible to detect a link on the one hand between these attitudes and this development and on the other between the spirit and the letter of the guarantee offered by the Big Three. However, NATO experience shows that a nuclear guarantee is difficult to separate from conventional guarantees,[37] while the latter have a more independent existence.

In any case, the real solution is the creation and organisation of an international peace-keeping force. But such a force would not be viable without the agreement of the two Super-Powers. In the meantime and

[34a] *Hearings 1969*, p. 452.
[35] *Hearings 1968*, p. 88.
[36] A. F. Neidle, *American Journal of International Law*, 1963, pp. 60–62.
[37] M. Wilbrich, *Foreign Affairs*, July 1966, pp. 683–92.

without losing sight of this aim, the security guarantee just examined here offers advantages and disadvantages and raises many question marks. Still it does exist, and, as some States have recognised, a guarantee even if it is imperfect and open to doubt is better than no guarantee at all.[38] Agreement by the two Super-Powers over collaboration in the security field, however vague it may be, is a fact without precedent since the end of the Second World War, if only because of its psychological and political importance.[39] Naturally, the duration, importance and consequences of this agreement will depend on the course of events and the consolidation of *détente*. If *détente* does continue, the two Super-Powers will necessarily be forced to strengthen general security and to reduce present instability due to frontier and other conflicts.

Certainly, neither of the two Super-Powers can be expected to put itself on the side of the law, and each will try to impose its will in what it considers its sphere of interest. None the less, any rational organisation of international society implies collaboration between the Big Two who in their turn must be subjected to the effective and constructive pressure of small and medium States. However, the difficulty of the problem is illustrated by the fact that the Conference of non-nuclear States held in August–September 1968 proved itself incapable of adopting a single resolution on the security problem,[39a] thus showing that under present conditions of international relations, it was very difficult to use other means and methods than those envisaged by Resolution 255 of the Security Council and the declarations of intent upon which it was based.

III. THE ATTITUDE OF INDIA

Unfortunately, as we shall see, the attitude of India, one of the most important non-nuclear States, does not inspire great optimism. On 15 March 1968, Mrs Gandhi announced that India would not sign the Treaty. Shortly afterwards, some West German politicians tried to establish a common front against the Non-Proliferation Treaty between their country and India.[40] However, as has been quite rightly demonstrated, the positions

[38] S/PV. 1431 (Paraguay and Senegal).
[39] Mr Dean Rusk insisted on this point: *Hearings 1968*, pp. 40–48. Mr Nitze, assistant Defence Secretary, felt that the guarantee reflected the great interest the United States and the Soviet Union had in common to prevent nuclear aggression or the threat of such aggression. ibid., p. 56.
[39a] With the exception of a recommendation adopted at West Germany's initiative which limits itself to recalling a certain number of legal principles laid down in the Charter. See Note 23 of the Conclusion.
[40] *Hindustan Times*, 9 April 1968 (referred to hereafter as *H.T.*).

of the two countries were far from identical. India appeared to demand, as a condition for acceding to the Treaty, the adoption of nuclear disarmament measures, but would have settled for partial measures. West Germany on the other hand demanded guarantees from the United States and a more friendly attitude from the Soviet Union. The Indian position varied considerably over guarantees; in the last phase of drawing up the Treaty, she insisted on the role the Security Council must fulfil outside and independently from the Non-Proliferation Treaty.[41] New Delhi's attitude was also important because it determined that of Pakistan which said it did not wish to sign the Treaty as long as India did not sign.[42]

In the past, as is well known, the Indian government has been one of the fiercest opponents of the nuclear bomb, declaring that India will never manufacture atomic weapons. This attitude could be traced back directly to the moralistic character of Nehru's foreign policy. Tension with China introduced new factors, and after the explosion of the first Chinese bomb, Prime Minister Shastri said in November 1964 that India would not proceed to manufacture a bomb which would absorb economic resources that were too important to her. But the word "never" disappeared and it is thought that India must now have knowledge of nuclear technology in all its aspects.[43] In London in December of the same year, Shastri campaigned for a common front of non-nuclear States against the use of atomic weapons as well as a guarantee from nuclear States to all non-nuclear States.[44] However, as the nature of the guarantees that the three nuclear States were offering to the non-nuclear States became clear, India became colder and colder towards the Treaty.[45] What had happened during this time was that internal pressures by groups who were against limiting the country's freedom of action had grown stronger and the government had to take them into account.[46] On 15 March 1968, before Parliament, Mrs Gandhi denounced the draft Treaty which she found unsatisfactory. For his part Mr S. Singh, deputy Foreign Minister, said the security guarantee could not be sufficient compensation for the promise that the non-nuclear States had to make in signing the Treaty. At the same time, several members of parliament were against accession on the grounds of

---

[41] *The Economist*, 1 June 1968. See also the statement of the Indian delegate. S/PV. 1433.
[42] *The Times*, 24 April 1968; *H.T.*, 25 and 26 April 1968.
[43] *Keesing's Contemporary Archives*, Vol. XV, p. 20567.
[44] ibid., p. 20799.
[45] In May 1965, in the Geneva Committee, India asked for guarantees under UN auspices, which indicated in the opinion of some observers that she had lost interest in them. *New York Times*, 5 May 1965.
[46] *The Economist*, 16 March 1968.

national independence.[47] A little later Mrs Gandhi was to use the same
argument as well as stressing India's well-known interests and her national
security. She made a call for unity, faced by the pressures likely to be
exerted upon India by the two Super-Powers, who could go so far as to
stop all forms of aid.[48] In May, on the occasion of a visit to Australia, the
Indian Prime Minister said that her country did not wish to prevent
nuclear States which considered it opportune, from signing the Treaty.
Yet China would never sign, and the draft Treaty, which in her opinion
created new divisions in the world, gave no security whatever to India, in
that the guarantees given by the nuclear States were not automatic. But
when she was asked what sort of guarantees she wanted, Mrs Gandhi did
not reply.[49]

The Indian government's position has remained the same for some time:
no accession to the Treaty; development of nuclear energy for exclusively
peaceful purposes. It has been stated that the latter undertaking, national
and unilateral in character, has no need to be internationalised.[50] But the
fluctuations and instability of Indian internal politics remove much of the
credibility of this "national undertaking", even supposing it ever had
credibility for other States. In fact the Indian attitude is purely negative
and has everything wrong with it. Some Indian military spokesmen have
come out against accession to the Treaty on the grounds that no security
guarantee is worthy of confidence, and that the country had to develop its
own economic and technological independence. Others have pointed out
the inconsistency which exists between non-accession to the Treaty and
the official statement that India will not manufacture nuclear weapons. It
is absurd, so they say, to reserve a right – at the price of a certain loss of
prestige – that one has no intention of exercising. For economic, scientific
and technological reasons, it is impossible for India to risk isolating herself
and adopt the motto "go it alone . . . ".[51]

In order to get more security – and there are no absolutes here – India
might possibly try to conclude a bilateral Treaty with one of the Super-
Powers who might promise to intervene immediately and automatically.
Under such a Treaty, and in order to whittle down its promise, the
guarantor State would have to maintain troops and bases on Indian territory. Such a situation would demand, or even presuppose, a basic change in
Indian foreign (and domestic) policy. In fact since 1964, India had the

[47] H.T., 15 March 1968.
[48] H.T., 6 April 1968.
[49] H.T., 23 May 1968; Le Monde, 24 May 1968.
[50] See the statement of 24 January 1970 in H.T., 25 January 1970.
[51] See the very interesting confrontation between Generals Som Dutt and J. S.
Paranjpe. H.T., 29 April 1968.

choice between two solutions: either to develop nuclear weapons, or to get a guarantee from one or several nuclear powers and give priority to economic development.[52] The first solution is the more difficult in that, compared to China, India is at a disadvantage over geographical situation, location of centres of population and industry,[53] economic difficulties, and backwardness in the field of military nuclear technology.[54] If she wanted to follow such a policy, India would have to go as far as adopting the French idea, which would be far too costly for her.[55] It seems that India's basic problem lies in her economic and political internal difficulties that could be exploited by foreign countries, rather than in any threatened aggression from outside. Even for her civil nuclear industry, India is largely dependent upon supplies and aid from outside. It may also be questioned whether countries supplying financial aid might not change their attitude to Indian appeals for help if the country were to divert funds to a military atomic programme. Lastly, the Indian position is not likely to strengthen the links between her and other non-aligned States.[56]

India has been unable to make a choice. Her prestige is the more vulnerable, internationally speaking. Her only promise, for the moment, not to manufacture nuclear weapons remains of doubtful value because of agitation by pressure groups against the country remaining non-nuclear. India is not capable of giving the world a scientific and military blueprint having the same importance and arousing the same keen interest as the blueprint for peace it offered world public opinion in the time of Gandhi and Nehru.[57]

[52] See the excellent articles in *H.T.*, 14 March and 12 June 1968.
[53] M. J. Desai, *Disarmament and Arms Control*, Autumn 1965, pp. 135–42. Taking these factors into account, India ought to make double the effort China is making in order to have available as effective a deterrent force.
[54] Bader, op. cit., pp. 66–75.
[55] Major-General D. K. Palit, a supporter of the bomb, answered the economic arguments used against him by quoting the advice of General Beaufre; it was necessary to follow the French example, begin a military programme and not exercise the final option (that is to say the decision whether or not to build the bomb) until later. *H.T.*, 2 March 1970. The trouble is that once a military programme has been started, you never see it stop half-way.
[56] This is clearly what the embarrassment in the Indo-Yugoslavian communiqué of 27 January 1968 indicates.
[57] Cf. *H.T.*, 13 April 1968. Opening a seminar devoted to these problems in 1966, the President of India also recognised a difference between accession to exclusively peaceful activities in the nuclear field and accession to the Non-Proliferation Treaty. During this seminar, it was recognised that it was in the common interest of the USA and the USSR not to build a dam against the Chinese presence, which would have relieved India. It was also admitted that if she began military manufacture, India would still have to make greater efforts in the conventional arms field. *International Studies*, October 1967, pp. 151–61.

9. COLLATERAL MEASURES

WE shall now examine what are called collateral measures, that is to say those that might be taken in the interests of peace in general but would demand certain sacrifices from nuclear States.

Etymologically speaking, we are talking about measures related to the aims of the Non-Proliferation Treaty and flowing more or less directly from this Treaty. In this sense it is legitimate to ask, as the Italian delegate did, whether the Treaty is itself a simple collateral measure or if it is an instrument marking the beginning of the construction of the new international community of the nuclear age.[1] We shall examine in succession the next stages in this construction and the setting up of a denuclearised zone.

I. THE NEXT STAGES

1. Various proposals

The Non-Proliferation Treaty is not a disarmament measure. Non-nuclear States acceding to it forgo activities they have not yet engaged in and in return ask nuclear States to take immediate disarmament measures. As far back as 1965, the eight non-aligned Powers said the Non-Proliferation Treaty was only one means of arriving at general and complete disarmament and in particular nuclear disarmament.[2] In 1966 they proposed that the Treaty be accompanied or followed by concrete measures among which should be the following: a complete stop on the production of fissile materials for military purposes; an embargo and gradual reduction in stocks of nuclear weapons, their launchers and vectors; a ban on the use of nuclear weapons. "These different measures could be incorporated in a Treaty as part of its provisions, not as a declaration of intent."[3]

According to Switzerland, the declaration of intent in the preamble ought to be inserted into the main body of the Treaty and be changed so as to cover more precise duties such as, for example, the stabilisation of atomic arsenals at their present levels.[4] This was an idea that had already been put forward by the United States in 1964, when they recommended

---

[1] A/C. 1/PV. 1565.
[2] ENDC/159.
[3] ENDC/178.
[4] ENDC/204.

a "cut-off", a halt to the production of fissile materials for atomic weapons purposes. This idea, as has been observed, was taken up by the eight non-aligned countries.

Signor Fanfani, for his part, thought it would be desirable to conclude an agreement, perhaps independently from the Treaty, under which (a) the nuclear Powers would from time to time transfer to non-nuclear States for peaceful purposes a suitable quantity of fissile material they had produced; (b) this material would be paid for at a reduced price, part of which would be handed over to the United Nations Development Fund; (c) the transfer of materials would be subject to control, in accordance with the provisions of the Non-Proliferation Treaty.[5] This system would reduce the quantity of fissile material available for military purposes in nuclear States. Also the idea in paragraph (b) would satisfy certain demands of non-nuclear States, that the non-proliferation agreement should speed up progress in atomic energy for peaceful purposes in developing countries, and facilitate the transfer to these countries of resources made available through disarmament measures. One of the Brazilian amendments tried to incorporate this principle into the Treaty, in the form of a legal undertaking by the nuclear States.

The draft of 24 August 1967 limited itself to stating in the preamble that signatory States: (a) intend to stop the nuclear arms race as soon as possible; (b) ask for the co-operation of all States with a view to achieving this objective; (c) wish to arrive at the conclusion of a general and complete disarmament Treaty, under strict and effective international control, involving a halt to the manufacture of nuclear weapons, the liquidation of all existing stocks, and the elimination of nuclear weapons and their vectors. Several non-nuclear States have felt that the aims stated in paragraph (c) ought to be incorporated into the body of the Treaty itself, in the form of a separate article. According to a Mexican proposal, each nuclear State Party to the Treaty would undertake to carry on negotiations in good faith with all possible diligence and perseverance, with a view to reaching agreement over the banning of all tests, the halting of atomic weapons manufacture, as well as the other aims listed in the preamble to the American-Soviet draft.[6] This was also the purpose of a Brazilian amendment which envisaged agreements towards stopping the nuclear arms race, and then the reduction and elimination of these weapons and their vectors.[7] On this point the Big Two made some concessions, which did not, however, go very far. The Draft of 18 January includes a new Article VI which repeats the Mexican proposal, in vaguer terms.

[5] ENDC/205 and PV. 318.
[6] ENDC/196.
[7] ENDC/201, Rev. 1.

In the final text, the provisions in the preamble were still further strengthened. The States Party stated their intention "to take effective steps towards nuclear disarmament". (Preamble, paragraph 8.) They also recalled that the Parties to the Moscow Treaty expressed their determination to achieve the discontinuance of all nuclear tests and to continue negotiations to this end. (Preamble, paragraph 10.) Lastly, according to Article VI of the Treaty, the Parties undertook to pursue negotiations with a view to stopping the nuclear arms race *at an early date*. These four words were inserted at the request of Sweden.[8] Article VI as it now stands distinguishes between measures regarding cessation of the nuclear arms race which must be taken at an early date, and nuclear disarmament to which – arguing *a contrario* – the same urgency is not attached. This is a realistic and reasonable position. Some wanted to go further. They demanded the insertion into the Treaty of a proper timetable (the date of the beginning of negotiations and the latest date by which they were to be concluded) and a list of questions upon which the negotiations should be based.[9] This would have imposed guidelines that were too rigid and completely unacceptable to the Super-Powers. Article VI includes a promise to negotiate, but not to conclude and it is difficult to see how the Parties could validly have committed themselves to reach agreement. A list of specific measures would have blocked agreement on other points capable of affording more fruitful possibilities of negotiation.[10]

Some countries, however, made their accession to the Treaty contingent upon a serious promise by the nuclear States to take real disarmament measures. Thus India had asked for a provision in the Treaty under which nuclear States would promise to stop producing new nuclear weapons.[11] Other States, such as France, and some writers[12] felt that only general disarmament could ensure the success of the Non-Proliferation Treaty. This line of reasoning, according to which countries refused to support the Treaty for the sole reason that it did not go as far as they had hoped was particularly shocking coming from a country like India which has always insisted on the need to put a stop to the nuclear arms race.[13] As for the French argument, one cannot do better than quote M. Jules Moch: "Our government, by rejecting partial practical measures so as not to be interrupted in building up its little *force de frappe*, acts as if it were bent upon stressing its support for general disarmament only because it knows this is

---

[8] ENDC/215.
[9] See for example A/C. 1/PV. 1566 (Uganda).
[10] Cf. ENDC/PV. 363 (Sweden).
[11] A/C. 1/PV. 1567.
[12] See for example D. Vital, *International Affairs*, 1968, pp. 419–33.
[13] See in this sense ENDC/PV. 378 (United States).

at present impossible. Is it trying to give itself an alibi before world opinion?"[14]

In fact, non-nuclear States have several different means of putting pressure upon nuclear States to force them to negotiate seriously and in good faith. Delay between ratification and accession can be put to good use for this purpose.[15] Article VIII (3) on the periodic conferences meant to consider the way the Treaty is working affords another field of action for non-nuclear States. Thus the Canadian delegate was quite right to affirm that non-nuclear States refusing to accede to the Treaty would lose all moral authority giving them the right to insist upon the nuclear powers stopping, then reducing and eliminating their nuclear weapons.[16]

Yet as early as 27 June 1968, Mr Gromyko, speaking for his government, said he was prepared to go ahead with an exchange of views on the limitation and reduction of strategic weapons both offensive and defensive, including anti-missile missiles (that is to say, the A.B.M.).[17] This change of attitude, which it certainly is, may be partly due to the adoption of the Non-Proliferation Treaty. We have already had occasion to discuss the possible effects of a nuclear arms race, especially in the anti-missile-missile field. It is possible to put up various hypotheses about this. For example, an agreement between the two Super-Powers aimed at stopping the manufacture of the A.B.M. might perhaps give them still more powerful motives to avoid surprises from other nuclear Powers and non-nuclear countries and to prevent other States from brandishing atomic weapons or threatening to use them. If they were to give up the A.B.M., the United States and the Soviet Union could not, any more than they can today, ignore or shut themselves away from the rest of the world. In any case, after some hesitation, the new US administration sat down with the Soviet Union at a conference table on 17 November 1969 to examine the limitation of offensive and defensive strategic nuclear weapons systems. For its part in 1969, the General Assembly invited the United States and the USSR to observe, as an urgent measure, a moratorium upon the continuation of tests and deployment of new offensive and defensive strategic nuclear weapons systems. This recommendation, incorporated into Resolution 2602A (XXIV) was passed by 82 votes to 0. There were 37 abstentions including the United States and the Soviet Union, which obviously does not give grounds for optimism.

On 5 July 1968 the Soviet Union put forward a work programme for

[14] *Le Monde*, 31 July 1968.
[15] Cf. ENDC/PV. 364 (Sweden).
[16] A/C. 1/PV. 1573.
[17] *The Times*, 28 June 1968.

stopping the arms race and for disarmament.[18] On 15 August 1968 the Co-Chairmen of the Geneva Committee, after a debate which took place within the organisation, agreed upon the following agenda: (1) new and effective measures for the halting, in the near future, of the nuclear arms race and for nuclear disarmament (stopping of tests, non-use of nuclear weapons, stopping the production of fissile materials for military purposes, stopping the manufacture of nuclear weapons, reduction and then elimination of nuclear stocks, denuclearised zones); (2) non-nuclear measures (chemical and bacteriological warfare, regional limitation of weapons); (3) other collateral measures (peaceful use of the sea-bed); (4) general and complete disarmament.[19]

This agenda was a compromise, which explains its vagueness as well as the total lack of an order of priority. It is worth noting that the Co-Chairmen whose job it was to draw up the agenda, took into account remarks made by the other members of the Committee and that they specifically recognised the right "of each delegation to raise and discuss any disarmament subject at any meeting of the Committee". The Committee will have to change its working methods, negotiate several matters at the same time, and no longer concentrate for years on a single problem, as it did between 1963 and 1968 over the Non-Proliferation Treaty. But it must not go from one extreme to another and by tackling many subjects fail to arrive at any concrete solution. In order to avoid this danger, the Mexican delegate proposed the formation of several restricted sub-committees, each appointed to deal with a particular problem.[20]

The Swedish delegate also listed the points she considered ought to have priority: (1) total test ban; (2) stopping the production of fissile materials for military purposes; (3) the problem of biological and chemical weapons; (4) the exclusively peaceful use of the sea-bed; (5) the question of the international control of peaceful nuclear explosions.[21]

It is impossible for us to study these different questions here. We must

[18] A/7134. This memorandum puts forward nine precise points for discussion which are listed in the order in which they were given: (1) banning the use of nuclear weapons; (2) measures aimed at stopping the production of nuclear weapons and reducing and eliminating stocks of these weapons; (3) limitation and, later, reduction of vectors for strategic weapons (this point covers the A.B.M.); (4) banning the flight of bombers carrying nuclear weapons beyond national frontiers and limiting the navigation areas of missile launching submarines; (5) banning underground tests of nuclear weapons; (6) banning the use of chemical and bacteriological weapons; (7) eliminating foreign military bases; (8) regional disarmament measures (reduction in the level of weapons at the regional level and denuclearised zones); (9) use of the sea and ocean bed for exclusively peaceful purposes. Of course, for completeness sake the Soviet note mentions general and complete disarmament.

[19] ENDC/PV. 390.   [20] ENDC/PV. 389.   [21] ENDC/PV. 383.

be satisfied with a brief examination of the test ban, chemical and biological weapons, international trade in conventional weapons, and the denuclearisation of the sea- and ocean-bed outside national territorial jurisdiction.

2. Total Test Ban

In a speech on 10 June 1963, President Kennedy announced he had reached agreement with the USSR and Great Britain to begin negotiations in Moscow at the highest level in the hope of speedy agreement upon a total test ban. It has already been explained why only a partial test ban Treaty was subsequently signed. However, the Parties to the Moscow Treaty declared in the Preamble and in Article I (1, B) that they would try to conclude a Treaty banning all tests including those carried out underground. For its part the General Assembly vainly sought the suspension of underground tests, the conclusion of a total test ban Treaty and the organisation of an international exchange of seismic data.[22] This shows how, in spite of the promises incorporated into its text, a partial test ban Treaty is in danger of retaining its incomplete character indefinitely.

From 1964 onwards, the number of tests carried out has tended rather to increase, the great majority being carried out underground.[23] In spite of protests by experts, in April 1968 the United States exploded in Nevada a device of the equivalent power of a million tons of T.N.T., that is to say fifty times the power of the Hiroshima bomb.[24] Sweden suffered – and protested to interested governments – about the growing frequency of radioactive fall-out from underground tests.[25]

On 15 September 1965, the eight non-aligned members of the Geneva conference demanded the conclusion of a Treaty banning underground tests, which might be facilitated by exchanges of scientific information and by improvement in techniques of detection and identification. In the meantime, the eight asked nuclear States to put a moratorium upon tests of all kinds.[26] The Soviet Union during 1965 had accepted the idea of this moratorium as well as a proposal by the United Arab Republic to extend the Moscow Treaty to cover underground tests with a seismic scale of

---

[22] Resolutions 2032 (XX), 2163 (XXI), 2343 (XXII), 2455 (XXIII) and 2604 (XXIV).
[23] From October 1963 until the end of 1968, the United States carried out 170 tests, the USSR 24, the UK 2, France 16 and China 8. See *SIPRI Yearbook of World Armaments and Disarmament, 1968/69*, p. 242.
[24] *The Times*, 23 April 1968 and *Hindustan Times*, 27 April 1968.
[25] ENDC/PV. 399. See also ENDC/404 (India) and ENDC/235.
[26] ENDC/159. It was a question not only of detecting a phenomenon, but also of deciding whether it was a natural earthquake or an artificial explosion.

over 4·75.[27] As for the United States, they said they were ready to conclude a general test ban Treaty with appropriate controls.[28]

On 17 August 1966, the eight non-aligned powers made a fresh proposal: (a) that underground tests over a certain level be banned altogether and others suspended until the conclusion of a general test ban Treaty; (b) that by international co-operation among national institutions, seismic information be improved (this has been called the Detection Club); (c) that a verification system by challenge be created, under which a party suspected to be guilty of violating the Treaty would be challenged to give all appropriate information and even to allow an on-the-spot inspection; in case of an unsatisfactory reply, any other Party would be able to denounce the Treaty; (d) that for cases where on-the-spot inspections were authorised, a list of impartial inspectors be deposited with the Secretary-General of the United Nations; (e) that experts recruited individually among citizens of neutral countries should examine the problem of identifying underground tests and give their opinion about this.[29]

The document just summarised reflects the efforts made by the Swedish delegation and its Chairman, Mrs Alva Myrdal. After much research, she demonstrated that detection and identification methods have been perfected to such an extent that it is possible now to envisage controls without on-the-spot inspections. In this case there would only be an extremely unlikely statistical probability of confusion between an earthquake and an underground test. As the potential violator could not be sure that the test would not be identified, control without inspection, even if it left a margin of uncertainty (a very small one it is true), would constitute a sufficient deterrent against any violation.[30]

Mrs Mydal believes that if the possibility of identification is perfected by the methods she suggests, false alerts will become rare; it could legitimately be said that there would not be more than one every ten years. "A decision over what constitutes adequate verification is without any doubt at all a political one, even if it has to be taken on the basis of completely adequate scientific and technical considerations."[30a] The Swedish delega-

[27] That is to say about 20,000 metric tons, which is equivalent to the force of the Hiroshima bomb. The most powerful bomb, the one tested by the Russians, was about 60 Megatons or 60 million metric tons.
[28] ENDC/160.
[29] ENDC/177.
[30] ENDC/191 and PV. 309, 315, 323, 332, 364, 385.
[30a] ENDC/PV. 399 and 415. On 1 April 1969 the Swedish delegation tabled a draft Treaty banning underground tests of nuclear weapons, ENDC/242. The draft included all underground tests, the only exception being explosions for peaceful purposes carried out under the special international agreement which had to be negotiated under the Non-Proliferation Treaty. It is worth quoting the text of

tion's argument was disputed on technical and political grounds by the American[31] and British[32] representatives. It is obvious, however, that no control system can offer a total or absolute guarantee. The United States themselves accepted, as far as the Non-Proliferation Treaty and the draft Treaty for the partial demilitarisation of the sea-bed were concerned, safeguard systems that were far from being watertight.

In April and June 1968, the Stockholm International Peace Research Institute[33] organised two conferences of seismological experts from ten countries.[34] Without going into details, one can say the experts were agreed on the fact that since 1963 detection and identification methods had much improved. Ordinary seismological instruments enabled the nature of explosions in hard rock to be detected and identified when the energy liberated was of the order of 20–60,000 metric tons. On the other hand, we probably did not yet have the means of detecting and identifying explosions of under 20,000 metric tons, particularly when they were carried out in a light soil or in large cavities in hard rock.[35] The experts did not

---

the draft of Art. II: "1. Each State Party to the present Treaty undertakes to co-operate in good faith to ensure the strict observation and execution of the present Treaty. 2. Each State Party to the present Treaty undertakes to co-operate in good faith in an effective international exchange of seismological data in order to facilitate the detection, identification and localisation of underground phenomena. 3. Each State Party to the present Treaty undertakes to co-operate in good faith in order to elucidate all phenomena relative to the aims of the present Treaty. In applying this provision each State Party to the Treaty is empowered: (a) to ask for information and to collect information given in reply; (b) to propose an inspection in its territory or in a territory placed under its jurisdiction, such inspection to be made in the manner prescribed by the inviting Party; (c) in cases where it considers insufficient information is available or has been put at its disposal under the series of preceding provisions, or any one of them, to put forward proposals concerning appropriate methods to elucidate the said phenomena. 4. Each State Party to the present Treaty may draw the attention of the Security Council of the United Nations and of other Parties to the Treaty that another Party has, in its opinion, not co-operated to the greatest possible degree in the elucidation of a particular phenomenon."

[31] ENDC/PV. 320. The American delegate put forward an interesting argument which shows the importance attached to world public opinion. Suppose, he said, there exists technical proof of a violation, a proof disputed by the violator and within the understanding only of seismological experts. A Party deciding to withdraw because of this violation would assume the responsibility for his act before public opinion. ENDC/PV. 401.

[32] ENDC/PV. 319.

[33] (SIPRI). This is a non-governmental international organisation created and financed by the Swedish Parliament. The controlling bodies and the staff are international.

[34] Canada, Czechoslovakia, France, India, Japan, Romania, Sweden, USSR, United Kingdom, U.S.A.

[35] ENDC/230.

examine in detail the possibilities of using large modern detection systems nor methods of detection by satellite, already widely used. They felt the use of statistical methods recommended by the Swedish delegation would enable identification procedures to be improved. A precise and effective international system for the exchange of information ought to be established. It is regrettable that an organisation as well endowed as the American Atomic Energy Commission has not made greater efforts in the field of detection and identification techniques.[36] Moreover, it may be questioned whether the two Super-Powers, and in particular the Soviet Union, are ready to make public the most modern detection and identification methods they use and the results they obtain.

A new proposal was made recently by Britain.[37] It was for the creation by Treaty of a special committee to examine complaints about violations of the total test ban. The committee would be made up of representatives of the three nuclear States, of three non-aligned countries and one member appointed by the Secretary-General of the United Nations or the Director-General of the IAEA.[38] Compulsory decisions would be taken by a majority of five votes and under these conditions the committee could arrange on-the-spot inspections each time such a measure seemed justified. Also, if it were impossible to conclude a total test ban Treaty immediately, the British proposal was for a step by step diminution, beginning by an agreed annual quota of underground test explosions of nuclear weapons. The quota system for tests would operate on a decreasing scale for a fixed number of years ending up with a nil quota. But the USSR did not want to accept the principle of the Committee. As for the annual quotas, they ought, in the opinion of some countries, also to include peaceful nuclear explosions.[39]

The UAR proposal, already referred to, to combine a ban on explosions over a certain power with a moratorium on explosions under this figure, has also been taken up again recently.[40] However, Mrs Myrdal has spelt out the technical difficulties of such a solution: explosions of the same power will be registered on seismographical instruments as having completely different intensity if they do not take place in the same kind of soil or rock. Under these conditions it looks as if the most realistic and rational solution would be to adopt the 1966 proposal of the eight non-aligned countries, with its system of verification by challenge.

[36] Cf. R. E. Lapp, *The New Priesthood* (New York, Evanston, London, Harper and Row, 1965), p. 210.
[37] ENDC/232; PV. 381 and 387. A variation was proposed by Japan. ENDC/PV. 424.
[38] Remember that the committee proposed by the non-aligned countries was to be made up of independent scientific personalities.
[39] Cf. ENDC/PV. 385 (Sweden).
[40] ENDC/PV. 383 (Czechoslovakia) and 402 (USSR).

A general test ban Treaty would contribute enormously towards stopping the arms race as it would prevent the development and testing of new weapons. In addition there exists a link between the conclusion of such a Treaty and the problem of peaceful nuclear explosions: the Treaty ought to except peaceful explosions carried out in conformity with appropriate international procedure and under the authorisation of an international organisation by countries which have signed the Non-Proliferation Treaty and the total ban Treaty.[41]

In 1969, the General Assembly, on Canada's initiative, adopted Resolution 2604A (XXIV) asking member States and certain other States for information "in the context of the creation of a world exchange of seismological data so as to facilitate the achievement of a complete ban on nuclear tests". This resolution touches upon a fundamental problem, the existence and efficacy of the "detection club" recommended in particular by Sweden. The Soviet Union, which had indicated it was ready to take part in an organised exchange of national seismological data voted, together with some of her allies, against the Resolution. In particular, she found fault with the previously mentioned resolution – often irrelevantly – because it asked for too wide and too detailed information, because it envisaged not only an exchange of seismological data but also data upon seismic observatories, because it imposed a rigid time limit on replies, because it envisaged the evaluation of data obtained through the exchange, by an international organisation, whilst in the Soviet Union's opinion this evaluation was a matter for each individual State, because it went against the principle of the purely voluntary communication of data, and because it did not include East Germany among those countries which asked for information.[41a] All these arguments in fact proved to what extent the Soviet Union was anxious not to admit any precedent whatsoever that could be used, directly or indirectly, against her arguments against allowing any inspection.

The difficulties therefore must not be underestimated. In 1963, when the United States Congress accepted the Partial Test Ban Treaty, it demanded at the same time that the underground tests necessary for the development and perfection of nuclear weapons be pursued with the utmost vigour. The USSR, as is well known, refuses any on-the-spot inspection and this refusal, in the eyes of the Americans, justifies the solution of the partial ban.[42] As far back as 1966, Mr Dean Rusk emphasised that on-the-

[41] ENDC/PV. 385 (Sweden), 391 (Burma), 399 and 415 (Sweden).
[41a] ENDC/PV. 429; A/C. 1/PV. 1699 and 1712.
[42] In 1960 the USSR accepted three annual inspections. The figure considered as an indispensable minimum by the West was seven. Faced with this refusal by the West, the USSR withdrew their offer in 1963 and now are no longer willing to consider any inspection which they put in the same category as espionage.

spot inspection was necessary to give a feeling of security and confidence to those adhering to the future total Test Ban Treaty.[43] But certain American politicians protested against such a rigid position, against the refusal to run a small risk in exchange for a big political advantage.[44] It seems that in 1966, the American government envisaged the conclusion of a Treaty banning (without inspection) underground tests of over 20,000 metric tons, but that it gave up the idea because of opposition from certain quarters. Even if methods of detection and identification offered total security, Congress would, it appears, be against the conclusion of a total test ban Treaty for psychological, political and perhaps economic reasons.[45] Such pessimism is not entirely justified. Everything depends on the effectiveness of the education and information programme that the executive would have to carry out for members of Congress. After all, President Kennedy succeeded quite easily in getting the Moscow Treaty ratified by a Congress that was hesitant at first.

3. Chemical and bacteriological (or biological) weapons

The Geneva Protocol of 1925 (signed 17 June 1925) bans the use in time of war of bacteriological agents and "asphyxiating, poisonous or other gases, and of all analogous liquids, materials or devices". In the middle of 1969, sixty-seven States were Party to the Protocol. Among those not party to it, the most important are the United States and Japan.[46]

On 6 August 1968, the British delegation to the Geneva Conference put forward a working document,[47] that can be summarised as follows: the 1925 Geneva Protocol is not a very satisfactory document; (a) certain States have not adhered (principally the United States and Japan); (b) certain adherent States have reserved the right to use the banned weapons against non-Party States or against States violating the Protocol and their allies; (c) there is uncertainty as to whether the norms laid down by the Protocol are customary or simply conventional; (d) there is a difference of interpretation over the word "gas", some countries maintaining that it only covers lethal agents; (e) the word "bacteriological" does not embrace the whole range of microbiological agents that might be used; (f) the terminology of the Protocol leaves in doubt the legality of using the banned

---

[43] *Hearings 1966*, p. 25.
[44] R. B. Russell, *The UN and US Security Policy* (Washington, Brookings Institution, 1968), p. 93.
[45] W. B. Bader, *The US and the Spread of Nuclear Weapons* (New York, Pegasus, 1968), pp. 122–24; also M. Wright, *Disarm and Verify* (London, Chatto and Windus), 1964 pp. 118–29.
[46] *SIPRI Yearbook of World Armaments and Disarmament* pp. 334–36.
[47] ENDC/231.

weapons in the event of hostilities not equivalent to a war in the technical sense of the term. Therefore the United Kingdom proposed to separate the two categories of weapons and to conclude a new Convention banning microbiological methods of warfare, which would complete the Geneva Protocol without replacing it. The proposal is justified by the peculiarly horrible character of these methods, by the indignation their use would arouse and by the fact that they have never been used until now. There would therefore be, in this field, a possibility of arriving quickly at results acceptable to a very great number of States. The new Convention would also ban the production of microbiological agents for military purposes and all research for such purposes. Existing stocks would be destroyed. "All interested civil medical and health services will have access to all research work giving rise to allegations that the duties imposed by the Convention are not being respected. This research work ought if necessary to be made the subject of an international enquiry and the public ought to be admitted as observers, in so far as this is compatible with national security and the protection of industrial and commercial processes." Also it is envisaged "that a group of competent experts, created under the aegis of the United Nations, should carry out an enquiry into the allegations of a party to the Convention claiming that another party has infringed the duties laid down by the Convention. The Convention would include a provision under which Parties would unreservedly promise to co-operate in an enquiry, and any failure to respect this duty or any other duty imposed by the Convention would be communicated to the Security Council."

It appears that the British proposal arose out of a desire to influence the United States who are using in Viet-Nam agents banned by the Geneva Protocol, at least according to the interpretation given to the Protocol by the majority of academics and governments. In addition, the British government wanted to calm the public indignation that had been provoked in Britain by information about the activities of the microbiological research centre at Porton Down. It is under the exclusive control of the Defence Ministry, carries out its work and research in secret, and supplies information and products to the United States. This state of affairs was the subject of strong criticism from Labour MPs and from eminent scientists, twenty-one of whom, including eight Nobel Prize winners, sent a letter of protest to the Prime Minister in May 1968.[48] In any case, this example shows that the pressure of public opinion can cause governments to take positive action on the international level. And more recently when the British

[48] *The Times*, 6, 7, 8, 27, 28 June 1968; *The Observer*, 16 June 1968; *The Economist*, 20 July 1968. See also questions and answers in the House of Commons 27 June, 1 and 4 July 1968.

government went over completely to the American view that the Geneva Protocol does not cover tear gases, this attitude can be clearly put down to a desire to continue using gases of this type in Northern Ireland.

In any case the British proposal was criticised from many quarters, and finally the Geneva Committee agreed to recommend that the General Assembly ask the Secretary-General to appoint a group of experts to study the effects of the possible use of chemical and bacteriological forms of warfare. This report was published in July 1969 and it is worth giving a quick summary of it. The experts begin by stressing that the Geneva Protocol "established a custom and thence a norm of international law and, in practice, most States have adhered to the principle by which they will not have recourse to such weapons".[49] Of course there are differences between C and B weapons, the latter being considered as living organisms reproducing themselves and having more powerful and less rapid effects than the former.[50] But the two categories of weapons have many common characteristics: their effects are unforeseeable and civilians are even more vulnerable to them than the military;[51] protection against both categories of weapons is well nigh impossible or illusory;[52] they can be disseminated by the same vectors.[53] "A chemical and bacteriological (biological) war would thus pave the way to hostilities which it might become difficult, if not impossible, to contain, and all to a greater extent than has been the case in any previous war. Now the concept of hostilities that it is impossible to contain is incompatible with the concept of military security[54] ... " "As the effects of chemical and bacteriological (biological) weapons are unforeseeable, to different degrees, both from the point of view of their extent and their duration and as no secure protection can be envisaged against these effects, the universal elimination of these weapons would not prejudice the security of any country."[55] The experts give yet another reason for not separating the two categories of weapons: "an agent considered today as biological could tomorrow, given the progress of scientific knowledge, be classed as a chemical agent".[56] Already there is complete disagreement over the nature of the toxins that experts classify as chemical substances (for although they are produced by living organisms they do not reproduce themselves).

[49] A/7575, para. 7.
[50] ibid., paras. 17 et seqq.
[51] ibid., paras. 10 and 367.
[52] ibid., paras. 104 and 374.
[53] ibid., para. 346.
[54] ibid., para. 368.
[55] ibid., para. 374.
[56] ibid., para. 19.

Much has been said about C and B weapons – particularly B weapons – describing them as the weapons of the poor. On this point the report is fairly equivocal. It shows that the production of a single agent and its use by means of a simple launching method would not be expensive, but that a proper weapons system (that is to say "all the material and personnel as well as the necessary organisation to maintain and operate a military installation") would demand "large resources and considerable means for its operation and maintenance".[57]

As far as the distinction between lethal and non-lethal agents is concerned, the report shows that it is often difficult to establish. "An attack using any given lethal agent will not have fatal consequences for every individual, whilst an attack by an incapacitating agent may kill a certain number, such as young children and people weakened by malnutrition, illness or old age, as well as a great number of those who find themselves in special situations, such as for example those who have been exposed to radiation."[58] Deaths have been observed after exposure to tear and irritant gases.[59] Herbicides, defoliants and crop-destroying substances may have permanent and as yet unknown effects upon the ecological balance. Already 16 per cent of the forest area of South Viet-Nam has been destroyed between 1963 and 1968, which may have incalculable effects upon the climate, environment, fauna, and flora.[60] A report by the WHO published on 21 November 1969 shows the dangers resulting from absorption through food and water of chemical products used as weapons. It makes public the results of a preliminary laboratory study: mice and rats treated with one of the defoliant agents used gave birth to an abnormally high number of deformed young. In October 1969 Mr Lee DuBridge, scientific adviser to President Nixon, recognised the dangers resulting from the use of these substances.[61]

Of course, tear and irritant gases are used in civil disorder and riot by a great number of national police forces. It is impossible to draw any conclusion as to the legitimacy of using them in international armed conflict. "It is true that considerable efforts have been made in the course of the last few years to perfect chemical agents whose aim is not to kill but to diminish a man's ability to fight. Such agents are used by the civil power in many countries to put down disorders and combat riots. But during military operations they would inevitably be used in addition to

[57] ibid., para. 36 and in general Chapters I and V.
[58] ibid., para. 20.
[59] ibid., para. 150. See also S. M. Hersh, *Chemical and Biological Warfare* (London, MacGibbon and Kee, 1968), pp. 182–86.
[60] ibid., paras. 31, 300, 305–13, 355–64, 371.
[61] *The Observer*, 8 March 1970.

other forms of attack and their total effect might be fatal."[62] In addition, "once the first step towards this form of warfare has been taken, escalation is probable and no one knows where this may lead";[63] whether we are dealing with incapacitating agents or lethal agents, "as soon as they began to be used, there would be a grave danger of escalation, not only as far as the use of the same type of weapon is concerned but also that of other categories of weapons".[64] Let us add our opinion that if the use by the police of certain substances can be considered legitimate, it does not follow at all that it is authorised in international relations, the field covered by the Geneva Protocol. It is worth recalling that the 1963 Moscow Treaty makes the same kind of distinction: it bans certain kinds of nuclear tests only in so far as they might cause radioactive fall-out outside national frontiers.

Does the Geneva Protocol only cover lethal agents or incapacitating agents as well? The question is all the more important as on 25 November 1969 President Nixon stated that the United States "as has often been repeated will not be the first to use lethal chemical weapons and extends this renunciation to being first to use chemical paralysing products". The administration will submit to the Senate for advice and consent the ratification of the 1925 Geneva Protocol.[65] So this statement does not cover tear, irritating or blister gas, nor herbicides, defoliants or other crop-destroying substances.

Now as Mr Philip Noel-Baker, Nobel Peace Prize-winner, has recalled (he was a member of the British delegation in 1925 and was one of the authors of the British memorandum presented on 18 November 1930 to the preparatory Disarmament Commission) everyone admitted in 1925 that the Protocol covered *all* chemical substances (it was said in Geneva: "perhaps one day some criminal lunatic will invent something which will destroy animals and crops") and in 1930 Britain strongly supported the same argument believing that the Protocol ban covered tear gases.[66] For her part, Mrs Myrdal told the First Commission of the General Assembly: "it follows clearly from reading the verbatim report of the 1925 Conference and still more from the reports of the League of Nations Disarmament Conference in 1932 and 1933 and of the preparatory commissions, that

[62] ibid., para. 4.
[63] ibid., para. 13.
[64] ibid., para. 368.
[65] A/C. 1/PV. 1699. The United States also renounced the use of lethal biological weapons and agents and other means of biological warfare. On 15 February 1970, in a supplementary statement, President Nixon announced that this renunciation extended to toxins.
[66] *The Times*, 6 December 1969.

both Parties to the 1925 Protocol and those who did not adhere to it were convinced that the ban which had just been included in the Protocol and which was increasingly considered as the expression of a universally valid law, was a total ban. The question whether tear gases were included was also discussed and settled very explicitly. In a memorandum presented to the Preparatory Commission of the 1932 Conference, the British delegation adopted the firm position that the expression "other gases" in the Geneva Protocol included tear gases. The French delegation which represented the depositary government confirmed immediately that the words "ou similaires" in the French text had the same meaning. The delegations from Romania, Yugoslavia, Japan, China, the Soviet Union, Italy, Canada, Czechoslovakia, Turkey and Spain were fully in support of the British position. No delegation rejected this position. The United States verbally expressed reservations over the use of tear gases by the police and the question was left to the Disarmament Conference for a final decision, which was what happened. In a unanimous report of the Special Committee of the 1932 Conference, the ban was defined as including "tear-producing, irritant and blister substances". It was also decided that the term applied "not only to substances harmful to human beings", but also "to chemical substances in general". These definitions which, we have confirmed following the discussion in the Preparatory Commission applied in particular to the Geneva Protocol, met no opposition from any of the delegations. I would add that the United States and the Soviet Union took part in these discussions.[67]

Some non-aligned countries have also formally confirmed this interpretation, as in his introduction to the experts' report, U Thant asks United Nations members to reaffirm "clearly that the ban laid down in the Geneva Protocol applies to the use in warfare of all bacteriological and biological agents (including tear gases and other irritants) existing now or capable of being developed in the future".

It was in this spirit that the Assembly adopted on 16 December 1969 Resolution 2603A (XXIV) which states, in substance, that the rule laid down by the Geneva Protocol is a customary rule, since (a) the majority of States then in existence acceded to the Protocol; (b) since this time other States have become Party; (c) others have stated their desire to conform to its aims and principles which have been widely respected in practice; and (d) the Assembly, no one voting against, invited all States to conform strictly to its aims and principles of the Geneva Protocol.[68]

The resolution adopted by 80 votes to 3 (Australia, the United States

[67] A/C. 1/PV. 1695.
[68] This passage refers to Resolution 2162B (XXI).

and Portugal) with 36 abstentions took a clear stand in favour of the widest interpretation of the ban.[69] Those abstaining who spoke in the First Commission did not oppose the basic argument (with the exception of the Netherlands and the United Kingdom). They criticised the interpretation by the Assembly of a Protocol which it belonged to the Parties to interpret. This argument loses much of its value if it is admitted we are dealing with a customary norm (although from the legal point of view the text of the Resolution contains some bad drafting). In any case, on 10 December 1969, in the First Commission, the French delegation, whose abstention was motivated by the aforementioned considerations, confirmed France's traditional position: "The 1925 Protocol had in our opinion a very general scope. Such is still our position. . . . We have always said that the 1925 text left no doubt on this point".

Let us return now to the British proposal which was later duly transformed into a draft Convention.[70] This draft unconditionally bans the use of biological means of warfare, the production of these means and research for such production. Existing stocks should be destroyed. No control was envisaged. Any Party which felt that forbidden methods were being used against it could complain to the Secretary-General of the United Nations who would immediately have to set up an enquiry and give the result to the Security Council. Any Party which had reason to believe that the provisions relative to production, research or destruction of stocks had been violated, could complain to the Security Council, which could then ask the Secretary-General to carry out an enquiry. All this adds very little to the rights already enjoyed by member States and organisations of the United Nations (except the general authority given to and the duty imposed upon the Secretary-General to carry out an enquiry immediately in case of complaint by a State against which biological means of warfare had been used).

The British draft has been criticised for uselessly repeating the ban on biological warfare, which was already covered by the Geneva Protocol,

---

[69] "*Declares* as contrary to the generally accepted rules of international law, such as have been laid down in the Protocol concerning the prohibition of use in war of asphyxiating, toxic or similar gases, and bacteriological means, signed in Geneva on 17 June 1925, the use in international armed conflict of (a) any chemical agent for use in war – chemical substances whether in gaseous, liquid or solid state – because of their direct toxic effect on man, animals or plants; (b) any biological agent for use in war – living organisms, whatever their nature, or infectious products deriving from them – intended to cause illness or death of people, animals or plants, and whose effects depend on their ability to multiply in the person, animal or plant attacked."

[70] ENDC/255 (10/7/69) and 255/Rev. 1. Corr. 1. (26/8/69). In a statement on 25 November 1969, President Nixon gave conditional support to this proposal.

thus weakening the scope of the latter instrument. It is true that the Protocol only applies to the Parties and is full of reservations. But if one agrees with the great majority of academics and governments that there is now a customary norm, these limitations have no real validity or meaning. Also, in spite of precautions taken in drafting the British proposal,[71] it may have drawbacks in that it introduces uncertainty into the meaning of the Geneva Protocol; its adoption might lead to a multiplication of undertakings by States on the same subject, which would raise doubts about the similarity and exact meaning of these undertakings.

On the other hand, the British proposal does mark considerable progress, in that it bans the development, testing, manufacture and stockpiling of B weapons. But why separate these from C weapons? We have summarised the British argument above. It does not appear convincing. Stockpiling and holding of both B and C weapons raise delicate security problems. In spite of precautions, accidents harmful to animals and man can happen, as the example of C weapons in the United States shows only too well. A ban on manufacture might strengthen the Geneva Protocol and give all countries a greater sense of security, on condition that this ban refers both to B weapons which have never been used until now and C weapons which have been used and are at present being used in Viet-Nam. The report of the United Nations experts shows, as has been recalled, that it is difficult to distinguish between the two categories of weapons which belong to separate categories. They are linked together in the 1925 Geneva Protocol, in other international instruments (such as the Paris Treaty of 23 October 1954 and the Austrian State Treaty of 15 May 1955), in Disarmament proposals submitted by the United States and the Soviet Union, in relevant Resolutions of the United Nations General Assembly, and in military manuals in most countries. Also, if a new Convention were to be adopted referring exclusively to B weapons, it might even encourage a C weapons arms race. It was for this reason that the Soviet Union and her allies tabled a proposal at the General Assembly banning the development, manufacture, stockpiling and acquisition of chemical and bacteriological (biological) weapons. This draft contains no provisions for control or complaint except this: "States Party to the Convention undertake to consult each other and to co-operate with each other in resolving problems which might eventually arise over the application of the provisions in the present Convention".[72]

---

[71] The draft provides that nothing it contains limits the duties undertaken by States under the 1925 Geneva Protocol and that each Party promises never to use biological methods of warfare "provided that it has not already made undertakings to this effect by Treaty or other instruments in force banning the use of chemical and biological methods of warfare".

[72] A/7655.

The General Assembly, by an overwhelming majority, decided that the new Convention ought to include both B and C weapons and it sent back the two drafts, British and Russian, to the Geneva Committee asking it to try urgently to reach agreement upon the two draft Conventions (Russian and British) and to submit a report to the 25th session of the Assembly on progress made in all aspects of the question.[73]

It would seem that the new draft ought to leave out the ban on use, already covered by the Geneva Protocol. Among other problems to be solved will be that of control. On this, Mrs Myrdal proposed that the WHO should be asked to collect and publish information about B and C weapons from government and scientific sources, and to ask questions when the information given showed any suspicious gaps; an on-the-spot inspection system would be established by reciprocal laboratory visits made by academics and scientific experts.[74]

On this point it is worth mentioning the voluntary inspection system for laboratories working on microbiological research and manufacture. This experiment was made by Pugwash scientists from Sweden, Denmark, Austria and Czechoslovakia. Visits were made at the invitation of laboratory directors after the competent authorities of the host country had been informed. It appears that as a result of this experiment which has been going on since 1964, such inspections would make it possible to prevent work being carried out in secret and in most cases to detect violations of any agreement particularly those relating to publicity and research.[75] In the control field, progress might be made thanks to new research by the Pugwash group and SIPRI in Stockholm. Besides, it seems to the author that if future Conventions were to be concluded covering B and C weapons, they ought to include a provision under which no citizen of any Party should be penalised or suffer damage as a result of the communication of information by him to competent international organisations about the application of the Conventional norms. For it is most important in a field such as this, that experts and technicians belonging to each Party should be able to contribute directly towards safeguarding the Treaty and to inform the international organisations directly of all their observations giving even the slightest indication of a Treaty violation. Moreover the system of inspection by challenge, recommended by Sweden in the context of a total nuclear test ban, could also be introduced. If one State Party has reason to believe that another party has violated the Convention, it has the right to demand

---

[73] Resolution 2603 B III (XXIV).
[74] ENDC/PV. 391.
[75] See the letter from Mrs Patricia Lindon, Assistant Secretary-General of the Pugwash Conference, *The Times*, 3 July 1968.

an immediate inspection. If the State under suspicion refuses the inspection, the plaintiff State has the right to denounce the Convention with immediate effect.

4. Conventional arms trade

Quite different problems are raised over trade in conventional weapons. Much has been said in the past about the activities of private arms traffickers. Now there exists also that of governments, certain of which have created Ministries officially concerned with promoting arms sales abroad. Those who denounce the immorality of such trade and its evil character find their argument countered by the economic and technical advantages resulting from the manufacture and export of conventional weapons.[76] Every industrialised country says it cannot give up the trading advantages as long as other countries carry on this trade.[77] Some countries, such as the United States, try to lay down restrictive conditions under which arms sold may be used, but these conditions are rarely respected.[78] Developing countries play off the arms exporting Powers against each other, profit by their competition, obtain new deliveries, and burden their already slender resources with new debts. Often the exporting country is obliged for political reasons to increase the number of its clients. Thus the Soviet Union, supplier to India, was forced to supply Pakistan as well in order not to get involved in a dispute with the latter. But her relations are as strained with India.[79]

Thus on the political, economic and military level an agreement limiting or ending the arms trade would represent immense progress. But it is doubtful if this could be achieved without eliminating the causes of tension and conflict, or at least some of them. In any case it would demand agreement between the supplying and importing countries. If a certain number of countries continue to want to buy arms they will find sellers attracted by the prospect of profits and the desire to gain political advantages.

It would, however, be possible to adopt a preliminary measure: to instruct a section of the UN Secretariat to publish an annual report on arms deliveries based on all available information. At the same time States would undertake to present periodically complete data on their arms exports, whatever their origin or source, with a foreign destination, or a given region or several regions. For a preliminary period then, States

[76] This was the argument defended in the Commons on 17 July 1968 by Mr Denis Healey, Labour Defence Minister.
[77] Cf. Katzenbach, Department of State Bulletin, 11 December 1967, pp. 794–98.
[78] US Senate, *Arms Sale and Foreign Policy*, Hearings before the Committee on Foreign Relations, 1967.
[79] Cf. *The Economist*, 13 July 1968; *The Times*, 29 June, 9 and 12 July 1968.

would have the chance to limit the geographical range of their obligations. It would be best if corresponding duties could be agreed over the communication of information on arms sales and imports. The United States have just stated they would accept "measures enforcing arms suppliers to communicate or register their arms deliveries to a certain area".[80] Unfortunately, here also the chances of progress seem slight. At the 23rd Session of the General Assembly, a very modest proposal by Denmark had to be withdrawn due to the reticence of a great number of States, and particularly of developing and non-aligned States which imagined they saw a discriminatory measure against them. And yet it was only a proposal to ask the Secretary-General to consult member States on their position concerning an eventual undertaking to register with the Secretary-General all imports and exports of conventional arms.[81]

5. The denuclearisation of the sea- and ocean-bed

(a) History

It was due to the initiative of the Maltese delegation that the United Nations General Assembly examined at its 22nd Session (1967) "the question of reserving for exclusively peaceful purposes the sea- and ocean-bed as well as its subsoil under the high seas beyond the limits of actual national jurisdiction, and exploiting their resources in the interests of humanity". By its Resolution 2340 (XXII) the Assembly set up a Special Committee to study different aspects of the question thus defined. The Committee and its judicial sub-committee discussed the exclusively peaceful use of the sea- and ocean-bed. In its first report the special Committee observed that the majority of delegations represented supported the argument that "the concept of peaceful use completely excluded military use". According to others "if one wanted to tackle the problems realistically, one had to declare and accept the principle that the said zone must be used exclusively for peaceful purposes, and one should allow military activities undertaken for peaceful purposes or with peaceful intent which were compatible with the UN Charter and the duties imposed by international laws. The general aim had to be to avoid extending the arms race to the sea- and ocean-bed."[82] According to this last argument "there was no general ban upon military activities on the high seas, and no proposal had even been made for such a ban".[83] The Soviet Union had submitted a

---

[80] ENDC/228.
[81] A/C. 1/L. 444/Rev. 1; A/C. 1/PV. 1616, 1624, 1629, 1630.
[82] *Report of the Special Committee*, General Assembly, 23rd Session, Official Documents, A/7230, para. 47.
[83] ibid., para. 48.

proposal recommending the use of the sea- and ocean-bed for exclusively peaceful purposes and a ban on its use for military purposes.[84] India repeated the expression "for exclusively peaceful purposes" adding, however, "the activities of States in relation to the exploration and use of the sea- and ocean-bed will take place in accordance with international law, including the United Nations Charter, with a view to maintaining peace and international security and helping international co-operation and understanding".[85] For their part the United States envisaged "the limitation of armaments on the sea- and ocean-bed" and requested a definition of "the essential factors for a practical, controllable and effective international agreement which would prevent this new environment being used for the siting of weapons of mass destruction".[86]

By Resolution 2467 A (XXIII) the Assembly set up the Committee on the Peaceful Uses of the Sea-Bed and the Ocean Floor. It was to study in particular: (a) the principles and legal norms necessary to ensure the exploitation of the sea-bed's resources for the benefit of humanity; (b) in the context of its title, and taking into account international research and negotiation over disarmament, the exclusive reservation for peaceful purposes of the sea- and ocean-bed without prejudice to the limits which might be agreed in this respect. The new committee did not reach generally acceptable conclusions on the point which concerns us. The legal working group observed that under the heading "reservation for exclusively peaceful uses", it was proposed to ban, according to country: (a) use for military purposes; (b) all military activities and all use for military purposes; (c) use for other than peaceful purposes.[87] In the summary of its work, the judicial sub-committee observed that a common denominator emerged out of a declaration of principle stating that the zone will be reserved for exclusively peaceful purposes; "on the other hand there was no agreement upon the wording of passages in the draft declaration about the geographical limits of applicability of this principle and about the extent of banned activities".[88]

From the beginning of 1969, the Geneva Committee considered ways of demilitarising the sea- and ocean-bed. On 18 March 1969, the Soviet Union tabled a draft Treaty on the subject.[89] A counter-proposal was

[84] ibid., para. 57.
[85] ibid., para. 58.
[86] ibid., para. 59.
[87] *Report of the Peaceful Uses Committee*, General Assembly, 24th Session, supplement 22 (A/7622), p. 54.
[87] *Report of the Peaceful Uses Committee*, General Assembly, Official Documents, 24th Session, supplement 22 (A/7622), p. 54.
[88] ibid., pp. 46–47.
[89] ENDC/240.

tabled by the United States on 22 May 1969.[90] The two Super-Powers agreed on a joint draft which saw the light of day on 7 October 1969.[91] Taking into account certain proposals by other members of the Committee, they slightly modified their draft which was published in its revised form on 30 October 1969.[92]

The report of the Committee, where the text in question appeared, was then discussed in the First Commission of the General Assembly where many States criticised both the draft and the procedure adopted, saying in particular that the two Super-Powers seemed to want to force a decision at any price, without giving time to the Assembly to study the problem in depth and to make itself heard. The Assembly finally adopted Resolution 2602F (XXIV) by which it "welcomed the fact that the draft Treaty had been presented to the General Assembly in its current session" and "invited the Disarmament Committee Conference to take into account all proposals and suggestions that had been made during the present session of the General Assembly and to continue its work on this question in order to be able to submit the text of a draft Treaty for the scrutiny of the General Assembly".

(b) Demilitarisation or denuclearisation

It is not possible to discuss here the problem of the legal status of the high seas from the point of view of military use. We have shown the divergence of opinion which exists about this in the Committee on the Peaceful Uses of the Sea-Bed and Ocean Floor. As for the continental shelf, the divergences are just as great. Judge Ammoun recently stated: "for two obvious reasons – the economic aims and rights of riparian States, and respect, as far as necessary, for the freedom of the high seas – utilisation of the continental shelf, as well as of the high seas, is excluded from military use".[93] But the preparatory work and the text of the 1958 Convention on the Continental Shelf are far from being clear about this.[94] In the Peaceful Uses Committee some delegates "expressed the opinion that it was hardly probable that States would not take into account their own security needs from the simple fact that the Convention remained silent or imprecise about this".[95]

In any case, interest in the demilitarisation of the sea-bed is all the greater as military use lies not in the realm of speculation but of reality,[96]

[90] ENDC/249.
[91] ENDC/269.
[92] ENDC/269, Rev. 1.
[93] ICJ *Reports*, 1969, p. 118.
[94] Cf. A/AC. 135/19, Add. 1, paras. 60–70.
[95] A/7622, para. 45.
[96] W. T. Burke, *Towards a Better Use of the Oceans*, SIPRI Monograph (Stockholm, Almqvist and Wiksell, 1969), p. 83.

and as peaceful and military use of this environment may prove to be incompatible, making it necessary to establish an order of priority.[97] It appears that ever greater efforts and sums of money are being devoted to oceanographic research which always has military applications, if only in part.[98] The sea or ocean environment gives better camouflage and because of this encourages States to perfect means of detection that remain underwater or fixed to the ocean- or sea-bed. Mines of the traditional sort are well known. Experiments are surely taking place with Sonar detection networks anchored to the sea-bed, scrambling devices, false echo sounding devices, etc. Fixed submarine bases are on the cards together with a launching system based on the continental shelf and enabling missiles or anti-missile-missiles to be used. These bases which present-day satellites cannot reveal or detect could be developed under the sea-bed or anchored to it. The feasibility of underwater silos is also being studied, living quarters under the sea or fixed to the sea-bed, hiding places for stocking particularly important materials, as well as the establishment of an ultra-modern communication and surveillance system. As Mrs Myrdal remarked, "an installation set up for civil purposes, such as a set-up for the extraction of petroleum, could be combined with a military installation, such as a missile base or an observation post".[99]

The United States, because of their geographical position and their strategic doctrine as well as their technical lead, are particularly interested in perfecting means of detection and sonar systems. This explains right from the start the divergent opinions of the Big Two. This divergence, as the Indian delegate correctly observed, reflects the differences existing between the naval warfare strategy of the authors of the two drafts.[100] The Soviet draft of 18 March 1969 would have banned "use for military purposes of the sea- and ocean-bed and its subsoil . . . " (Article I). On the other hand, under the American draft of 22 May, each Party would have undertaken "not to instal or place fixed nuclear weapons or other fixed weapons of mass destruction, or fixed launching platforms for such weapons upon, in or under the sea- and ocean-bed . . . " (Article I). The difference is clear – in the first case it was a question of demilitarisation, in the second, of denuclearisation.

---

[97] R. Bierzanek, ibid. p. 143.
[98] *SIPRI Yearbook of World Armaments and Disarmament, 1968/69* (Stockholm, Almqvist and Wiksell, 1969), pp. 97–98, 109–11.
[99] ENDC/PV. 405. See also the speech by the delegate from Equatorial Guinea. A/C/1/PV. 1676; F. E. Bothwell, *Bulletin of Atomic Scientists*, October 1969, pp. 21–22 and the report of the UN Secretary-General A/AC 135/28 dated 10 July 1968.
[100] ENDC/PV. 428.

In schematic form, the American argument is as follows. The expression "use for military purposes" is much too vague. Regarding Resolution 2467A (XXIII) inviting the Peaceful Uses Committee to study the reservation for exclusively peaceful purposes of the sea- and ocean-bed, the United States has always insisted that only specifically excepted activities should be banned.[101] In other words, everything not expressly forbidden would be permitted; the Soviet draft would have banned alarm and detection systems installed on the sea-bed and defensive anti-submarine weapons which the United States cannot do without; installations for improving communications and navigation, as these installations often fulfil military and civil needs at the same time; scientific research work when, as is very often the case, it is helped or carried out by military personnel using military equipment other than weapons.[102] There is no possibility now, or even in the near future, of using the sea-bed for military activities of the traditional kind, such as to create security dangers for States. There is no danger either in the immediate future, of a classic arms race which it would hardly be worth while situating in this environment. What is true is that certain systems can operate simultaneously for nuclear and conventional weapons, for example launching platforms. This is in no sense an argument for a general ban; the difficulty must be solved by banning the installation of such platforms.[103] Moreover, a general ban would raise insoluble control problems, whilst it is relatively easy to detect nuclear installations. The precedent of the 1959 Antarctic Treaty is often quoted, which only allows peaceful activities (Article I). But this instrument refers to a zone where there had been no military activity and where nobody had any interest in such activities. As for the precedent of the 1967 Treaty on Outer Space, its Article IV says Parties "shall use the Moon and other celestial bodies exclusively for peaceful purposes". But this provision established a distinction between on the one hand the Moon and celestial bodies where Man had not yet landed, and where no kind of military activity existed, and on the other hand outer space already being explored where the ban only refers to nuclear weapons and weapons of mass destruction. Now outer space could very well be compared to the sea-bed. Finally the United States stated that the Treaty ought to be able to be amended easily, and be flexible, and in that way, if need arose, the scope of the ban might one day be extended.

The Soviet Union, for its part, argued otherwise, along the following lines. A classic arms race is quite possible. Indicators are: NATO's long-

---

[101] ENDC/PV. 411. See, along the same lines, the criticism by the UK delegate, ENDC/PV. 404.
[102] ENDC/PV. 397 and 421.   [103] ENDC/PV. 411 and 421.

term plans; the perfection of mines and underwater missiles; the very fact that the United States considers the need for future amendment. If it were considered sufficient to ban only weapons of mass destruction, this would be contrary to Resolutions 2340 (XXII) and 2467 A (XXIII). The American argument about control is not relevant: in the event of a partial ban, it would be necessary to verify existing military installations in order to find out whether they are concealing weapons of mass destruction and States will hesitate to submit to this procedure, which will enable the verifying State to discover their military secrets. A total ban would mean no more military installations, everything would become crystal clear. The solution adopted in the Antarctic Treaty should therefore be followed; the fact that the sea-bed is beginning to be used for military purposes proves how urgent the problem is and is an extra argument in favour of the Soviet view. It is not possible to distinguish between offensive and defensive weapons for exclusively defensive weapons do not exist. However, installations not having a direct military purpose would be allowed, together with communications systems of help to navigation and scientific research, even when they are operated by military personnel and using military equipment.[104]

In the Geneva Committee, the group of non-aligned countries was clearly in favour of a total ban. This position can be explained by that adopted by most of them elsewhere, when they insisted on qualifying the sea- and ocean-bed as the "common patrimony of humanity".[105] Thus Mrs Myrdal stated: "if our ultimate goal is to continue to leave the sea-bed open to international use for peaceful purposes, as well as to ensure the freedom of the high seas – which, after all, is the generally admitted purpose – the sea-bed ought not to be strewn with different sorts of installations for military purposes. However, if general agreement were finally reached on a ban including a small number of exceptions, these ought to be clearly defined and stated in the Treaty. The Antarctic Treaty and the Treaty on Outer Space might again make a useful guide in the choice of appropriate wording."[106] Later the Swedish delegate returned to her argument, recommending a general ban, with an exception for constructions and installations having a purely defensive and passive function (for example, means of communication, aids to navigation, surveillance and detection gear). The meaning of this exception, covered by a general form of words, would have to be defined during discussions.[107] So we come

[104] ENDC/PV. 400, 406, 409, 423.
[105] A/7622, paras. 19–27.
[106] ENDC/PV. 405; also ENDC/PV. 421 (UAR).
[107] ENDC/PV. 422; also ENDC/PV. 426 (Mexico); 428 (India); 430 (Nigeria).

back to the same idea: only what was expressly allowed would be permitted.

Canada, the least committed of the Western Powers, put forward a compromise proposal. The Russian draft was too radical in that it prevented defensive measures. That of the United States was not radical enough as it would "confer respectability on the siting of conventional weapons, a legal authorisation which they would not otherwise benefit from, and would give rise to possible disputes over the right of protection of the installations in question". Thus Canada proposed a ban on (a) nuclear weapons; (b) weapons of mass destruction; (c) storage containers, launching platforms and installations associated with nuclear weapons or with weapons of mass destruction; (d) other undersea weapons, bases or fortifications with the help of which or from which military action might be taken against the territory, the territorial waters or the air space (or against objects therein) of another State.[108]

Finally the joint draft presented by the United States and the Soviet Union adopted the American argument. It banned Parties from placing or installing on the sea- and ocean-bed nuclear weapon devices or other types of weapons of mass destruction, as well as constructions, launch installations, or other installations expressly conceived for storing, testing or using such weapons. The Parties "undertake not to help, encourage or incite any State to commit forbidden acts . . . and not to take part in such acts". (Article I).

So there was a partial ban not stated in the wisest terms. The phrase "other types of weapons of mass destruction" was criticised first of all for imprecision, and it was felt that it ought to be clearly defined.[109] According to one of the Co-Chairmen, the expression covered C, B and radioactive weapons.[110]

The draft mentioned devices, constructions, launching installations and other installations. Strictly speaking then, the text would not prevent a State from placing a nuclear warhead on the sea-bed except that it would be hard to see for what reason it should do so. The word "expressly" is restrictive in character and might allow many ways of getting round the Treaty. However, one of the Co-Chairmen said that nuclear mines anchored or placed on the sea-bed would be banned. It would be difficult to distinguish a nuclear mine from a non-nuclear one. In any case floating mines are not mentioned by the draft. Elsewhere, "the Treaty would not apply to research at commercial installations not expressly built for the stocking, testing or use of weapons of mass destruction. Also, installations

[108] ENDC/PV. 424. See also 410.
[109] ENDC/PV. 444 (United Kingdom).
[110] ENDC/PV. 397 (United States).

expressly designed for the use of nuclear weapons or weapons of mass destruction would not escape the Treaty ban even if they might also be used for conventional weapons."[111] The least that can be said is that the Treaty ought to have been more clearly drafted to express the intention of its authors. However, the ban on launching platforms and vectors is important: it prevents a State Party from making preparations for a sudden withdrawal from the Treaty.[112]

Submarines or vessels able to navigate at depth above the sea-bed are allowed and would not violate the Treaty if they were anchored or temporarily at rest on the sea-bed.[113] The ban then is upon installations, constructions, containers, vectors, "whose main method of deployment or operation demands physical contact with the sea-bed"[114] as well as upon "vehicles carrying weapons of mass destruction or designed to receive them, and only able to navigate when in contact with the sea-bed"[115]. This would refer to caterpillar or other tracked vehicles carrying nuclear weapons or other tracked weapons of destruction.[116] This last interpretation seems to us more exact than the preceding one which, however, came from the Co-Chairman. Tracked vehicles are neither installations nor constructions, but devices, and these are only banned when they are fitted with nuclear weapons or other weapons of mass destruction.

It is worth noting another official comment on the text, according to which the Treaty "would not prevent peaceful uses of nuclear energy. The ban it imposes is in no way aimed at preventing nuclear explosions carried out for peaceful purposes, nor at preventing practical applications of nuclear reactors, scientific research, and peaceful applications of nuclear energy, in accordance with obligations arising out of other Treaties."[117] Now, up to the present time there has been a general refusal to distinguish nuclear weapons from other nuclear explosives, arms tests from experiments carried out with the help of explosive devices. The reason is simple: a distinction can hardly be made in the present state of nuclear technology.

The 1968 Non-Proliferation Treaty covers nuclear weapons or other explosive nuclear devices. The 1963 Moscow Treaty bans all experimental nuclear weapons explosions or *any other nuclear explosion*, in particular underwater, including the high seas. The new American–Soviet draft does not mention explosive nuclear devices. This fact and the comment quoted

[111] CCD/PV. 440 (United States).
[112] ENDC/PV. 397 (United States).
[113] CCD/PV. 440 (United States).
[114] ENDC/PV. 397 (United States).
[115] CCD/PV. 444 (United States).
[116] ibid. (United Kingdom).
[117] CCD/PV. 440 (United States).

above are disturbing.[118] Peaceful nuclear explosions would only be allowed by amendment to the Moscow Treaty, and only ought to be so by an international organisation, under its control or safeguard.

It appears that most countries in favour of a total ban would resign themselves to the idea of a partial ban, on condition they got some firm promises about its later extension. The Co-Chairmen inserted into the preamble a paragraph in which they state their conviction that their text only marks an interim stage and their determination to continue negotiations with a view to other measures enabling the sea- and ocean-bed to be excluded from the arms race. They also accepted the insertion into the text of an article borrowed from the Non-Proliferation Treaty: a revision conference will meet five years after the entry into force of the Treaty to examine how it is working and to ensure that the aims stated in the preamble and the Treaty provisions are being duly observed.

But these concessions seemed insufficient to many States. Mrs Myrdal observed: "we know, alas, by experience, that a partial ban Treaty does not necessarily lead to the conclusion of a total ban Treaty. What is worse, a partial ban Treaty may be interpreted as allowing what is not expressly banned." And to force the two Super-Powers to start new negotiations immediately,[119] the Swedish delegation, supported by many others asked for the insertion into the text of the Treaty of an Article in these terms: "Each Party to the Treaty undertakes to pursue negotiations in good faith on other measures towards a more general ban on the use for military purposes of the sea- and ocean-bed as well as its subsoil".[120]

(c) The zone affected

According to the Soviet proposal, the ban would apply "beyond the twelve mile territorial waters limit for coastal States". According to the American draft, only the sea-bed within a three mile strip parallel to the coast would escape denuclearisation. The Soviet delegate justified his position by observing that most States had fixed the width of their territorial waters beyond three miles. If it were desired to reduce the width of the zone exempted from the ban to less than twelve miles, verification measures would become difficult for States with territorial waters twelve miles wide, since ships and planes carrying out verification would have to ask the permission of the coastal State in order to penetrate inside this zone.[121]

As for the United States, their delegate recalled that the partial ban

[118] Cf. CCD/PV. 445 (UAR).
[119] CCD/PV. 443.
[120] CCD/271. Cf. Art. VI of the Non-Proliferation Treaty.
[121] ENDC/PV. 423.

would apply only to the sea-bed and not to the waters above it. In comparison with the twelve mile limit, the three mile limit would add two million square miles to the area covered by the ban. It is also more practical: let us suppose that a State has fixed the width of its territorial waters at six miles and the strip exempted from the ban extends to twelve miles. In this case a non-coastal State could site nuclear weapons on the sea-bed at a distance of between six and twelve miles from the coast.[122] As for tracing base lines, the principles laid down by the Geneva Convention of 1958 on territorial waters and the contiguous zone ought to be followed. On this last point, the two Super-Powers seemed to be in agreement from the beginning.[123]

As for the position of other States, it is worth mentioning the "maximalist" argument of Japan, who asked for the full application of the ban right from the coastline. In this case, although there would be verification problems, they would not be more complicated than those resolved by the Non-Proliferation Treaty.[124]

Italy and Brazil felt that the extent of the zone exempted from the ban ought to be defined in terms of the scope of this ban: if it were a question of demilitarisation, this zone ought to be greater than if just denuclearisation were decided upon. In the latter case, the width of the zone could be fixed at twelve miles, but if demilitarisation were chosen, bathymetric measurements would have to be taken, not distance from the coast.[125] The underlying idea is that the continental shelf ought to be able to be used for military activities of the classic variety, and especially for defence activities. Other States, like Nigeria and Sweden, have protested against any other attempt to link the extent of the zone exempted from the Treaty to the existence of a continental shelf. In their opinion, this would be an unjust and discriminatory measure.[126] "If, for example, parts of the continental shelf over which coastal States today claim limited national sovereignty were to be excluded from the demilitarised zone, none of the seas surrounding my country's coastline, neither the Baltic, nor the Eastern parts of the North Sea would be covered by the agreement . . . ".[127] Also, Nigeria[128] and Japan[129] felt that if there were two parties with coastlines opposite or adjacent to each other and the distance between the two coasts were less

[122] ENDC/PV. 397 and 414.
[123] ENDC/PV. 490 and 414.
[124] ENDC/PV. 420.
[125] ENDC/PV. 410, 423, 441.
[126] ENDC/PV. 411 (Nigeria).
[127] ENDC/PV. 405 (Sweden).
[128] ENDC/247 and ENDC/PV. 411.
[129] CCD/PV. 442.

than twenty-four miles (in other words if the twelve miles zone bisected a similar zone and these zones belonged to adhering States), these two States would have to give up their right to use these zones for military purposes. This proposal did not appear to gain the approval of the majority.

Canada, preoccupied by the length of its own coastline, proposed the creation of a two hundred mile wide strip measured from the outer limits of the zone outside the jurisdiction of the Treaty. Within this strip, only the coastal State, to the exclusion of all others, could carry on defensive military activities not banned by the Treaty.[130] This proposal was not accepted by the Co-Chairmen, any more than the preceding one.

The Co-Chairmen, in their first joint draft of 7 October 1969 defined as follows the limits of the zone where the Treaty was to apply: the sea- and ocean-bed and their subsoil beyond the maximum contiguous zone defined in the 1958 Geneva Convention on Territorial Waters and the Contiguous Zone. (Article 1). The outer limit of this contiguous zone would be measured in accordance with the provisions of Section II of the Geneva Convention and of international law. (Article 2).

These provisions aroused much criticism. They really meant that the Soviet argument had prevailed. The width of the zone outside the Treaty jurisdiction was therefore fixed at twelve miles. But, it was alleged, the formula adopted for Article I would allow a non-coastal State to site nuclear weapons on the sea-bed situated within the contiguous zone of the coastal State, particularly when the latter fixed the width of its territorial waters at less than twelve miles.[131]

The second joint draft of 30 October replied to these criticisms by taking up, in a manner which was not perhaps the most fortunate, an idea put forward by the Swedes:[132] "Undertakings given in paragraph 1 of the present Article apply also within the contiguous zone mentioned in this paragraph; if it is only within the said zone they do not apply to the coastal State". (Article 1, new paragraph 2.) It is evident that this authorisation cannot mean that a State adhering to the Non-Proliferation Treaty is freed from its obligations. It is true, however, that the Treaty does not prevent a State possessing nuclear weapons from depositing such weapons on the territory of another State, on condition that it keeps them in its care, possession and control. But can the sea- and ocean-bed, even within the contiguous zone, be considered the territory of the coastal State?[133]

[130] ENDC/PV. 424.
[131] CCD/PV. 441 (Italy), 442 (Japan), 444 (UAR).
[132] ENDC/PV. 422.
[133] Most States answer in the negative, feeling that it forms part of the common patrimony of the human race. See for example Argentina A/C. 1/PV. 1695. The idea of the contiguous zone refers to waters and not to the sea- and ocean-bed.

But the tenor of Articles 1 and 2 raises still further objections. Why refer in a Treaty to another Treaty which has been ratified only by some States and which might undergo modification in the future, and why not state clearly and simply in figures the width of the strip exempted?[134] The Latin American States in particular, who go so far as to fix the width of their territorial waters at two hundred miles, protested against Articles 1 and 2. Doubtless Article 2 does say that the Treaty in no way affects the positions, rights and claims of States as to the waters situated along their coasts or as to the sea- and ocean-bed. But the Latin American countries are mistrustful; in their opinion, the draft Treaty on the sea-bed has nothing to do with the contiguous zone nor with the Geneva Convention to which it refers: the zone and the Convention cover only the waters near the surface. If the reference to the Convention were to be maintained "we should be obliged to conclude that the mention of the Geneva Convention has only one meaning and that is to prejudge the issue of how wide territorial waters ought to be".[135]

(d) Control

The Soviet draft said: "All installations and constructions situated on the sea- or ocean-bed, or in their subsoil are accessible, on a reciprocal basis, to the representatives of other States Party to the present Treaty for the purpose of ensuring that States which have placed such elements there carry out the obligations assumed by them under the present Treaty" (Article 2). It referred therefore to control by the State themselves, national not international control. The ambiguity of the idea of reciprocity has been pointed out: does it mean that the installations are accessible (a) to other Parties who also have such installations, or (b) to all Parties adhering to the Treaty on a non-discriminatory basis?[136] The text of the Article would support the first interpretation. The Soviet delegate's statement does not completely clarify the situation as it would allow the alternative interpretation: "In case of conclusion of an agreement for a total ban on all military activity on the sea- and ocean-bed, control over the carrying out of the agreement by the parties shall be based on the principle of free access to installations situated on the sea-bed".[137]

The Swedish delegation proposed that if a total ban proved impractical, and if exceptions were allowed, military arrangements carried out by one Party should be notified by it to other Parties.[138] This was not the method

---

[134] CCD/PV. 445 (UAR).
[135] A/C. 1/PV. 1695 (Argentina) and 1696 (Ecuador).
[136] ENDC/PV. 405 (Sweden).
[137] ENDC/PV. 400.   [138] ENDC/PV. 405.

adopted by the American draft which does not even talk about the principle of a total ban, and which allows acts not specifically banned. Article 3 of this draft gave to any party the benefit of observing activities carried out on the sea- and ocean-bed by other Parties "without interfering in these activities or in any other way threatening rights recognised under international law, including the freedom of the high seas". In cases where observation was not enough as a method of control, Parties undertook the duty of consultation and co-operation "to try and resolve these matters". As a matter of fact this text allowed nothing more than what all States already enjoy, that is to say the right of observation on the high seas.

The first joint draft repeated the wording of the American draft except that the word "observation" was replaced by "verification" and that this was only to be exercised where activities of a State Party raised doubts about the execution of the duties it had undertaken under the Treaty. Parties agreed to consult and collaborate "in order to eliminate any doubt as to the execution of obligations assumed under the Treaty". In addition, a Party could exercise the right of verification, either by itself, or with the aid of another Party. In fact, if the wording was tighter, the substance remained basically the same. The same could be said of the second joint draft which introduced a new idea: if the above mentioned consultation and collaboration failed to eliminate doubt the Parties could, in accordance with the United Nations Charter, inform the Security Council. As one delegate remarked, it is curious, to say the least, that so little attention has been paid to the right that States already possess under the Charter.[139]

Let us now examine the three main objections raised against these drafts. First of all in the present state of world affairs, at a time when lack of equality among States is seen most clearly in the technological field, the draft Treaty only restricts the two Super-Powers. They alone have the necessary means to carry out verification. Of course, the Soviet delegate did say that the Treaty gives all parties the same right of taking part in control operations.[140] But this is only the equality in words so often denounced by Marxists. The Canadian delegate expressed many countries' opinion when he said an acceptable verification system "must (a) give all signatories the certainty that it will allow detection of any important Treaty violation with minimum delay by providing irrefutable proof, (b) follow and strengthen the existing law of the sea, to the extent that it protects

---

[139] See CCD/PV. 447 (Canada).
[140] CCD/PV. 440.

the interests of coastal States".[141] It has thus been the opinion of some States that effective and concrete rights had to be given to Parties and that each adherent State ought to have the right, in order to carry out a verification, of requesting and obtaining the help of a technologically advanced Party. We have seen that this idea, in a watered-down form, was retained in the joint draft, which really imposes no duty on any Party to supply any help requested. The American Co-Chairman felt he could go further. In his opinion, a more binding solution would have raised delicate problems over the examination of the basis of the complaint (an examination which costs money and involves risks) and the establishment of priorities (a country might receive requests from several others and want to keep the material – costly and rare – for its own use). "Equipment and technical staff for specialised activities of this sort are lacking, and States having them ought to examine in detail all Treaty provisions proposed to control their use". In addition, the United States could not take upon itself obligations to help, "given the present state of technology and the fluctuating political relations among many countries capable of becoming Parties to the Treaty".[142] To which the Indian delegate replied that a country which had sufficient financial means to set up installations on the sea-bed, of course has enough money to cover the expense of the help it might be asked to provide.[143]

Few States went as far as to envisage an international organisation exercising control in the immediate future,[144] a procedure that the two Co-Chairmen considered complicated, costly and impossible to achieve in the present state of technology, a field reserved for few countries.[145] But many voices were raised asking for the principle of international responsibility to be followed from now on.[146] Ceylon asked for verification based upon a system of notification by which all military activities and control would be communicated to an international organisation and, through it, to all Parties. According to Ceylon, the international organisation ought to play the role of watchdog over the whole area outside national jurisdiction.[147] This idea was at the back of the Canadian proposal which in its revised and weakened form said that any Party might request help from another,

---

[141] CCD/PV. 441.
[142] ENDC/PV. 421 and CCD/PV. 443.
[143] ENDC/PV. 428.
[144] India, however, did envisage giving control to the UN (ibid.), Nigeria to an international organisation specially to be set up (ENDC/PV. 411) and Ghana to IAEA (A/C. 1/PV. 1702).
[145] ENDC/PV. 421 and CCD/PV. 443 (United States), ENDC/PV. 409 (USSR).
[146] CCD/PV. 445 (Pakistan and Yugoslavia).
[147] A/C. 1/PV. 1707.

directly or indirectly by calling upon the good offices of an appropriate international body such as the Secretary-General's office of the United Nations.[148]

It is worth mentioning yet another idea put forward both by Mexico[149] and the United States:[150] States having common interests in certain regions could conclude appropriate arrangements or agreements for mutual help towards verification activities. But it must be asked whether in the present state of technology this method would not lead to a consolidation and enlargement of blocs since mutual aid agreements between poor and backward countries would be meaningless and carry no real weight.

The second important objection was over the nature of control. If the text of the joint draft was rather vague, its meaning has become clearer thanks to explanations by the American Co-Chairman. In fact the term verification covers two ideas: observation and inspection. On this, the American delegate felt it was the right to observe and consult which mattered. More extensive operations would prove difficult, expensive and dangerous for the verifying State and for those inside the installation to be verified. In any case if an adhering State wanted to violate the Treaty, it would not do so to put a nuclear weapon on the sea-bed but to set up a large scale apparatus which could be easily observed. According to the United States, Article III of the joint draft, about control, "does not imply a right of access to installations on the sea-bed which are not contrary to the purposes of the Treaty, nor a duty to reveal activities on the sea-bed which are not contrary to the purposes of the Treaty".[151] The United States understands "right of access" as "the right to go inside an installation and the right to open equipment". This right seems neither practical nor necessary. On the other hand, the possibility of contacting the object in question is understood, in the sense that "in accordance with the principle of the freedom of the high seas, parties may have access – and close access – to the area where an installation or device is situated, on condition that this does not interfere in any way with the activities of the State in question". So what is meant is adequate observation (which is considered effective

---

[148] A/C. 1/992. See a similar amendment by Brazil A/C. 1/993, Rev. 1. The original Canadian proposal actually said: "in order for this verification to be possible under non-discriminatory conditions, to all States Party to the Treaty, each State Party to the Treaty may ask another State Party to the Treaty to help it to verify the carrying out of the duties arising out of the Treaty". CCD/270. This text too did not entail any duty for the State receiving the request. However, any intervention by the Secretary-General under a duty to obtain results seemed to the Super-Powers to amount to inadmissible moral pressure.

[149] ENDC/PV. 426.

[150] CCD/PV. 443.

[151] CCD/PV. 440. See also ENDC/PV. 414, 421.

even from five hundred metres away) taking into account the activities that putting nuclear weapons on the sea-bed would demand, and taking into account also the size and operation of installations specially constructed to take nuclear weapons or other weapons of mass destruction.[152]

For once therefore, the roles were reversed; controls demanded by the USSR went further than those conceded by the United States. The latter tried to prove that it was not necessary to use the same verification procedure in different situations. "The United States has always sought to set up verification procedure appropriate to each individual measure."[153] The Italian delegate replied to this argument: "We cannot fully support the argument that each Treaty involves different control requirements and that consequently it is not possible to adopt the same rules in each case. We feel, on the contrary, that similar criteria are desirable in order to avoid any imbalance."[154]

A large number of States insisted on the fact that verification ought to include at the same time observation and inspection through access. This was the key to any effective control.[155] According to the United Kingdom, siting and verification procedures must become easier in the future. This is why the revision conference will have to pay special attention to the eventual modification of verification procedure.[156] Many other countries expressed their anxiety over these provisions and the interpretation the American delegate gave them. According to these countries, the emphasis put upon observation is such as to favour the two Super-Powers who alone have the necessary means to carry out proper observations and to interpret the data and results. A small Power, supposing it asks for and gets the necessary help, would only be able to verify by direct access. Verification by observation will always be unsatisfactory as long as the observation is carried out, with very advanced technical means, by another State which is the only one or one of the few able to interpret them. Refusal of access also means as a result that the Super-Powers will not be subject to control by others. In addition, these Super-Powers, under cover of continuous observation, will watch over the peaceful activities carried out by other States on the sea-bed, on the continental shelf and at sea, beyond the

---

[152] CCD/PV. 443.
[153] ibid.
[154] CCD/PV. 447.
[155] CCD/PV. 445 (Yugoslavia) and 447 (Canada).
[156] A/C. 1/PV. 1694. Referring to the information sessions organised for the Geneva Committee by the American delegation, the Canadian representative remarked that in future the multiplication of drilling installations and underwater engineering on the sea-bed will make it difficult to detect eventual violations of the Treaty without inspection. ENDC/PV. 424.

twelve mile limit.[157] To quote the Indian delegate: "How can the right of verification be exercised if a Power having nuclear weapons is allowed to refuse disclosure of its activities on the sea-bed or to refuse access to its installations on the sea-bed? How can it be known what is put on the sea-bed if there is no possibility of observing it closely enough to determine whether there are nuclear weapons or other weapons of mass destruction there? To be completely subject to the discretion of a nuclear weapon State is not good enough."[158]

The third important objection came from a large number of countries which wanted to protect the rights of coastal States over their continental shelf. This last objection seemed to indicate some contradiction in the minds of those who having criticised the operational extent of controls, too limited in their opinion, now wanted their geographical limitation. The contradiction was only apparent; in both cases the majority of maritime States were simply defending themselves from what they considered possible encroachments by the Super-Powers. Some anxiety was thus expressed over the undue embarrassment that might be caused to coastal States by a constant close watch upon their peaceful activities.[159] This is all the more true since, as the American delegate admitted, observation can give positive results, even if the United States do respect the five hundred metre security zone mentioned in paragraphs 2 and 3 of Article 5 of the 1958 Geneva Convention on the Continental Shelf. Also, many States feared that under the pretext of verification, a technologically advanced Power might interfere in the exploitation of the natural resources of the continental shelf belonging to others, or itself exploit these resources or still worse site nuclear weapons there. A coastal State must therefore have the effective and concrete right to verify objects placed on its continental shelf, but other States would only enjoy restricted verification rights over the shelf.[160] Some States which felt that Article III of the joint draft gave no new rights in relation to existing international law, wanted to go further.[161] Others found cause for suspicion: logically, Article III ought to be taken out if it really added nothing new; if it were left in, it was because it did go further than existing law and it was capable of prejudicing the acknowledged rights of a State over a continental shelf.[162] The

---

[157] CCD/PV. 444 and 445.
[158] CCD/PV. 444.
[159] CCD/PV. 444 (Ethiopia).
[160] ENDC/PV. 423 (Brazil); CCD/PV. 434 (Romania), 441 (Canada), 445 (Argentina, Yugoslavia), 447 (Canada); A/C. 1/PV. 1694 (United Kingdom), 1705 (Chile).
[161] ENDC/PV. 430 (Ethiopia).
[162] CCD/PV. 444 (Brazil).

American Co-Chairman was not convincing when he opposed the proposals for prior notification of verification to the coastal State and participation by this State in verification operations. According to the argument he put forward, notification and participation of this kind would violate international law. On the high seas it is in fact impossible to distinguish whether a vessel is carrying out activities unrelated to the Treaty, activities which are permitted under international law unless specifically excluded, or whether it is carrying out verification operations which, under the Treaty would be subject to notice and participation. The freedom of the high seas would be threatened since the coastal State might take advantage of the Treaty provision and exercise control over the activities of any ship or submarine positioned near its continental shelf. It is also difficult, contrary to some suggestions, to distinguish simple observations from other operations such as photography, diving without touching the sea-bed, and so on. The American Co-Chairman recalled that the right of access and the right of protecting to an undue degree the continental shelf claimed by the same countries might prove incompatible. "If the right of access to installations were to be recognised by the Treaty, it would evidently be easier to prevent, or complicate in one way or another the activities of coastal States on the continental shelf."[163]

This line of reasoning did not prevent Canada from tabling a new draft article about control,[164] a draft that was later modified.[165] Basically, Canada proposed to distinguish between observation and other verification methods. Observation would be carried on freely in accordance with international law. If observation proved to be insufficient, the suspecting Party and the suspected Party would be advised of these consultations and co-operation, and would be able to participate. Thus the idea of notice and joint participation was retained and made applicable to the Party under suspicion, to Parties whose territories were in the area of the suspected activities as well as to any other Party so requesting. It is easy to see the complications and difficulties to be met with in practice. The second Canadian text stated in addition, that all verification activities would be carried on "taking duly into account the sovereign or exclusive rights that international law grants to coastal States over the natural resources of their continental shelf". The first version of the Canadian proposal was much more precise and specific.

The continental shelf was Brazil's special preoccupation. She also tabled two successive versions of an amendment to Article III.[166] This amendment also covered notice and joint participation but went much further than

[163] CCD/PV. 443.   [164] CCD/270.   [165] A/C. 1/992.
[166] ENDC/264; A/C. 1/993/Rev. 1/Corr. 1.

Canada's. It stated that "all verification carried out in areas under the national jurisdiction of a State Party will have to take due account of the sovereign rights of coastal States". So even simple observation may be made impossible; the fears expressed by the American Co-Chairman are thus confirmed. In any case, even observations must be previously notified to the coastal State having the right to be associated with it. The cumulative effect of the expressions "national jurisdiction" and "sovereign rights"[167] could be to remove all meaning from the twelve mile limit established by the Treaty (as is well known, Brazil is one of the countries whose territorial waters extend well beyond twelve miles).

The refusal of the General Assembly to approve the joint draft reflects the growing annoyance of small and medium Powers at what they feel is the offhand and undemocratic attitude of the Super-Powers which offends them in a field where the effects of technological inequality are felt particularly keenly. This largely explains the pressure in the Geneva Committee and the General Assembly for a total ban and control that was more egalitarian, and more restrictive upon the freedom of action of the Super-Powers and less upon that of other Powers. This is why most members of the Geneva Committee requested the insertion into the joint draft of a provision taken from the Non-Proliferation Treaty about periodical revision conferences, and the modification of the amendment provision which in the first version gave nuclear Powers a sort of right of veto over future amendments. These two demands were satisfied. But one can also detect a sort of legalistic and unconstructive perfectionism. Thus Brazil asked for provisions for the settlement of disputes to be incorporated into the Treaty. Perhaps the author of the proposal realised it was the first time such provisions were included in a Treaty negotiated by the Geneva Committee, but he justified his proposal by a rather fallacious argument according to which "never before had the Committee actually prepared a Treaty or taken part in the preparation of a Treaty providing for foreign control in areas under the national jurisdiction of States".[168]

In any case it was the first time that the General Assembly decided to

---

[167] According to Art. 2 of the 1958 Convention on the continental shelf, the coastal State exercises sovereign rights over the continental shelf for exploration purposes and for the exploitation of its natural resources. As Judge Ammoun said, the rights that States exercise over the continental shelf are functional, limited by economic aims. The freedom of the high seas must only be affected to the extent that the fulfilment of these purposes demands. ICJ *Reports 1969*, p. 118. For its part the Court distinguished between territorial waters under the sovereign jurisdiction of the State and the continental shelf. In this case, the State has no jurisdiction over the waters lying above and only has jurisdiction on the sea bed for purposes of exploration or exploitation. ibid., p. 37.

[168] CCD/267.

send back to the Geneva Committee a draft treaty tabled together by both Super-Powers. That was an important new fact. The American delegation insisted on the psychological and political importance of an agreement which was to shelter from nuclear weapons a new region representing three-quarters of the earth's surface, and an agreement which extended the area of arms control. "One cannot support the argument that an arms control measure is only desirable if it halts the arms race that has already begun or if it stops an arms race about to begin."[169] The Brazilian representative thought that even a text which placed immediate restrictions only upon the two Super-Powers would represent a limited yet considerable measure of military restraint and would thus serve the interests of peace.[170] A little later the same delegate showed more anxiety; in his opinion, the Treaty distracted attention from the more serious and essential problem of nuclear disarmament. Negotiations about the Treaty were essentially bilateral (between the Big Two), they "tended towards the hypothetical instead of bearing on real situations", and neglected the interests of small States.[171] It is open to question whether it is in the interest of these States to oppose on principle the partial agreements made between the United States and the USSR. In any case it does not seem that such an attitude is general. For the majority of States an extra delay and a new effort to improve the Treaty were necessary for they involved no risk. As the Mexican delegate said: "the only danger ... would be if the nuclear Powers were in a hurry to install apparatus including nuclear weapons on the sea- and ocean-bed. But that hardly seems probable given that the two main nuclear Powers have agreed on a Treaty banning such installations, which proves conclusively that they have concluded it would be contrary to their own security and excessively burdensome to engage in a new arms race in the depths of the sea."[172]

II. THE DENUCLEARISATION OF LATIN AMERICA

The idea of the denuclearisation of certain parts of the world has been current for some time now. It may be explained by the relative ease with which non-nuclear countries can reach agreement among themselves not to change their status. Such agreements are among equals. Nuclear States

[169] ENDC/PV. 397 and A/C. 1/PV. 1691. In order to justify his argument the American representative referred in particular to the Declaration and the Treaty on the principles governing outer space.
[170] ENDC/PV. 423. This comment was made about the American draft and before the Big Two agreed on a joint text.
[171] CCD/PV. 444.
[172] A/C. 1/995.

in this case are simply asked to promise to respect the agreement reached by others and not to use nuclear weapons against them.

The creation of denuclearised zones answers another need: international security, on a world scale, is difficult to organise, and efforts at the regional level may prove more fruitful in the short run. The establishment of zones is thus a partial measure, geographically, a gradual way of solving the security problem. But if this method is only applicable to fixed and clearly defined regions, it does allow more radical steps to be taken than those in the Non-Proliferation Treaty. Denuclearisation is by definition and in principle incompatible with keeping atomic weapons in the zone in question even if they belong to and are put under the exclusive control of a country outside the zone.

In order for regional denuclearisation to succeed, there must not be any serious tension, nor any fundamental disagreement between States in the region in question. The States must not belong to rival alliances. A fairly high degree of regional co-operation, agreement and homogeneity is also required. This explains the failure of certain regional denuclearisation plans – the Nehru plan of 1958, the Unden plan of 1961, the Kekkonen plan of 1963, the Soviet plan of 1963 on the denuclearisation of the Mediterranean area, and so on.[173] The denuclearisation of Africa, by means of an international Treaty and under the auspices of the United Nations was demanded by the 21 July 1964 declaration of African Heads of State, then on 25 May 1965 by the Addis Ababa meeting and also by the Heads of State and Government of non-aligned nations at their second conference in Cairo on 10 October 1964.[174] The idea was taken up and approved by the General Assembly of the United Nations;[175] its failure was due to divisions within Africa and above all to the existence of a "white" Africa.

As far as Europe is concerned, the Rapacki plan of October 1957 for the denuclearisation of the two Germanies, Poland and Czechoslovakia is well known. Such a plan was not acceptable to the West for, in their opinion, it would have threatened the military balance by eliminating tactical nuclear weapons from West Germany while allowing the Soviet Union on the borders of NATO to keep them on her territory. Whatever opinions are held about this argument, the subject of so much discussion, the Gomulka plan, put forward on 28 December 1963 and 29 February 1964 could have had a more favourable reception. The plan was for a freeze of the nuclear *status quo* in the four countries mentioned above. Governments

[173] Cf. W. B. Bader, op. cit., pp. 115–17, A/CONF. 35/DOC. 9.
[174] ENDC/180.
[175] Resolution 2033 (XX).

having armed forces within the proposed zone would have promised not to manufacture nuclear weapons and not to import new weapons. A joint NATO–Warsaw Pact Committee would have exercised control over factories in the four countries as well as at frontiers, sea and airports. The application of the Gomulka plan, which the British Labour Party had approved before it got into power, would have created confidence in a particularly sensitive area. The plan would also have been suitable for further development.[176] But for political reasons, West Germany did not want to accept the plan. This was regrettable. The German threat, real or imaginary, was in the end one of the "justifications" of and one of the reasons for the Russian aggression against Czechoslovakia in August 1968.

The Non-Proliferation Treaty includes in its final version Article VII which recognises – rather uselessly, but at the request of certain Latin American countries – the right of any group of States "to conclude regional Treaties with a view to guaranteeing a total ban on nuclear weapons within their respective territories". But until now, only the Latin American countries have succeeded in concluding a denuclearisation Treaty.

The Heads of State of five Latin American republics meeting on 29 April 1963 announced they had agreed "to conclude a multilateral Latin American agreement by which their countries would promise not to manufacture, receive, stock, or test nuclear weapons".

The United Nations General Assembly in its resolution 1911 (XVIII) approved this statement and expressed the hope that a satisfactory agreement could be drawn up. At the end of November 1964, a preliminary meeting on the denuclearisation of Latin America was held in Mexico.[177] A preparatory commission met in Mexico from 15 March 1965. On 12 February 1967 it approved the Treaty banning nuclear weapons in Latin America (also known as the Tlatelolco Treaty), open to signature on 14 February 1967.[178] We have space here only for a quick and superficial examination of this Treaty.

How was it drawn up? Since it was a regional agreement, there was no reason for it to be negotiated within the United Nations. The Organization of American States was not an ideal framework either, since it included a nuclear State, the United States, and one State in the region, Cuba, which

[176] Cf. A/5827, 1964; K. D. Lapter in *Disarmament and Arms Control*, Summer 1964, pp. 299–309; K. Malcuzynski, *Le Plan Gomulka* (Warsaw, Western Press Agency, 1965).

[177] UN Doc., A/5824.

[178] A/6663, also ENDC/186. For other sessions of the preparatory Commission cf. A/5912, A/5985 and A/6328.

it was hoped would join, was excluded.[179] So a special organisation was set up, the Preparatory Commission for the Denuclearisation of Latin America (COPREDAL) comprising all the independent countries in Latin America (with the exception of Guyana) as well as Jamaica and Trinidad and Tobago. No nuclear State was a member. States outside the continent internationally responsible for territories situated in the continent were not admitted as members either.[180]

The Preparatory Commission showed the importance it attached to the opinion of the United Nations by adopting a final resolution requesting member States to ask for the matter to be put on the agenda of the General Assembly in order to put before the world organisation "the meaning and scope of the Treaty provisions".[181] On 5 December 1967, the Assembly approved by 82 votes to nil and 28 abstentions a resolution welcoming the new Treaty "with special satisfaction".[182]

Why did the Latin American States want to adopt a regional Treaty covering the same field as the future Non-Proliferation Treaty? The answer is evident. The general Treaty had not yet been concluded and the regional Treaty was conceived, according to its own preamble, "as a means of reaching general disarmament later on". A still more important consideration: the regional Treaty went further than the draft Non-Proliferation Treaty or the Treaty itself. In addition, the regional Treaty is the sovereign and exclusive work of the Powers in the region. Real equality among the States taking part marked the drawing-up stage, in which nuclear States did not take part. The Pakistan delegate emphasised this: "The Treaty is the first disarmament Treaty whose conclusion is entirely due to the initiative of a group of States which do not have nuclear weapons and which are considered to be developing countries."[183]

States outside the continent are not admitted as Parties to the Treaty. They may, by adhering to Additional Protocol I apply denuclearisation, as defined by Articles 1, 3, 5, and 13 of the Treaty, to the territories for

---

[179] On this point and others cf. P. Barnes, "Latin America: the first Nuclear-Free Zone?", *Bulletin of Atomic Scientists*, December 1966, pp. 37–40.

[180] Many countries outside the continent were represented by observers at COPREDAL meetings. The Netherlands, which is internationally responsible for territories situated in the continent, asked if it could take part with the same rights as member States. But the Commission decided that extra-continental States, even if they were responsible for territories within the continent, would not be party to the Treaty, so that their presence was not indispensable.

[181] A/6676.

[182] The large number of abstentions reflects the mistrust of the Soviet bloc as well as the indignation aroused by the refusal of COPREDAL to accept Guyana as a party to the Treaty, because of the existing conflict between her and Venezuela. We shall return to this point.

[183] A/C. 1/PV. 1510, 27 October 1967.

which they are *de jure* or *de facto* internationally responsible. Until now, two States have signed Additional Protocol I – the United Kingdom and the Netherlands. The nuclear Powers, for their part, are called upon not to adhere to the Treaty, but to sign and ratify Additional Protocol II. By so doing, they promise: (1) to respect the Treaty provisions; (2) not to contribute in the area in question to the carrying out of acts violating the obligations laid down in Article I of the main body of the Treaty; (3) not to resort either to the use of nuclear weapons or the threat of their use against States for which this Treaty is in force. On this last point, the obligations undertaken by the nuclear Powers go much further than those arising out of Security Council Resolution 255 and the declarations of intent on which this Resolution is based. It is a question here not of the application of the principle of "no first use", but of a limited renunciation (with regard to certain countries) of the use of nuclear weapons.

The drawbacks to the procedure adopted cannot be concealed; for example the Soviet delegate stated that his country's attitude would depend on that of the other nuclear Powers.[184] Much time may go by before a common will emerges under these conditions. Also no real negotiations took place between COPREDAL and the nuclear States. However, the latter did have the opportunity – which only two of them took up – to submit their views on the first drafts in writing. Originally COPREDAL did not intend to resort to the technique of Additional Protocols, but wanted a General Assembly resolution approving the Treaty. This resolution would have stated that all States voting in favour automatically promised not to take either directly or indirectly any step likely to compromise respect for the obligations assumed under the Treaty. The United States criticised this method because it would have made a General Assembly resolution mandatory.[185]

Whatever the reason, none of the nuclear Powers has been in a hurry to adhere to the Protocol. China is against it.[186] France, which had answered on 4 May 1966 the protests of the Presidents of Peru, Ecuador and Colombia against the French nuclear tests in the Pacific,[187] sent a note to the Mexican government on 26 July of the same year. France stated that she "welcomed all attempts to limit the proliferation of nuclear weapons when this was at the initiative of interested Parties. It was from this point

---

[184] A/C. 1/PV. 1509.

[185] Information on these problems can be found in the report of the third session of COPREDAL, A/6328, and also in the book published by the Mexican Foreign Minister A. G. Robles, *The Denuclearisation of Latin America* (Carnegie Foundation for International Peace, 1967), pp. 131–32, 151.

[186] *New York Times*, 2 October 1966 and Robles, op. cit., pp. 154–58.

[187] *La documentation française*, N.E.D., 3384–3387, 29 April 1967, p. 92.

of view that the French government would communicate its intention not to take any initiative that might encourage Latin American States to promote nuclear activities of a military character in their territories." And the note added that "the activities of the Space Centre in Guyana only concern tests of space rockets and satellite launches". It looks as if France does not intend to sign either Additional Protocol.[188] The Soviet Union for its part, criticised the Treaty on more than one point. As for the United States, they had stated in their note of 10 December 1965 that they would support the creation of denuclearised zones "when the initiative for the creation of such zones originates in the same region, when this zone includes all States in the region whose participation is considered important, when the creation of this zone does not disturb the necessary security agreements, and when there are provisions for an enquiry if there are suspicions of violations of the agreement".[189] All these conditions appear to be fulfilled. Only Cuba holds out against adherence to the agreement, on the grounds that she cannot do so as long as the United States are not disposed to return the Guantanamo base and to accept the provisions of the Treaty for the Virgin Islands and Puerto Rico.[190] Now the United States had stated that the Treaty provisions could not apply to the Virgin Islands, Puerto Rico or the Guantanamo base. Yet Washington signed Additional Protocol II on 1 April 1968. The first nuclear State to sign on 20 December 1967, was the United Kingdom. These two signatures have not been followed by others up to the time of writing.[190a] But it may be questioned whether the adhesion of nuclear States to Additional Protocol II is absolutely necessary to the success of the regional Treaty. The moral weight of the undertaking made by States in the region is such that the undertaking will apply *erga omnes* provided that the majority of these States adhere to the Treaty.

Why has the first denuclearised zone been established in Latin America? The 1962 crisis over the temporary installation of nuclear weapons in Cuba made countries in the region conscious of the danger threatening them and the need to meet it as long as none of them had nuclear weapons. Most of them wanted to be pioneers and to create a precedent. On the other hand no serious conflict or threat of a conflict exists in the region. So much could not be said for Africa, where the problems of South Africa, Rhodesia

---

[188] For the French note of 26 July 1966, see Robles, op. cit., pp. 141–42.

[189] A/C. 1/PV. 1507.

[190] Cuba also refused to take part in the Preparatory Commission. The United States declares that the non-adherence of Cuba will not for this fact alone stop her signing Additional Protocol II.

[190a] The General Assembly invited nuclear States to sign and ratify Additional Protocol II as quickly as possible. Resolutions 2286 (XXII) 2456B (XXIII).

and the Portuguese colonies seem to have no short-term solution. Besides no country in the continent seems to be today on the point of becoming able to manufacture nuclear weapons. Finally, the preamble to the Treaty indicates another reason. The governments of signatory States are convinced that the Treaty will constitute a means of preventing their peoples wasting their limited resources on nuclear arms.

Article I of the Treaty lays down the duties of the contracting Parties which, in more detailed and expanded form, correspond to those assumed by non-nuclear States Party to the Non-Proliferation Treaty. The former Treaty, in contrast to the latter, does not divide States into nuclear and non-nuclear; as has been observed, nuclear States did not take part in drafting the text and are called upon to undertake duties by signing an Additional Protocol, not the Treaty itself.

The duties undertaken under Article I are more precise and extensive than those defined by Article II of the Non-Proliferation Treaty. The regional Treaty prohibits the *testing, use,* manufacture, production or acquisition of any nuclear weapon even indirectly and even on behalf of third Parties. *Receipt, deposit, installation, setting up* or *possession* of any nuclear weapon even through third Parties fall under the same ban. Parties to the Treaty also undertake to give up the carrying out, *encouragement* or authorisation of the use, testing, manufacture, production, possession or control of nuclear weapons and any *participation* in such activities. It can be seen therefore that the duties of States Party to the regional Treaty are greater than those of non-nuclear States Party to the Non-Proliferation Treaty. The latter, in contrast to the former, may permit a nuclear State to deposit nuclear weapons on their territory, on condition that these weapons remain under the control of the nuclear State. In the same way, by adhering to Additional Protocol II a nuclear State would give up the possibility of depositing nuclear weapons on the territory of a State Party to the regional Treaty, a right that nuclear States Party to the Non-Proliferation Treaty retain with regard to non-nuclear States Party to this Treaty in so far as the latter do not undertake stricter duties under other Treaties.

Article I concerning duties contains an important omission: the word "transport" is left out. The Preparatory Commission, in an interpretative statement, felt that "if the transporter is one of the contracting Parties" transport is prohibited as Article I bans "the possession, in whatever form, of any nuclear weapon, directly or indirectly, on their own behalf, on behalf of a third Party, or in any other way". If the transporter is a State not Party to the Treaty, transport becomes transit. In this case, and to the extent that there is no overland transit, which is forbidden, it is up to the territorial State to allow or to refuse transit, unless a Treaty between the States in question makes other arrangements. The problem arises over the Panama Canal. Since 25 September 1965 the United States have recognised Panamanian sovereignty over the Canal Zone. In their Note dated 10 September 1965 to COPREDAL, they said they were ready to accept that the Canal Zone be covered by the Treaty on condition that transit rights were not affected. These rights, moreover, arise out of the agreements binding the United States and Panama. Now transit includes deposit which is forbidden by the Treaty. It seems therefore that under these conditions adhesion by Panama would raise some difficulties.[191]

Another problem arises over explosions for peaceful purposes which have already been discussed. It arises here because of the interpretation of Articles 5 and 18 of the Treaty. In contrast to the Non-Proliferation Treaty, the regional Treaty does define nuclear weapons. This is the definition given in Article 5: "any device capable of releasing nuclear energy in an uncontrolled manner and which has a group of characteristics that are appropriate for use for warlike purposes".[192] But there is no practical difference between this device and a weapon capable of being used in explosions for peaceful purposes. Now according to Article 18, the contracting parties may carry out explosions for peaceful purposes even when they use with this end in view "devices similar to those used in nuclear weapons" provided that they do not infringe the other Treaty provisions and in particular those in Articles 1 and 5. They must inform the Organisation set up by the Treaty as well as the IAEA about the explosions and provide them with the specified information and enable them to carry out observation and verification.

It seems difficult to reconcile these provisions with Articles 1, 5, and 18. In order to make logical sense out of these provisions seen as a whole one could take the meaning of the word "similar" for a start. This term covers several concepts and is open to widely different interpretations – two of which – diametrically opposed – should be mentioned. According to

---

[191] The Argentine delegation asked that the following statement be inserted in the final record of COPREDAL: "the Argentine delegation is convinced that it is necessary to ban the transport (including the transit) of nuclear weapons within the territorial jurisdiction of the contracting Parties, considering that to allow transport would be contrary to the spirit of the Treaty whose object is the denuclearisation of Latin America . . . ".

[192] The definition which figured in the draft which emerged from the second session of COPREDAL was inspired by that in the arms control protocol of the WEU Treaty of 23 October 1954, and was much more comprehensive than the final text of Art. 5. It is worth noting that the latter does not cover nuclear-propelled warships, not armed with nuclear weapons, according to an interpretation contained in the British Note of 24 August 1966.

Mexico, Article 18 means "that explosions for peaceful purposes may only be carried out by the Parties if these explosions do not necessitate the use of nuclear weapons as defined by Article 5".[193] Lord Caradon, speaking for the United Kingdom took the same view. In his opinion, the Treaty did not permit the parties to carry out nuclear explosions for peaceful purposes as long as new technical progress did not make possible the development of devices for peaceful explosions which could not be used as weapons.[194]

On the other hand, according to an official Brazilian statement, Article 18 "allows signatory States to carry out, alone or in association with third Parties, nuclear explosions for peaceful purposes, including explosions triggered off by devices similar to those used in nuclear weapons".[195] In fact, as far as Brazil is concerned, it looks as if the word "similar" means "identical". Yet the USSR strongly criticised the ambiguity of Article 18. Although the Treaty does not allow adhesion with reservations, the United Kingdom would be perfectly in order to attach Lord Caradon's interpretative declaration to its adhesion.[196] It should be added that Lord Caradon expressed the wish that his statement would be followed by *similar* statements from other nuclear Powers. There again one comes across the difficulties caused by the adhesion of powers to a Treaty in the drafting of which they have not taken part.

Having said all this, one must admit that an analysis of the preparatory work leaves no doubt over the true meaning of the provisions just examined. The definition of nuclear weapons was wider and more comprehensive in the first drafts than in the final text. The United States insisted during the drafting period and particularly in their Note of 29 August 1966 that the ban should also apply to "other nuclear explosive devices". They did not win the point. Also, the draft prepared by COPREDAL during its second session included stricter provisions by which the contracting parties were not to carry out any peaceful nuclear explosion without observing the provisions of the Moscow Treaty and obtaining the permission of the Organisation set up by the Treaty. These provisions are not included in the final text. It would appear therefore that Brazil was interpreting the text correctly.[197] Again, according to Article 18, Parties must give prior

---

[193] A/C. 1/PV. 1504 and ENDC/PV. 374.
[194] A/C. 1/PV. 1508.
[195] ibid.
[196] Cf. the speech by Mr Garcia Robles, A/C. 1/PV. 1511. According to Art. 27, "the present Treaty cannot be made subject to reservations". This provision applies to Additional Protocol II.
[197] This interpretation was officially confirmed by Brazil when it ratified the Treaty (29 January 1968).

notice to the Organisation to be created, and to the IAEA, of any planned peaceful explosion and they must provide the required information about it "with the notice that circumstances demand". Neither the Organisation nor the IAEA are called upon to authorise the explosion which they thus have no power to prevent. Besides, Article 18 allows Parties to carry out explosions or to collaborate with third Parties for this purpose. The system adopted by Articles I, II and V of the Non-Proliferation Treaty is quite different. This, in practice, prohibits non-nuclear States from carrying out explosions, but enables nuclear States to provide other parties, under conditions laid down by the Treaty, with assistance and services for peaceful explosions.

By signing Additional Protocol II, nuclear States promise "not to have recourse to the use of nuclear weapons nor to the threat of their use against contracting Parties to the Treaty". It is useful to remember that the Assembly in its 1966 Resolution – 2153A (XXI) – asked the nuclear powers to make such an undertaking towards third Parties to a regional denuclearisation Treaty. It will be observed that such an undertaking is much more limited than a declaration by all nuclear States promising not to be the first to use nuclear weapons.

What is the scope of the undertaking given in Additional Protocol II? Mainly psychological. The provision under examination here was intended to reward Latin American States Party to the Treaty, to give them a privileged position and to increase their feeling of security. At the same time a basic distinction was made between nuclear weapons and classical weapons which marks an attempt to educate world public opinion in order to make it understand the meaning of this distinction and the monstrous nature of nuclear weapons. Besides, the undertaking in Additional Protocol II tended to depreciate these weapons as status symbols and symbols of international prestige, and to demonstrate their reduced usefulness in the conduct of foreign relations and the solution of international conflicts.

A nuclear State having signed Additional Protocol II may renounce it at any time in accordance with Article 30 of the Treaty which applies *expressis verbis* in this case. There is an omission in Additional Protocol II in the undertaking by nuclear Powers. Signatories of the Protocol promise to carry out certain acts and to refrain from certain others in relation to contracting Parties. The text does not cover the territories affected by Additional Protocol I in relation to which it would be equitable for the nuclear Powers to give the same undertaking.[198] This omission could be

[198] It refers to territories for which extra-continental Powers are internationally responsible.

rectified by appropriate declarations signed at the time of adhesion for each of the States affected by Additional Protocol II.

An "Agency for the Prohibition of Nuclear Weapons in Latin America" was set up with the task of ensuring that the Treaty obligations are respected (Article 7). The Agency includes a General Conference, a Council[199] and a Secretariat (Article 8). The General Conference, which has the power to make agreements with governments and international organisations and bodies, is empowered to examine and resolve questions raised within the ambit of the Treaty and to carry out research for the better accomplishment of the aims of the Treaty (Article 9). But within a fixed period, each contracting Party has to negotiate and subsequently conclude multilateral or bilateral agreements with the IAEA for the application of its safeguards system to their nuclear activities (Article 13).[200] Thus the two systems, regional and universal, were combined. But the first, less important than the second which it only helped to complete and reinforce, was vaguer and based mainly upon the Parties' periodic relations. The second was more specific, more precise, based upon agreements in due and proper form by which the IAEA carried out special inspections (Article 16, 1(a)). However, two cases were foreseen when the Regional Body would carry out inspections: (i) at the proper request of a Party which suspected another Party of carrying on clandestine activities; (ii) at the invitation of a Party suspected or accused of having violated the Treaty (Article 16, 1(b)). A study of the preparatory work shows that the IAEA would exercise its powers in the field normally reserved for it – namely control of the exclusively civil use of material, equipment and nuclear installations. The Regional Body on the other hand would concentrate on policing the ban on the introduction or import of nuclear weapons. It was also agreed that it would exercise surveillance over peaceful explosions. Taking into account the provisions and interpretation of Article V of the Non-Proliferation Treaty, it appears this task will fall on the shoulders of the IAEA. It could be otherwise for a State Party to the denuclearisation Treaty but not adhering to the Non-Proliferation Treaty, which perfected a nuclear explosion by itself. This is fairly improbable in the foreseeable future.

---

[199] Comprising five members elected by the General Conference taking into account the principle of equitable geographical representation.

[200] During the drafting of the Treaty, a more progressive and quicker technique was envisaged: without actually excluding the possibility of bilateral agreements, a standard type of agreement would be concluded between the regional body and the IAEA and it would apply to the contracting parties. But States less enthusiastic about the Treaty aims sabotaged this idea. Cf. on the progressive argument the speech of the Mexican Foreign Minister on 19 April 1966, Robles, op. cit., pp. 47–56.

In any case it must be stressed that the Regional Body's safeguards system covers a much wider field than the system set up by the Non-Proliferation Treaty. It has to ensure not only that peaceful nuclear activities are not misused for military purposes but also that Parties do not carry on any of the forbidden activities with the help of equipment or weapons brought in from outside (Article 12).

It appears that a State Party to the denuclearisation Treaty not carrying on any atomic activities would not be bound to negotiate with the IAEA the conclusion of the agreement mentioned in Article 13. A State simultaneously Party to the two Treaties would logically only negotiate a single agreement with the IAEA.

On 6 September 1968, Mexico concluded an agreement with the IAEA over the application of safeguards within the framework of the Treaty banning nuclear weapons in Latin America.[201] It is possible here to give only a very superficial idea of this text which is, moreover, based upon the IAEA's safeguards document. But what must be emphasised is that this does not refer only to the regulations actually in force but also to the text as modified in the future by the Board of Governors. This fact is important but its value as a precedent is limited for it was specifically stated while the agreement was under discussion that it could in no circumstances serve as a precedent even within the framework of the regional Treaty.[202]

According to the agreement, the safeguards apply to all nuclear activities, main installations, equipment and nuclear material (except ores) held, produced, treated or imported. Mexico notifies the IAEA from time to time of its activities, production and imports and the IAEA keeps an up-to-date inventory of these. A new and interesting concept, taking into account the fact that it is a bilateral agreement is that of the exporting State (in relation to Mexico). The exporting State, although not party to the Treaty, is bound to confirm Mexico's import declaration. It may also ask for information about that part of the inventory which contains Mexico's import declarations. As the Chairman (the Canadian representative) said: "This concept might be an interesting means of encouraging co-operation between importing and exporting States and the Agency with a view to fulfilling the conditions of an agreement: despite the absence of a legal obligation by the exporting State it would obviously help to strengthen the Agency's safeguard system. Consequently this arrangement must be encouraged."

Mexico recognises the IAEA's right to keep one or more resident inspectors on its territory. Conflicts between the Parties are resolved by

[201] INFCIRC/118.
[202] GOV/OR. 403.

compulsory arbitration, but the Board of Governors (except as far as financial provisions are concerned) can take immediate executive decisions, which is important particularly when it is a question of the violation of the agreement by a State Party. Lastly, as far as financial matters are concerned, it appears that the agreement adopts the practice of transferred safeguard agreements (that is to say agreements by which the IAEA assumes responsibility for safeguards exercised by an exporting State in the context of a bilateral agreement it has concluded with an importing State). The Agency is thus responsible for the expenses of the agreement. It is understood, however, that Mexico will pay the expenses entailed in the drawing up and running of accounts, or the preparation of reports, information and data relating to plans as well as the expenses of an official to be appointed to accompany the Agency inspectors.

To return to the regional Treaty, it should be noted that States adhering to Additional Protocol I or Additional Protocol II cannot become members of the organisation to be set up. But States bound by Additional Protocol I must negotiate agreements with the IAEA to apply Agency safeguards to the nuclear activities they might undertake in the territories for which they are responsible and which are situated in the zone covered by the Treaty.

Two other points are worth stressing. The financial aspects of control were only dealt with in relation to special inspections. Expenses arising out of these were to be met by the Party or Parties requesting the enquiry, but in special circumstances the Board could decide to charge these expenses to the Regional Body (Article 16 (2)).

What are the sanctions in case of violation of the duties undertaken? The results of special inspections are communicated to the United Nations (for both the General Assembly and the Security Council) and may be submitted to an extraordinary session of a General Conference of the Organisation (Article 16, 6 and 7). The Conference may make recommendations to the Party or Parties in question and report to the United Nations. When it observes a Treaty violation, the Conference must address its recommendations to member States, and if it feels that the violation constitutes a danger to peace and security, may inform the General Assembly and the Security Council, the Council of the OAS and the IAEA (Article 20). It will thus fall to these three organisations (or to one or two of them) to take concrete steps in cases where serious violations are observed. At the same time, the IAEA may at its own initiative apply the provisions of Article XII, C of its own Statute.

Thus in the control field, the Treaty adopts a happy solution which allows it to reconcile regionalism with the technical know-how, the experience and the ability of the IAEA. As the Secretary-General of the

United Nations said: "For the first time in history, a denuclearised zone has been created by Treaty in an inhabited part of the globe. In the disarmament field, it is the first Treaty to establish an efficient control system entrusted to a permanent supervisory body. The safeguard system set up within the framework of the International Atomic Energy Agency aims at ensuring that atomic energy is not diverted from the peaceful ends it must serve, to military use; besides, a special inspection system for preventing abuses has been planned in case there might be a risk of secret activities which could escape the IAEA's safeguard system.[203]

Who may adhere to the Treaty? Article 25 tells us. The Treaty is indefinitely open to signature to all Latin American Republics as well as to other sovereign States of the Western Hemisphere whose whole territory is situated south of Latitude 35° North. The same facility is offered to States situated within this geographical area, which might become independent in the future, provided that their admission is approved by General Conference.

The Treaty, moreover, forbids the adhesion of any country whose territory was, before 14 February 1967, the object of a dispute between one or several Latin American countries and an extra-continental country, as long as the dispute has not been peacefully resolved (Article 25). This provision was invoked to prevent Guyana's adhesion. There exists a territorial dispute between this country and Venezuela dating from the time when Guyana was still a British colony. As there is also a dispute between the two countries over the interpretation of Article 25(2), the first General Conference of the Agency for the Prohibition of nuclear weapons in Latin America (OPANAL) decided on 8 September 1969, to set up a good offices committee of three to take steps towards finding a solution to the dispute.[204]

States internationally responsible for territories situated within the geographical zone covered may not become contracting Parties. They are invited to sign Additional Protocol I and in essence promise to obey the duties laid down in Article 1 and to accept the IAEA's safeguards system by concluding with it the agreements mentioned in Article 13.

The provisions concerning the entry into force of the Treaty (Article 28) gave rise to particularly difficult negotiations. Some countries, in particular Brazil, supported by Argentina, Colombia and Venezuela, wanted to make entry into force subject to many complex conditions. Others, led by Mexico, wanted on the contrary to facilitate entry into force as much as possible. Finally, a rather lame compromise was reached. As a general rule, entry into force is conditional upon the fulfilment of the following: ratifica-

[203] General Assembly. Official Documents of the XXIst session, Supplement no. 1A.
[204] A/7681, p. 13.

tion of the Treaty by all countries affected by Article 25; signature and ratification of Additional Protocol I by all States able to do so; signature and ratification of Additional Protocol II by all nuclear States; conclusion with the IAEA of the agreements laid down in Article 13 (Article 28 (1)). However, each signatory State has the right to renounce totally or partially the previously mentioned conditions (Article 28 (2)). As soon as the Treaty enters into force among eleven States (having taken advantage of this possibility of renunciation) the depositary government will call them together in order to set up the body created by the Treaty (Article 28(3)).

During the summer of 1969, the Treaty entered into force, fourteen States having ratified it by renouncing the conditions laid down in Article 25, paragraph 1. The first General Conference of OPANAL, which took a certain number of administrative and legal decisions, met in Mexico City from 2 to 9 September 1969.[205]

Amendments may be proposed by any contracting Party. Such proposals entail a meeting of the signatories followed by the summoning of the General Conference of the Agency which has to decide by a two-thirds majority. Entry into force of amendments is governed by the conditions laid down in Article 28 (1 and 2) concerning the entry into force of the Treaty itself.

The Treaty is of unlimited duration. It may be renounced by any Party which "feels that events relating to the content of the Treaty or the provisions of Additional Protocols I and II annexed to it, threatening its supreme interests or the peace and security of one or more contracting Parties, have taken place or are about to take place". The renunciation must be notified three months in advance to the Secretary-General of the Agency, who communicates it to all Parties, to the Secretary-General of the UN (for the General Assembly and the Security Council) and to the Secretary-General of the OAS (Article 30). Here again we find, although in a vaguer and freer form, the Non-Proliferation Treaty formula.

The Latin American States insisted on putting a clause in the Treaty about the settlement of disputes. The clause adopted is more like a declaration of intent than a legal undertaking.[206]

---

[205] A/7681. The fourteen States were as follows: Barbados, Bolivia, Costa Rica, Dominican Republic, Ecuador, El Salvador, Haiti, Honduras, Jamaica, Mexico, Nicaragua, Paraguay, Peru, and Uruguay. As can be seen, the names of several important countries in the region are missing from this list.

[206] This is the text of Art. 24: "Unless the Parties concerned agree upon another mode of peaceful settlement, any question or dispute concerning the interpretation or application of this Treaty which is not settled shall be referred to the International Court of Justice with the prior consent of the parties to the controversy".

Finally, a word must be said about the zone of application of the Treaty. According to Article 3, "the term territory includes territorial waters, air space and any other place where the State exercises its sovereignty, in accordance with its legislation". In its Note of 29 August 1966, the United States unsuccessfully asked for the last five words, capable of raising so many delicate problems in inter-State relations, to be struck out. Britain, in its Note of 24 August 1966, protested against the interpretation according to which Article 3 covered the Continental Shelf, which, it said, was contrary to the Geneva Convention of 29 April 1958.

Under Article 4, as soon as the Treaty enters into force it will apply to certain parts of the high seas to the East and West of Latin America.[207] There is thus created a margin of regional security against, for example, tests such as those recently conducted by France. But some States, such as the Soviet Union, expressed surprise that a group of States should claim the unilateral modification of the legal status of international waters. The Mexican delegate explained that only nuclear powers had the interest and ability to site nuclear weapons within the zone marked out. By adhering to Additional Protocol II they would undertake not to do so, and from then on it would not be a condition *ultra vires*. Such an undertaking, the Mexican delegate added, "would only be a very modest counterpart to the decision taken by States signatory to the Tlatelolco Treaty to ban for ever nuclear weapons in a highly populated area of more than twenty million square kilometres".[208]

In any case, the Treaty does not prevent the transport on the high seas of nuclear weapons by Powers possessing them. But the provision we have just examined, inspired no doubt by perfectly respectable considerations, none the less might make the adhesion of nuclear Powers – and in consequence the entry into force of the Treaty – more difficult.

The delegate from Uruguay attacked "nuclear neo-colonialism".[209] This quest for a basis of equality explains the ambiguous provisions relating to peaceful explosions as well as the exaggerated demand for the adhesion of all Powers as a condition for the entry into force of the Treaty. It was another sort of egalitarianism, only a pretext perhaps, which was responsible for the provision making entry into force conditional upon ratification by all States in the region which were capable of adhering. Taken literally and applied inflexibly (we have seen that this condition like others can be renounced) the text in question might prevent the entry into force of the Treaty since Cuba has no intention of adhering. Happily, the Treaty did

[207] Cf. the explanation of the Mexican delegate A/C. 1/PV. 1504.
[208] A/C. 1/PV. 1511.
[209] A/C. 1/PV. 1509.

enter into force all the same and the Agency does work, but it is to be regretted that important countries such as Argentina and Brazil have not yet joined.

In spite of its imperfections, the Tlatelolco Treaty does mark an important step and gives a salutary example by banning unconditionally for the first time nuclear weapons in a populated area. Compared with the Non-Proliferation Treaty, it only refers to a single region, but it does set out to ban nuclear weapons completely from that region. It is better drafted, and includes precise definitions of these weapons, which is not the case in the Non-Proliferation Treaty. It establishes a new and autonomous regional body, at the same time creating appropriate relations between this body and the IAEA. Finally, it expresses the equality of the Parties and cannot be the subject on this account of any of the criticisms made against the Non-Proliferation Treaty.[210]

[210] Cf. A/C. 1/PV. 1569 (Mexico).

CONCLUSION

The Treaty on the Non-Proliferation of Nuclear Weapons was opened to signature on 1 July 1968. Since then two events have taken place: the invasion of Czechoslovakia by the troops of five countries belonging to the Warsaw Pact, and the meeting in Geneva from 29 August to 27 September 1968 of the Conference of non-nuclear States. Certainly neither of these two events seriously changed the basis of the problem, such as it has been described in the preceding pages. In spite of the obstacles, the sceptics were wrong; the Treaty came into force on 5 March 1970.

*　　*　　*　　*

A historical glance at the agreements concluded since 1947 and at disarmament negotiations gives an idea of the way the subject evolved. It went from the general, from the global, to the particular, to the partial; from a total system to fragmentary measures.

This tendency can be discerned both *ratione personae* and *ratione materiae*. Under the 1947 Peace Treaties, the Paris Agreements of 23 October 1954 and the 1955 Austrian State Treaty, some countries individually and more or less unreservedly renounced nuclear weapons. The Treaties of 1 December 1959 and 27 January 1967 denuclearised the Antarctic and Outer Space, whilst that of 14 February 1967 did the same for Latin America. The Moscow Treaty was a partial measure in two ways: it referred only to tests, and then only to tests carried out in certain environments.

These measures, or at least some of them, reflect the growing community of interest being established between the two Super-Powers, both subjectively and objectively. As the exceptional nature of nuclear weapons comes to be more generally recognised, there is a conscious attempt to turn them from the subject into the object of international relations and the law of nations. This series of Treaties of which the latest is that of non-proliferation, does not strictly speaking envisage disarmament measures, but all these instruments in some measure limit the freedom of action of the Parties and bring more logic into international relations. They are the consequence of *détente* which they, in turn, stimulate. Agreement and *détente* react on and influence each other in a sort of circular process.

Public opinion, worried about the genetic and physical health risks

214

which may arise from nuclear tests, played a considerable role in the conclusion of the Moscow Treaty. It could have as much influence on other questions if it were sufficiently informed on problems which are as important but which arouse less strong feelings.

Some of the instruments examined in Chapter 1 and the processes by which they saw the light of day, show the real lack of equality among States which in our chosen field is particularly striking and which inevitably shows up in the Treaties. The texts are often obscure, their terms are badly defined and ambiguous. This can be explained by the nature of the problems covered, by the delicate and difficult nature of agreement between the Super-Powers, an agreement which conditions the existence and balance of agreed norms of conduct. But legality and legal perfectionism take a back seat here. What matters is the existence of a Treaty system, a powerful means of educating and influencing the Super-Powers – and others – to accept a minimum of common life and laws.

*　　*　　*　　*

The Non-Proliferation Treaty has some of the characteristics of previous Treaties. It excels neither in precision nor in clarity of thought: as has been shown, the expression "non-proliferation" is in fact wrongly used.

However, the Treaty does translate into legal language (often defective) a non-proliferation policy that has for some years been applied in different ways by the Super-Powers. Empirical measures taken at the beginning were tried and found wanting; in the end it was felt that only a Treaty could produce the necessary security and safeguards. This Treaty without being the exclusive work of the Big Two, is the concrete proof of their agreement in a limited yet important field. It is the result of a compromise and it is only necessary to read the proposals in the Appendix to realise that each of the Super-Powers made concessions during the negotiations, the Soviet Union perhaps more than the United States.

Numerous arguments have been put forward for and against proliferation. It seems to the author that proliferation would lead to more insecurity in international relations, more fear – a bad counsellor – between States and governments, and in particular between the Super-Powers. In the armaments field, General Staffs always work on the least favourable hypothesis (and show what unbridled imaginations they have in this field) without succeeding in getting greater security through extra expense and new manufactures. For once it would be a good idea to apply this kind of thinking to peace, and, if in doubt at least to admit the possibility of the danger that would result from proliferation. Even if this danger is objectively considered to be small, it is impossible to ignore the attitude of the Super-Powers who for years have been showing signs of alarm at the possible consequences of proliferation. Proliferation brings an element of unreason into inter-State relations. It also helps to create imbalance, given the financial and economic demands of nuclear weaponry. And in our age, it is advance in the economic and social field that gathers prestige and is copied.

It is becoming more and more clear (and the example of the Big Two is convincing) that an arms race, an increase in military expenditure, and the manufacture of ever more sophisticated weapons, instead of creating more security, in fact both objectively and subjectively only augment the general feelings of insecurity.

By studying the relations of a small or medium Power with a State of the same size or a great Power, we have arrived at the conclusion that nuclear armament is not a rational or effective solution and that one cannot have faith in it. The aggression against Czechoslovakia on 21 August 1968 only confirms this observation. The Czechs would not have been more tempted to commit suicide with nuclear weapons than with conventional weapons. It was through passive resistance based on the unity and will of the people that the Czechs had initial success but alas, this was quickly nullified by the vacillations of their leaders and the plots of those loyal to the invader.

*   *   *   *

Since 1945, there has been a dual tendency on the institutional level. On the one hand, disarmament and related questions have tended more and more to by-pass the Security Council and become a matter for the General Assembly. Paradoxically, this tendency has only grown stronger as the two Super-Powers have got on better terms with each other. On the other hand, the Super-Powers have tended to negotiate as much as possible within the Geneva Committee – before witnesses – that is to say a negotiating body outside the United Nations, a body that has to remain small if it is to be effective, and whose composition had to reflect a certain geographical and political balance.

The Assembly plays the part of a discussion and pressure group. At the last moment, it got modifications in the text of the Non-Proliferation Treaty, without these affecting the basis of the Treaty. It temporarily blocked the Big Two's draft Treaty banning the siting of nuclear weapons and other weapons of mass destruction on the sea- and ocean-bed. It acts as spokesman for public opinion by making recommendations to nuclear States and repeating them frequently.

The negotiating body is the Geneva Committee. Its members were not elected but co-opted by the Big Two. Its composition, the result of difficult bargaining and a delicate balance, is tripartite, the same as subsidiary bodies of the General Assembly working in the economic field. However, in the Geneva Committee, the third group has as common denominator not economic under-development but non-alignment. And it does not constitute the majority.

The Committee ought to improve its working methods, have its own budget, and appoint highly qualified experts, chosen without reference to nationality. More homogeneity and cohesion among the non-aligned group would enable it to be more influential. But it is worth remarking that the role of the Committee has become continually stronger and that in the last Treaty it was more important than in the Moscow Treaty. Committee members ought to be more conscious that they have the vital task of coaxing agreement out of the Big Two who in turn would be well advised to show more consideration for the members of the negotiating body.

So the continuation in existence of the Committee and the extension of its influence seem necessary. This is not a contradiction of proposals for summit meetings of the nuclear States in so far as these meetings would be another forum where attempts could be made to advance the cause of disarmament and connected matters.

It is worth saying a word or two here about the recent Geneva Conference of non-nuclear weapon States. The UN Secretary-General expressed the hope that "the Conference will strengthen co-operation between nuclear and non-nuclear States and will facilitate the application of the provisions of the Non-Proliferation Treaty".[1] The Conference, which scarcely dealt with the Treaty, did not fulfil this expectation. It demonstrated the fragility and the risks of a meeting where there is no real dialogue between nuclear Powers and non-nuclear States. The former were present as observers at the Conference, trying to defend their interests in the lobbies, but refusing to speak during the sessions, although they had the right to do so.[1a] Demagogy and blackmail by some developing countries and even some European States, such as West Germany and Italy, were much in evidence. Thus these two latter countries scorning both political reality and legal rules unsuccessfully proposed that the Conference got down to defining the technical terms appearing in the Non-Proliferation Treaty.[2] In addition Italy put forward the idea of institutionalising the Conference of non-aligned States as a subsidiary organ of the General Assembly.[3] In

[1] A/CONF. 35/SR. 1.
[1a] *Hearings 1969*, p. 450.
[2] A/CONF. 35/SR. 4 and A/CONF. 35/C. 2/SR. 6.
[3] A/CONF. 35/C. 2/1.

the end this proposal was not put to a vote.[4] How could it be imagined that the single fact of being non-nuclear could constitute a sufficient common denominator for a group of States? What have countries like Italy, West Germany and Japan got in common even in the nuclear field, politically or economically, with the great majority of developing countries which only think of cashing in politically on their renunciation of atomic weapons and which have no nuclear industry? Luckily, after a month's debate, the Conference agreed to carry some fairly harmless resolutions which, if they did not bring anything new, did not compromise anything. It is just as well that attempts to get the General Assembly to call a new meeting of non-nuclear States have failed until now. These attempts have, moreover, met with the determined opposition of the Super-Powers.[4a]

*   *   *   *

A study of the preparatory work and the attitude of States has shown us the superiority of the Treaty over unilateral undertakings or diplomatic pressure. This is true in spite of the imperfections, ambiguities and gaps in the Non-Proliferation Treaty. These faults may, moreover, diminish and even disappear during the operation and "running in" of the Treaty system and the summoning of periodic conferences.

The Treaty does not go as far as the Treaty governing the denuclearisation of Latin America. It does not ban the placing on the territory of a non-nuclear State of atomic weapons belonging to a nuclear State and remaining under its control. This raises the whole problem of access to these weapons by non-nuclear States, and we have seen that on this point the Soviet Union which originally was opposed to such access has changed its attitude. During the Conference of non-nuclear States, certain countries tried unsuccessfully to come back to this point.[5]

If the Treaty confirms the lack of equality among the Parties, it is not the first to have this characteristic. Those who in the name of political and legal perfection, support "all or nothing at all" do a disservice to the cause of international collaboration. Moreover, one must reject the false idea that anything considered advantageous by one group of States is necessarily harmful to others. By acceding to the Treaty, non-nuclear States are not

[4] Cf. A/CONF. 35/6, para. 4.
[4a] *Hearings 1969*, pp. 477–79.
[5] Thus according to Ghana, a non-nuclear State ought to be defined as "a State that not only does not possess nuclear weapons, but has given up the right to acquire them and has banned the installation, transport, transit, use and control of these weapons by a third party in its territory or the territories it controls". A/CONF. 35/C. 1/S.R. 9.

helping the Super-Powers: they are giving significant help to international collaboration and organisation.

In the context of non-proliferation, the West German attitude is of capital importance. At the Conference of non-nuclear States, Herr Brandt said that "the Federal Republic has, with regard to the partners in the alliance to which she belongs, given up the manufacture of atomic weapons and has obeyed the requisite international controls. She aspires neither to have atomic weapons at her disposal, nor to possess them, at the national level."[6] The restriction implied in the latter sentence will be noted. None the less Bonn used the pretext of the invasion of Czechoslovakia to put off its decision over the Non-Proliferation Treaty. The feverish activity of the Federal Republic at the Conference of non-nuclear States has also been noted, and the support given to her by Italy and Japan, a combination which can only recall unpleasant memories.[7]

In reality, the Soviet intervention, however criminal it was, may safeguard the ideological and political *status quo* domestically as well as internationally. West Germany, as Chancellor Kiesinger again recalled on 18 July 1968, wants to change the *status quo*. It is all very well for her to say she wants to do this peacefully, for she arouses the mistrust and fear of a conservative Power like the Soviet Union is at present; those who know Russia realise to what extent this fear is real. It is by trying to reduce, and then little by little eliminate this fear that we shall perhaps arrive at a new stage of *détente*. Looked at in this way, the German refusal, even temporary, was not a sign of political maturity. The Soviet action was a sign of weakness and added nothing to Soviet military power, on the contrary it weakened it (Soviet troops cannot count upon the armies of the other Eastern countries, which in case of any serious trouble will at best be passive). As the British politician, Mr Enoch Powell, rightly said in a speech on 9 September 1968, the events in Czechoslovakia proved the falsity of the theory of nuclear dissuasion as the basis of the balance of power in Europe. As conventional forces are more or less evenly balanced between the two blocs in Europe, who would contemplate nuclear suicide, even supposing anyone had seriously thought about it?[8] So Bonn's decision to sign the Treaty was a relief. Let us hope that ratification will not be long delayed, as soon as the problems of relations between the IAEA and Euratom are settled.

[6] A/CONF. 35/SR. 3.

[7] Cf. *The Economist*, 28 September 1968 and *The Times*, 17 September 1968.

[8] This attitude is in contrast to that of Herr Willy Brandt. According to him, "as long as nuclear weapons are not eliminated from all parts, they will not be able to be banned as a means of dissuasion and legitimate collective defence". A/CONF. 35/SR. 3.

*   *   *   *

The provisions in the Treaty about control are also undeniably discriminating as they apply only to non-nuclear Parties. The resulting lack of equality has been mitigated in practice by unilateral undertakings by London and Washington. Besides, it is worth recalling that under bilateral agreements, control is exercised by the supplier over most deliveries made in the nuclear field.

Controls laid down in Article III of the Non-Proliferation Treaty are international and democratic in character. They must allow the free development of co-operation in the peaceful use of nuclear energy. The IAEA, created more than ten years ago, which already has a competent staff and some experience, is the institution which naturally springs to mind for the organisation of controls. The problem of Euratom does not appear to raise insurmountable difficulties at least in so far as such difficulties are not due to hidden political motives.

Fears about the industrial espionage that controls might encourage are, it appears to the author, much exaggerated. Nothing could better illustrate the differences in attitude and intent among non-nuclear States. Developing countries demand access to nuclear technology and know-how, even that covered by commercial secrecy, whilst West Germany, Italy, and Japan, to mention only these three, all want to protect their industries and technology and to invoke commercial secrecy.

None the less, at the Conference of non-nuclear States in Geneva, a certain number of countries proposed the creation within the IAEA of a formal safeguards organisation which would be less exclusive in membership than that of the Board of Governors. At the same time the Agency was also requested to try and simplify its control methods and limit their scope.[9] This proposal did not obtain the required number of votes. It was, moreover, more reasonable to make the system laid down under Article III of the Treaty work and get it applied by the Agency, before trying to amend it.[10] The German Federal Republic, which also requested the simplification of controls, recognised, in a working document that a big research, development and test programme was necessary to draw up the rules of a new safeguards system.[11]

---

[9] A/CONF. 35/L. 1, L. 2, and Rev. 1, L. 9 and Rev. 1, L. 12, L. 14, L. 16, L. 17, L. 18, L. 19; A/CONF. 35/5, para. 6, 10, 14, 15 – F and G. Following requests for more democratic methods in the selection of the Board of Governors of the Agency, it is at present studying the revision of Art. VI of the Statutes defining the composition of the Board. See GC(XXIII)/RES/261.

[10] See the relevant remarks of the UAR delegate, A/CONF. 35/C. 2/SR. 7.

[11] A/CONF. 35/C. 1/1.

As far as the peaceful uses of nuclear energy are concerned, most States taking part in the recent Geneva Conference seemed to believe they could barter their renunciation of atomic weapons – which they judged a sacrifice – for considerable technological and financial rewards from nuclear States. Now as we have observed, non-nuclear States like Canada, Sweden and India have been able to make important progress in the field of peaceful uses. Non-nuclear countries which protest against all forms of pressure have themselves actually tried to put pressure upon nuclear States forgetting that accession to the Treaty ought to encourage the spread of peaceful collaboration and not vice-versa.

In reality, the mirage of advanced technology may bring serious dangers. M. René Dumont has several times criticised the tendency of certain developing countries to want to mechanise their agriculture at all costs, when in the immediate future technically less advanced methods would be more economic and, taking local conditions into account, more logical.

It is also worth recalling that what holds up the development of nuclear industry in a developing country is not military or industrial secrecy covering manufacture in advanced countries (certain of which are in fact not nuclear) but lack of cash, technicians and experts. Developing countries thus have every interest in working together and creating common research institutes. The IAEA ought each year to publicise these efforts and discuss them by putting them in the context of a general plan for preventing the waste of resources that are still scarce. It might also each year usefully examine the extent and methods of international co-operation, the prices and conditions of sale of materials supplied by private companies and governments. This kind of publicity and periodical examination would also be generally reassuring to all concerned.[12] Technical assistance ought to be developed by helping in the training in advanced countries of technicians and experts from developing countries and sending qualified staff to these countries.

During the Geneva Conference of non-nuclear States, an attempt was made to list the countries which might benefit from aid, assistance and co-operation in the field of peaceful uses, and, in particular in the allocation of fissile material. The majority of those taking part (and this position was adopted in one of the Conference Resolutions) felt that they ought to include non-nuclear weapon States who accepted the application of the safeguards envisaged in Article III of the Non-Proliferation Treaty. In other words, the Conference accepted the principle that the Agency's

[12] Perhaps not to private companies. Years ago, the oil companies tried to prevent publication of a paper by the UN Economic Commission for Europe on the price structure of refined petroleum in Europe.

safeguards system ought to cover all peaceful nuclear activities of non-nuclear States, whatever they might be.

The defining of these countries raised two problems. Firstly, Article III of the Treaty gives the Agency certain powers over and above those it normally has, which are to be defined in an agreement to be concluded by it with the Parties to the Treaty. We know that under Article III(2) no State Party to the Non-Proliferation Treaty may carry out certain deliveries to any non-nuclear State unless the source or fissile materials delivered or manufactured from these deliveries are subject to the safeguards required by the said Article. In this case then, the safeguards system covers a narrower field than when it applies to non-nuclear States Party to the Treaty. The Treaty cannot be modified by the Conference of nuclear States. Article III(2) of course does not mention the agreements that the Agency has to conclude with non-nuclear States not Party to the Treaty to which States Party to the Treaty might make deliveries. But this provision gives the Agency powers in a field with which it is thoroughly familiar and which it has exercised for a long time. As it is, the Agency will simply have to apply the rules we have already analysed that are laid down in its safeguards document.

Secondly, Article IV(2) of the Treaty gives, as far as co-operation in the field of peaceful use is concerned, some sort of priority to States Party, but it does not specifically mention the States which would be subject to the controls mentioned in Article III without adhering to the Treaty.[13] Also, according to a working paper on peaceful explosions, presented by Mexico, States benefiting from services and aid in this field would be those adhering to the Non-Proliferation Treaty or the Tlatelolco Treaty, or those making any other special or regional arrangement for banning nuclear weapons on their respective territories.[14]

In the field of peaceful uses, there was much insistence at the Geneva conference, upon equal access by all States to nuclear technology and fissile materials, and some would have liked nuclear States to make firm promises about this. Here again it may be questioned whether the multiplication of costly installations is a desirable aim.

Equal access would have raised other delicate problems. So the resolution that was passed insisted on "access to special fissionable materials on a commercial basis" and on the granting by nuclear States of fissile materials for peaceful programmes of non-nuclear States which are subject to the

---

[13] It is worth mentioning that attempts to reach a definition, analysed here, can be explained, at least in part by the curious state of hostility between Pakistan and India, the latter being rather reluctant over controls.

[14] A/CONF. 35/Doc. 15, annex II, art. 3.

safeguards of Article III. It is evident that progress in co-operation in the field of peaceful uses depends upon the availability of material supplied commercially and without discrimination. The latter phrase appears, moreover, in Article IV(1), but in rather an ambiguous context. In any case, the Agency ought to establish a sort of draft plan of future needs of fissile materials, then reach an understanding with nuclear States, and even some non-nuclear States, to get firm guarantees of the delivery of these materials which it would then resell to user States, according to the plan drawn up. The Conference of non-nuclear States envisaged the creation by the IAEA of a "bank" of special fissionable materials. Different sections of the Agency discussed the matter. But it does not look as if the real problem arises out of any shortage of fissile materials. The materials offered to the Agency over ten years ago – for research reactors it is true – have hardly been touched and more than 5,000 kg of uranium 235 are still available. Most countries seem to prefer bilateral exchanges.[14a]

The financial problem is very important as we have seen. The creation of a special Nuclear Energy Fund has been proposed.[15] It is questionable, however, whether this is a realistic idea. Funds grow in number, but contributions are a different matter. It seems easier to get aid from advanced countries for individual well conceived projects.

Quite rightly, the Geneva Conference invited the IAEA to stimulate and improve the exchange of information. In addition increased possibilities for training ought to be offered to technicians and experts from developing countries. The Agency could recruit on a permanent basis, a group of eminent experts and technicians whose experience would always be available to backward countries. It would fall upon these countries to get together and form joint public companies, both commercial and industrial, and to obtain through the Agency for these companies the maximum of information, in accordance with the ideas developed in Chapter 6 (II).

As far as peaceful explosions are concerned, a problem arises over the impossibility of establishing at present a basic difference between devices used in these explosions and nuclear weapons. Also, although the Moscow Treaty did not define underground tests, a test whose effects could be felt above ground could not be considered as such; this kind of test is therefore banned. In addition, the Moscow Treaty bans tests, even underground, when they cause radioactive fall-out outside the territories of the State

[14a] See A/7677/Add. 2.
[15] Some went as far as to give details of how to calculate the contribution of nuclear States: four times their ordinary contribution to the Agency budget (A/CONF. 35/C. 2/SR. 3 – Belgium) or a fixed percentage of their expenditure upon the manufacture of nuclear fuel (A/CONF. 35/C. 2/SR. 6 – Pakistan).

under whose jurisdiction or control such an explosion takes place. Finally, certain countries, and particularly the eight non-aligned States, wanted to link the application of Article V of the Non-Proliferation Treaty with a general and complete test ban, which would result in an effective slowing down of the arms race.[16] According to this hypothesis, no explosion could take place in the territory of any State without the permission of an international organisation. This attitude is quite logical and in conformity with the preamble and Article VI of the Non-Proliferation Treaty. Italy, however, took a different point of view: she proposed a distinction between the rules for underground nuclear explosions for peaceful purposes and those of tests for military purposes, the latter continuing for the moment without restriction.[17] The Geneva Conference adopted the opinion of the eight non-aligned by an overwhelming majority.

It seems to the author that developing countries delude themselves about the use of nuclear explosions for peaceful purposes in the near future. Also, we have shown that there are ways of minimising the inconveniencies resulting from the monopoly held by the Super-Powers in this branch of technology.

The institutional problem was tackled by the Geneva Conference both in relation to peaceful uses in general and nuclear explosions in particular. Certain countries strongly blamed the composition of the Board of Governors of the IAEA which was in their opinion, old-fashioned and aristocratic.[18]

For this reason, and also doubtless for others, Italy[19] and Mexico[20]

[16] ENDC/235. This memorandum was dated 26 August 1968. One of the eight non-aligned, Mexico, in view of the Conference of non-nuclear States, tabled a working document on 22 August which is not quite compatible with the point of view expressed in the note by the eight.

[17] ENDC/234.

[18] See for example A/CONF. 35/C. 2/SR. 5 (Ghana) and SR. 9 (Pakistan). See note 9.

[19] A/CONF. 35/C. 2/2. This organisation (having the character either of a specialised institution, or of an independent body within the IAEA) would have the task of examining the requests of States wishing to carry out explosions, giving the necessary permission, supplying services, ensuring equal access for all States to nuclear technology, and helping the financing of explosion and civil engineering operations.

[20] A/CONF. 35/Doc. 15. This document proposes the creation of an independent body within the framework of the IAEA, with its own staff organisation, and in particular a Board of fourteen Afro-Asian States, six Latin American States and fourteen other States. The nuclear member States would of course be permanently included among these thirty-four. The body would carry out the duties resulting from Art. V of the Non-Proliferation Treaty and in particular examine requests, maintain international surveillance, and encourage and develop technical assistance and the exchange of information. According to the Mexican proposal, States supplying nuclear materials would be responsible for the cost

proposed the creation of a special organisation with certain powers in the field of peaceful explosions. The Conference preferred to recommend the Agency to study its possible work in this field. We have shown that because of the character of the new technology and the lack of technically skilled personnel it is not desirable to create a new organisation. Advantage must be taken of the Agency's experience and greater support must be given to it. This point of view was endorsed by the General Assembly.[21]

* * * *

The final clauses clearly illustrate the political significance of the legal technicalities. The provision about entry into force seems to be a happy compromise. Each State, if it so desires, can choose when to ratify the Treaty, in relation to ratification by any other State, and can even make contact with it for this purpose.

The advisability of the solution reached over the question of amendment is open to doubt. In fields as subject to change as those covered by the Treaty, maximum flexibility is required, and amendment procedure ought to have been made as easy as possible. Instead, revision conferences will necessarily allow non-nuclear States to put effective pressure upon nuclear States. Perhaps it would have been possible to limit the duration of the Treaty, because of the reticence of non-nuclear States.

The provision about withdrawal is at first sight very flexible and not unduly binding. But in practice it will prevent hasty decisions and it testifies, because of the very opposition it aroused, to the scope and strength of the Treaty bonds even when they appear to be unrestricting.

* * * *

Of the collateral measures, only one has been brought into effect up till now, that concerning the denuclearisation of Latin America.

It has been mentioned that the Treaty of Tlatelolco goes further than the Non-Proliferation Treaty. In particular it is the work only of non-nuclear States, who alone subscribe to the Treaty, which is thus completely free from discriminatory measures. However, a double problem remains: the adhesion of non-nuclear States to the Additional Protocol II and the

---

of transporting explosive devices to the territory of the receiving member State as well as for expenses arising out of preparatory engineering works and security and safety measures to be applied in the territory of this State. The supplier would be responsible for damage caused by the explosion upon the territory of the receiving State.

[21] Resolutions 2456C (XXIII) and 2605B (XXIV).

accession of States responsible for territories situated in the geographical zone covered by the Treaty to the Additional Protocol I.

Also, the denuclearisation Treaty set up a control system run by the world body, the IAEA, and by the regional body set up for this purpose. So regionalism and universality were both satisfied. If Article 13 of the Tlatelolco Treaty is less detailed than Article III of the Non-Proliferation Treaty, the agreements envisaged are of course identical to those which have to be concluded under Article III of the second Treaty. It will be noticed, however, that the regional Treaty, for obvious reasons, contains no provision similar to that contained in the same Article III according to which no State Party may supply any other State with material and equipment unless they are subject to the controls laid down by this same Article. Also, the controls set up by the Tlatelolco Treaty cover a much wider field for they are also aimed at the detection of clandestine activities and in particular at preventing the introduction or import of nuclear weapons. The special organisation set up, and its Secretary-General, are given wide ranging powers in this field.

There is some difference between the two Treaties over the question of nuclear explosives. The universal Treaty goes further than the regional one over this. But it is improbable that Latin American countries could carry out nuclear explosions by themselves and they will only be able to obtain the help of nuclear States under the conditions laid down by the Non-Proliferation Treaty.

It is worth stressing the fact that the Non-Proliferation Treaty is considered to give rise to new disarmament prospects. Only States Party to the Treaty will be able to exercise effective pressure upon adhering nuclear States to force them to adopt concrete measures in accordance with the preamble and with Article VI of the Treaty. States refusing to accede would thus be depriving themselves of a means of action towards reaching a goal which they themselves regard as essential.

The Conference of non-nuclear States, it ought to be remembered, asked the Super-Powers to begin negotiations "on the limitation of vector systems for strategic offensive nuclear weapons, and defence systems against ballistic missiles". It also suggested an order of priority for disarmament measures.[22]

[22] It asked "the General Assembly of the United Nations to recommend at its 23rd session, that the Committee of eighteen Disarmament Conference should begin negotiations at the latest by March 1969, with a view to:
(a) measures preventing any new development and any new perfection of nuclear weapons and their vectors;
(b) the conclusion of a total nuclear test ban Treaty, an initiative which would

*   *   *   *

Security guarantees raise complicated problems that are difficult to solve. The Geneva Conference of non-nuclear States was unable to pass a single resolution on this point.[23]

However, the question was widely discussed. Some States, such as West Germany and the Africans, stressed the need to cover the use or the threat of the use of conventional weapons.[24] Others asked for the conclusion of a universal Treaty giving guarantees to all and calling for a world conference for this purpose.[25]

According to Switzerland, the only solution was to adopt a protocol based upon the Additional Protocol II of the Tlatelolco Treaty.[26] Pakistan demanded unilateral guarantees given outside the framework of the United Nations Charter.[27]

All this proves that it was extremely difficult to find a solution capable of satisfying a wide number of States. It is evident that even the closest alliances do not give an absolute or automatic guarantee.[28] As has been properly shown, security guarantees can never depend upon legal formulae[29] as different categories of States have different exigencies, needs and situations.[30] And there is in addition a fundamental

---

mark an important step towards nuclear disarmament and rank high in the order of priorities;

(c) an agreement on an immediate halt to the production of fissile materials for armaments and a halt to the manufacture of nuclear weapons;

(d) the reduction, and subsequent elimination of all stocks of nuclear weapons and their vector systems."

[23] With the exception of a recommendation, tabled by West Germany, and adopted by fifty votes in favour to five against with twenty-five abstentions. This recommendation reaffirmed:

(a) the unalterable principle of a ban on the use of force;

(b) the right of all States to equality, sovereignty, territorial integrity, non-interference in their internal affairs, and free choice;

(c) the natural right of self-defence, recognised by Article 51 of the Charter and which, apart from measures taken or authorised by the Security Council, is the only exception to the ban on the use of force. By tabling this draft, Bonn was trying to reply to the Soviet argument based on Articles 53 and 107 of the Charter, claiming a right of intervention in Germany.

[24] A/CONF. 35/SR. 3 (West Germany) and SR. 6 (Uganda).

[25] A/CONF. 35/C. 1/L. 3 and 4; A/CONF. 35/5, para. 3, 11, 12.

[26] A/CONF. 35/SR. 8.

[27] A/CONF. 35/C. 1/SR. 2.

[28] This point was stressed by Assistant Secretary of State Katzenbach, according to whom even Art. V of the NATO Treaty which includes a special formula does not constitute an exception. *US Commitments to Foreign Powers*, US Senate, on Res. 151, August–September 1967, pp. 16, 75, 98, 157–8.

[29] A/CONF. 35/C. 1/SR. 8 (Mexico).

[30] A/CONF. 35/SR. 12 (Finland).

argument – the Non-Proliferation Treaty contributes to the security of all.

Following the invasion of Czechoslovakia by the Soviet Union and four other Warsaw Pact countries, Mr Nixon felt that the ratification of the Treaty ought to be delayed.[31] This was also the view of West Germany, Italy and Japan. This invasion certainly had two consequences on the international scene: (a) small and medium sized powers became more conscious of their weakness and vulnerability towards operations by the Super-Powers – they felt the real extent of the lack of equality; (b) statements and promises by the Super-Powers appeared even less credible than in the past.

But international order can only be built up with States as they actually are. It would really be a defeatist policy to make all progress towards co-operation between States, on a world scale, conditional upon them (or some of them) adopting attitudes more in conformity with morality and justice. In spite of the banditry and the violations of morality and law committed by one of them in Czechoslovakia and the other in Viet-Nam, only agreement between the Big Two will enable progress to be made on the road to disarmament and certain burning questions, such as the Middle East, to be solved. The Non-Proliferation Treaty is the symbol of a certain common understanding and co-operation between the Soviet Union and the United States, a link in the chain which is beginning to take shape. Now it is as well to look at the evidence: these two States more than any other suffer from fear, the fear of change, either at home or internationally.[32] The Non-Proliferation Treaty reassures both of them and may be considered a partial cure for this unhealthy fear. This is the area to look for consolidation of *détente* and agreement which perhaps in time will result in changes inside zones considered today as belonging to spheres of influence.

Such a concept is based on logic: the proof lies in the evolution and entry into force of the Non-Proliferation Treaty. President Nixon was forced to admit this in his letter to the Senate dated 5 February 1969: "I believe that ratification of the Treaty at this time would advance this Administration's policy of negotiation rather than confrontation with the USSR. Consonant with my purpose to strengthen the structure of peace, therefore, I urge the Senate's prompt consideration and positive action on this Treaty."[33]

But it is not only a question of the Big Two and the consequences of

[31] *International Herald Tribune,* 12 September 1968.
[32] The "domino theory" applied by the United States to South-East Asia is an example of this fear.
[33] *Hearings 1969*, p. 305.

their collaboration upon international society. It concerns the direct immediate interest of all countries. Both objective and subjective factors make it impossible for the armaments race to end in parity between the two Super-Powers. The balance of terror is only an ephemeral, momentary balance, always open to challenge.[34] However, progress towards disarmament will be infinitely long and difficult. The way lies through partial measures, arms control, and a better understanding between the two Super-Powers, helped by other Powers. The Non-Proliferation Treaty does form such a measure and it forms part of a process of educating public opinion, that cannot be halted or interrupted without harming the cause of peace. "The struggle to curb the proliferation of nuclear arms is not a bid to win Moscow's favours; it is a literally vital struggle, in which failure means greater danger for all."[35]

[34] See the well argued opinion of H. F. York, *Bulletin of Atomic Scientists*, March 1970, pp. 27–30.
[35] *The Economist*, 14 September 1968, p. 21.

APPENDIX I

US draft treaty to prevent the spread of nuclear weapons, 17 August 1965

The Parties to this Treaty,

Desiring to promote international peace and security,

Desiring in particular to refrain from taking steps which will extend and intensify the arms race,

Believing that the further spread of nuclear weapons will jeopardise these ends,

Recalling that resolution 1665 (XVI) of the General Assembly of the United Nations urges all States to co-operate for these purposes,

Desiring to achieve effective agreements to halt the nuclear arms race and to reduce armaments, including particularly nuclear arsenals,

Reaffirming their determination to achieve agreement on general and complete disarmament under effective international control,

Have agreed as follows:

ARTICLE 1

1. Each of the nuclear States Party to this Treaty undertakes not to transfer any nuclear weapons into the national control of any non-nuclear State, either directly, or indirectly through a military alliance, and each undertakes not to take any other action which would cause an increase in the total number of States and other organisations having independent power to use nuclear weapons.

2. Each of the nuclear States Party to this Treaty undertakes not to assist any non-nuclear State in the manufacture of nuclear weapons.

ARTICLE 2

1. Each of the non-nuclear States Party to this Treaty undertakes not to manufacture nuclear weapons; each undertakes not to seek or to receive the transfer of such weapons into its national control, either directly, or indirectly through a military alliance; and each undertakes not to take any other action which would cause an increase in the total number of States and other organisations having independent power to use nuclear weapons.

2. Each of the non-nuclear States Party to this Treaty undertakes not to seek or to receive assistance in the manufacture of nuclear weapons, or itself to grant such assistance.

ARTICLE 3

Each of the States Party to this Treaty undertakes to co-operate in facilitating the application of International Atomic Energy Agency or equivalent international safeguards to all peaceful nuclear activities.

ARTICLE 4

In this Treaty:

(a) "nuclear State" means a State possessing independent power to use nuclear weapons as of .... (date);

(b) "non-nuclear State" means any State which is not a nuclear State.

ARTICLE 5

1. This Treaty shall be open to all States for signature. Any State which does not sign this Treaty before its entry into force in accordance with paragraph 3 of this article may accede to it at any time.

2. This Treaty shall be subject to ratification by signatory States. Instruments of ratification and instruments of accession shall be deposited with the Governments of the United Kingdom of Great Britain and Northern Ireland, the Union of Soviet Socialist Republics and the United States of America, which are hereby designated the Depositary Governments.

3. This Treaty shall enter into force on the deposit of instruments of ratification by .... (a certain number of) Governments, including those of the United Kingdom of Great Britain and Northern Ireland, the Union of Soviet Socialist Republics and the United States of America.

4. For States whose instruments of ratification or accession are deposited subsequent to the entry into force of this Treaty, it shall enter into force on the date of the deposit of their instruments of ratification or accession.

5. The Depositary Governments shall promptly inform all signatory and acceding States of the date of each signature, the date of deposit of each instrument of ratification of an accession to this Treaty, and the date of its entry into force.

6. This Treaty shall be registered by the Depositary Governments pursuant to Article 102 of the Charter of the United Nations.

ARTICLE 6

1. This Treaty shall remain in force indefinitely subject to the right of any Party to the Treaty to withdraw from the Treaty if it decides that extraordinary events related to the subject matter of the Treaty have jeopardised the supreme interests of its country. It shall give notice of such withdrawal to all other signatory and acceding States and to the United Nations Security Council three

months in advance. Such notice shall include a statement of the extraordinary events it regards as having jeopardised its supreme interests.

2. .... years after the entry into force of this Treaty, a conference of Parties may be held at a date and place to be fixed by agreement of two-thirds of the Parties in order to review the operation of the Treaty.

ARTICLE 7

This Treaty, of which the Chinese, English, French, Russian and Spanish texts are equally authentic, shall be deposited in the archives of the Depositary Governments. Duly certified copies of this Treaty shall be transmitted by the Depositary Governments to the Governments of the signatory and acceding States.

IN WITNESS WHEREOF the undersigned, duly authorised, have signed this Treaty.

DONE in triplicate at the city of ...., the .... day of ...., one thousand nine hundred and ....

Amendments to the US draft treaty of 17 August 1965, presented on 21 March 1966

ARTICLE 1

Each of the nuclear-weapon States Party to this treaty undertakes:

1. Not to transfer nuclear weapons into the national control of any non-nuclear-weapon State, or into the control of any association of non-nuclear-weapon States.

2. Not to provide to any non-nuclear-weapon State or association of such States

   (a) assistance in the manufacture of nuclear weapons, in preparations for such manufacture, or in the testing of nuclear weapons; or

   (b) encouragement or inducement to manufacture or otherwise acquire its own nuclear weapons.

3. Not to take any other action which would cause an increase in the total number of States and associations of States having control of nuclear weapons.

4. Not to take any of the actions prohibited in the preceding paragraphs of this Article directly, or indirectly through third States or associations of States, or through units of the armed forces or military personnel of any State, even if such units or personnel are under the command of a military alliance.

ARTICLE 2

Each of the non-nuclear-weapon States Party to this treaty undertakes:

1. Not to manufacture nuclear weapons, and not to seek or to receive the transfer of nuclear weapons into its national control or into the control of any association of non-nuclear-weapon States of which it is a member.

2. Not to seek or receive, and not to provide, whether alone or in any association of non-nuclear-weapon States:

   (a) assistance in the manufacture of nuclear weapons, in preparations for such manufacture, or in the testing of nuclear weapons; or

   (b) encouragement or inducement to manufacture or otherwise acquire its own nuclear weapons.

3. Not to take any other action which would cause an increase in the total number of States and associations of States having control of nuclear weapons.

APPENDIX III

Soviet draft treaty on the non-proliferation of nuclear weapons, 24 September 1965

The States concluding this Treaty (hereinafter referred to as "the Parties to the Treaty"),

Considering the devastation that would be visited upon all mankind by a nuclear war and the consequent need to make every effort to avert the danger of such a war and to take measures to safeguard the security of peoples,

In conformity with the resolutions of the United Nations General Assembly calling for the conclusion of an agreement on the prevention of the wider dissemination of nuclear weapons.

Desiring the earliest possible attainment of agreement on the complete prohibition and elimination of all types of nuclear weapons within the framework of general and complete disarmament under strict international control,

Desiring to further the easing of international tension and the strengthening of trust between States, thus facilitating the conclusion of a treaty on general and complete disarmament.

Have agreed as follows:

ARTICLE 1

1. Parties to the Treaty possessing nuclear weapons undertake not to transfer such weapons in any form – directly or indirectly, through third States or groups of States – to the ownership or control of States or groups of States not possessing nuclear weapons and not to accord to such States or groups of States the right to participate in the ownership, control or use of nuclear weapons.

The said Parties to the Treaty shall not transfer nuclear weapons, or control over them or over their emplacement and use, to units of the armed forces or military personnel of States not possessing nuclear weapons, even if such units or personnel are under the command of a military alliance.

2. Parties to the Treaty possessing nuclear weapons undertake not to provide assistance – directly or indirectly, through third States or groups of States – to States not at present possessing nuclear weapons in the manufacture, in preparations for the manufacture or in the testing of such weapons and not to transmit to them any kind of manufacturing, research or other information or documentation which can be employed for purposes of the manufacture or use of nuclear weapons.

ARTICLE 2

1. Parties to the Treaty not possessing nuclear weapons undertake not to create, manufacture or prepare for the manufacture of nuclear weapons either independently or together with other States, in their own territory or in the territory of other States. They also undertake to refrain from obtaining nuclear weapons in any form – directly or indirectly, through third States or groups of States – for purposes of ownership, control or use and shall not participate in the ownership, control or use of such weapons or in testing them.

The said Parties to the Treaty shall not seek to acquire control over nuclear weapons or over their emplacement and use for units of their armed forces or personnel thereof, even if such units or personnel are under the command of a military alliance.

2. Parties to the Treaty not possessing nuclear weapons undertake not to obtain or seek to obtain, from States possessing nuclear weapons, assistance in the manufacture of such weapons or relevant manufacturing, research or other information or documentation which can be employed for purposes of the manufacture or use of nuclear weapons.

ARTICLE 3

The Parties to this Treaty shall refrain from offering any support, encouragement or inducement to States seeking to own, manufacture or exercise control over nuclear weapons.

ARTICLE 4

1. Any Party may propose amendments to this Treaty. The text of any proposed amendment shall be submitted to the Depositary Governments, which shall circulate it to all Parties to the Treaty. Thereupon, if requested to do so by one-third or more of the Parties, the Depositary Governments shall convene a conference, to which they shall invite all the Parties, to consider such amendment.

2. Any amendment to this Treaty must be approved by a majority of the votes of all the Parties to the Treaty, including the votes of all Parties possessing nuclear weapons. The amendment shall enter into force for all Parties upon the deposit of instruments of ratification by a majority of all the Parties, including the instruments of ratification of all Parties possessing nuclear weapons.

ARTICLE 5

1. This Treaty shall be open to all States for signature. Any State which does not sign the Treaty before its entry into force in accordance with paragraph 3 of the present article may accede to it at any time.

2. This Treaty shall be subject to ratification by signatory States. Instruments

of ratification and instruments of accession shall be deposited with the Governments of . . . , which are hereby designated the Depositary Governments.

3. This Treaty shall enter into force after its ratification by all Parties possessing nuclear weapons and the deposit of their instruments of ratification.

4. For States whose instruments of ratification or accession are deposited subsequent to the entry into force of this Treaty, it shall enter into force on the date of the deposit of their instruments of ratification or accession.

5. The Depositary Governments shall promptly inform all signatory and acceding States of the date of each signature, the date of deposit of each instrument of ratification of or accession to this Treaty, the date of its entry into force, and the date of receipt of any requests for conferences or other notices.

6. This Treaty shall be registered by the Depositary Governments pursuant to Article 102 of the Charter of the United Nations.

ARTICLE 6

This Treaty shall be of unlimited duration.

Each Party shall in exercising its national sovereignty have the right to withdraw from the Treaty if it decides that extraordinary events, related to the subject matter of this Treaty, have jeopardised the supreme interests of its country. It shall give notice of such withdrawal to all other Parties to the Treaty three months in advance.

ARTICLE 7

This Treaty, the Russian, English, French, Spanish and Chinese texts of which are equally authentic, shall be deposited in the archives of the Depositary Governments. Duly certified copies of this Treaty shall be transmitted by the Depositary Governments to the Governments of the signatory and acceding States.

In witness whereof the undersigned, duly authorised, have signed this Treaty.

Done in .... copies at the city of .... on the .... day of ....

Resolution 2373 (XXII) of the General Assembly, 12 June 1968

The General Assembly,

Recalling its Resolutions 2346 A (XXII) of 19 December 1967, 2153 A (XXI) of 17 November 1966, 2149 (XXI) of 4 November 1966, 2028 (XX) of 19 November 1965 and 1665 (XVI) of 4 December 1961,

Convinced of the urgency and great importance of preventing the spread of nuclear weapons and of intensifying international co-operation in the development of peaceful applications of atomic energy,

Having considered the report of the Conference of the Eighteen-Nation Committee on Disarmament, dated 14 March 1968,[1] and appreciative of the work of the Committee on the elaboration of the draft non-proliferation treaty, which is attached to that report,[2]

Convinced that, pursuant to the provisions of the Treaty, all signatories have the right to engage in research, production and use of nuclear energy for peaceful purposes and will be able to acquire source and special fissionable materials, as well as equipment for the processing, use and production of nuclear material for peaceful purposes,

Convinced further that an agreement to prevent the further proliferation of nuclear weapons must be followed as soon as possible by effective measures on the cessation of the nuclear arms race and on nuclear disarmament, and that the non-proliferation Treaty will contribute to this aim,

Affirming that in the interest of international peace and security both nuclear-weapon and non-nuclear-weapon States carry the responsibility of acting in accordance with the principles of the Charter of the United Nations that the sovereign equality of all States shall be respected, that the threat or use of force in international relations shall be refrained from and that international disputes shall be settled by peaceful means,

1. *Commends* the Treaty on the Non-Proliferation of Nuclear Weapons, the text of which is annexed to the present resolution;

2. *Requests* the Depositary Governments to open the Treaty for signature and ratification at the earliest possible date;

3. *Expresses the hope* for the widest possible adherence to the Treaty by both nuclear-weapon and non-nuclear-weapon States;

---

[1] A/7072. [2] *ibid*, Annex I.

4. *Requests* the Conference of the Eighteen-Nation Committee on Disarmament and the nuclear-weapon States urgently to pursue negotiations on effective measures relating to the cessation of the nuclear arms race at an early date and to nuclear disarmament, and on a Treaty on general and complete disarmament under strict and effective international control;

5. *Requests* the Conference of the Eighteen-Nation Committee on Disarmament to report on the progress of its work to the General Assembly at its twenty-third session.

APPENDIX V

Treaty on the Non-Proliferation of Nuclear Weapons

The States concluding this Treaty, hereinafter referred to as the "Parties to the Treaty",

Considering the devastation that would be visited upon all mankind by a nuclear war and the consequent need to make every effort to avert the danger of such a war and to take measures to safeguard the security of peoples,

Believing that the proliferation of nuclear weapons would seriously enhance the danger of nuclear war,

In conformity with resolutions of the United Nations General Assembly calling for the conclusion of an agreement on the prevention of wider dissemination of nuclear weapons,

Undertaking to co-operate in facilitating the application of International Atomic Energy Agency safeguards on peaceful nuclear activities,

Expressing their support for research, development and other efforts to further the application, within the framework of the International Atomic Energy Agency safeguards system, of the principle of safeguarding effectively the flow of source and special fissionable materials by use of instruments and other techniques at certain strategic points,

Affirming the principle that the benefits of peaceful applications of nuclear technology, including any technological by-products which may be derived by nuclear-weapon States from the development of nuclear explosive devices, should be available for peaceful purposes to all Parties to the Treaty, whether nuclear-weapon or non-nuclear-weapon States,

Convinced that, in furtherance of this principle, all Parties to the Treaty are entitled to participate in the fullest possible exchange of scientific information for, and to contribute alone or in co-operation with other States to, the further development of the applications of atomic energy for peaceful purposes,

Declaring their intention to achieve at the earliest possible date the cessation of the nuclear arms race and to undertake effective measures in the direction of nuclear disarmament,

Urging the co-operation of all States in the attainment of this objective,

Recalling the determination expressed by the Parties to the 1963 Treaty banning nuclear weapon tests in the atmosphere, in outer space and under water in its preamble to seek to achieve the discontinuance of all test explosions of nuclear weapons for all time and to continue negotiations to this end,

Desiring to further the easing of international tension and the strengthening of trust between States in order to facilitate the cessation of the manufacture of nuclear weapons, the liquidation of all their existing stockpiles, and the elimination from national arsenals of nuclear weapons and the means of their delivery pursuant to a Treaty on general and complete disarmament under strict and effective international control,

Recalling that, in accordance with the Charter of the United Nations, States must refrain in their international relations from the threat or use of force against the territorial integrity or political independence of any State, or in any other manner inconsistent with the purposes of the United Nations, and that the establishment and maintenance of international peace and security are to be promoted with the least diversion for armaments of the world's human and economic resources,

Have agreed as follows:

ARTICLE 1

Each nuclear-weapon State Party to the Treaty undertakes not to transfer to any recipient whatsoever nuclear weapons or other nuclear explosive devices or control over such weapons or explosive devices directly, or indirectly; and not in any way to assist, encourage, or induce any non-nuclear-weapon State to manufacture or otherwise acquire nuclear weapons or other nuclear explosive devices, or control over such weapons or explosive devices.

ARTICLE 2

Each non-nuclear-weapon State Party to the Treaty undertakes not to receive the transfer from any transferor whatsoever of nuclear weapons or other nuclear explosive devices or of control over such weapons or explosive devices directly, or indirectly; not to manufacture or otherwise acquire nuclear weapons or other nuclear explosive devices; and not to seek or receive any assistance in the manufacture of nuclear weapons or other nuclear explosive devices.

ARTICLE 3

1. Each non-nuclear-weapon State Party to the Treaty undertakes to accept safeguards, as set forth in an agreement to be negotiated and concluded with the International Atomic Energy Agency in accordance with the Statute of the International Atomic Energy Agency and the Agency's safeguards system, for the exclusive purpose of verification of the fulfilment of its obligations assumed under this Treaty with a view to preventing diversion of nuclear energy from peaceful uses to nuclear weapons or other nuclear explosive devices. Procedures for the safeguards required by this article shall be followed with respect to source or special fissionable material whether it is being produced, processed or used in any principal nuclear facility or is outside any such facility. The safeguards

required by this article shall be applied on all source or special fissionable material in all peaceful nuclear activities within the territory of such State, under its jurisdiction, or carried out under its control anywhere.

2. Each State Party to the Treaty undertakes not to provide: (*a*) source or special fissionable material, or (*b*) equipment or material especially designed or prepared for the processing, use or production of special fissionable material, to any non-nuclear-weapon State for peaceful purposes, unless the source or special fissionable material shall be subject to the safeguards required by this article.

3. The safeguards required by this article shall be implemented in a manner designed to comply with Article IV of this Treaty, and to avoid hampering the economic or technological development of the parties or international co-operation in the field of peaceful nuclear activities, including the international exchange of nuclear material and equipment for the processing, use or production of nuclear material for peaceful purposes in accordance with the provisions of this article and the principle of safeguarding set forth in the preamble.

4. Non-nuclear-weapon States Party to the Treaty shall conclude agreements with the International Atomic Energy Agency to meet the requirements of this article either individually or together with other States in accordance with the Statute of the International Atomic Energy Agency. Negotiation of such agreements shall commence within 180 days from the original entry into force of this Treaty. For States depositing their instruments of ratification or accession after the 180-day period, negotiation of such agreements shall commence not later than the date of such deposit. Such agreements shall enter into force not later than eighteen months after the date of initiation of negotiations.

ARTICLE 4

1. Nothing in this Treaty shall be interpreted as affecting the inalienable right of all the Parties to the Treaty to develop research, production and use of nuclear energy for peaceful purposes without discrimination and in conformity with Articles 1 and 2 of this Treaty.

2. All the Parties to the Treaty undertake to facilitate, and have the right to participate in, the fullest possible exchange of equipment, materials and scientific and technological information for the peaceful uses of nuclear energy. Parties to the Treaty in a position to do so shall also co-operate in contributing alone or together with other States or international organisations to the further development of the applications of nuclear energy for peaceful purposes, especially in the territories of non-nuclear-weapon States Party to the Treaty, with due consideration for the needs of the developing areas of the world.

ARTICLE 5

Each Party to this Treaty undertakes to take appropriate measures to ensure that, in accordance with this Treaty, under appropriate international observation and through appropriate international procedures, potential benefits from any peaceful applications of nuclear explosions will be made available to non-nuclear-weapon States Party to this Treaty on a non-discriminatory basis and that the charge to such Parties for the explosive devices used will be as low as possible and exclude any charge for research and development. Non-nuclear-weapon States Party to the Treaty shall be able to obtain such benefits, pursuant to a special international agreement or agreements, through an appropriate international body with adequate representation of non-nuclear-weapon States. Negotiations on this subject shall commence as soon as possible after the Treaty enters into force. Non-nuclear-weapon States Party to the Treaty so desiring may also obtain such benefits pursuant to bilateral agreements.

ARTICLE 6

Each of the Parties to the Treaty undertakes to pursue negotiations in good faith on effective measures relating to cessation of the nuclear arms race at an early date and to nuclear disarmament, and on a Treaty on general and complete disarmament under strict and effective international control.

ARTICLE 7

Nothing in this Treaty affects the right of any group of States to conclude regional treaties in order to assure the total absence of nuclear weapons in their respective territories.

ARTICLE 8

1. Any Party to the Treaty may propose amendments to this Treaty. The text of any proposed amendment shall be submitted to the Depositary Governments which shall circulate it to all Parties to the Treaty. Thereupon, if requested to do so by one-third or more of the Parties to the Treaty, the Depositary Governments shall convene a conference, to which they shall invite all the Parties to the Treaty, to consider such an amendment.

2. Any amendment to this Treaty must be approved by a majority of the votes of all the Parties to the Treaty, including the votes of all nuclear-weapon States Party to the Treaty and all other Parties which, on the date the amendment is circulated, are members of the Board of Governors of the International Atomic Energy Agency. The amendment shall enter into force for each Party that deposits its instrument of ratification of the amendment upon the deposit of such instruments of ratification by a majority of all the Parties, including the instruments of ratification of all nuclear-weapon States Party to the Treaty and all other Parties which, on the date the amendment is circulated, are members of the Board of Governors of the International Atomic Energy Agency. Thereafter, it shall enter into force for any other Party upon the deposit of its instrument of ratification of the amendment.

3. Five years after the entry into force of this Treaty, a conference of Parties to the Treaty shall be held in Geneva, Switzerland, in order to review the operation of this Treaty with a view to assuring that the purposes of the Preamble and the provisions of the Treaty are being realised. At intervals of five years thereafter, a majority of the Parties to the Treaty may obtain, by submitting a proposal to this effect to the Depositary Governments, the convening of further conferences with the same objectives of reviewing the operation of the Treaty.

ARTICLE 9

1. This Treaty shall be open to all States for signature. Any State which does not sign the Treaty before its entry into force in accordance with paragraph 3 of this article may accede to it at any time.

2. This Treaty shall be subject to ratification by signatory States. Instruments of ratification and instruments of accession shall be deposited with the Governments of the Union of Soviet Socialist Republics, the United Kingdom of Great Britain and Northern Ireland and the United States of America, which are hereby designated the Depositary Governments.

3. This Treaty shall enter into force after its ratification by the States, the Governments of which are designated Depositaries of the Treaty, and forty other States signatory to this Treaty and the deposit of their instruments of ratification. For the purposes of this Treaty, a nuclear-weapon State is one which has manufactured and exploded a nuclear weapon or other nuclear explosive device prior to 1 January 1967.

4. For States whose instruments of ratification or accession are deposited subsequent to the entry into force of this Treaty, it shall enter into force on the date of the deposit of their instruments of ratification or accession.

5. The Depositary Governments shall promptly inform all signatory and acceding States of the date of each signature, the date of deposit of each instrument of ratification or of accession, the date of the entry into force of this Treaty, and the date of receipt of any requests for convening a conference or other notices.

6. This Treaty shall be registered by the Depositary Governments pursuant to Article 102 of the Charter of the United Nations.

ARTICLE 10

1. Each Party shall in exercising its national sovereignty have the right to withdraw from the Treaty if it decides that extraordinary events, related to the subject-matter of this Treaty, have jeopardised the supreme interests of its country. It shall give notice of such withdrawal to all other Parties to the Treaty and to the United Nations Security Council three months in advance. Such notice shall include a statement of the extraordinary events it regards as having jeopardised its supreme interests.

2. Twenty-five years after the entry into force of the Treaty, a Conference shall be convened to decide whether the Treaty shall continue in force indefinitely, or shall be extended for an additional fixed period or periods. This decision shall be taken by a majority of the Parties to the Treaty.

ARTICLE 11

This Treaty, the English, Russian, French, Spanish and Chinese texts of which are equally authentic, shall be deposited in the archives of the Depositary Governments. Duly certified copies of this Treaty shall be transmitted by the Depositary Governments to the Governments of the signatory and acceding States.

In witness whereof the undersigned, duly authorised, have signed this Treaty.

Done in .... at .... this .... day of ....

APPENDIX VI

Declaration made in identical terms by the representatives of the USSR, the UK and the US to the 1430th Session of the Security Council, 17 June 1968

"The Government of the Union of Soviet Socialist Republics (of the United Kingdom, of the United States) notes with appreciation the desire expressed by a large number of States to subscribe to the Treaty on the non-proliferation of nuclear weapons.

"We welcome the willingness of these States to undertake not to receive the transfer from any transferor whatsoever of nuclear weapons or other nuclear explosive devices or of control over such weapons or explosive devices directly or indirectly; not to manufacture or otherwise acquire nuclear weapons or other nuclear explosive devices; and not to seek or receive any assistance in the manufacture of nuclear weapons or other nuclear explosive devices.

"The Union of Soviet Socialist Republics (of the United Kingdom, of the United States) also notes the concern of certain of these States that, in conjunction with their adherence to the treaty on the non-proliferation of nuclear weapons, appropriate measures should be undertaken to safeguard their security. Any act of aggression accompanied by the use of nuclear weapons would endanger the peace and security of all States.

"Bearing these considerations in mind, the Soviet Union (the United Kingdom, the United States) declares the following:

"Aggression with nuclear weapons, or the threat of such aggression, against a non-nuclear-weapon State would create a qualitatively new situation in which the nuclear-weapon States which are permanent members of the United Nations Security Council would have to act immediately through the Security Council to take the measures necessary to counter such aggression or to remove the threat of aggression in accordance with the United Nations Charter, which calls for taking

" ' . . . effective collective measures for the prevention and removal of threats to the peace, and for the suppression of acts of aggression or other breaches of the peace . . . '.

"Therefore, any State which commits aggression accompanied by the use of nuclear weapons or which threatens such aggression must be aware that its actions are to be countered effectively by measures to be taken in accordance with the United Nations Charter to suppress aggression or remove the threat of aggression.

"The Soviet Union (the United Kingdom, the United States) affirms its intentions, as a permanent member of the United Nations Security Council, to seek immediate Security Council action to provide assistance, in accordance with the Charter, to any non-nuclear-weapon State party to the treaty on the non-proliferation of nuclear weapons that is a victim of an act of aggression or an object of a threat of aggression in which nuclear weapons are used.

"The Soviet Union (the United Kingdom, the United States) reaffirms in particular the inherent right, recognised under Article 51 of the Charter, of individual and collective self-defence if an armed attack, including a nuclear attack, occurs against a Member of the United Nations, until the Security Council has taken measures necessary to maintain international peace and security.

"The vote of the Soviet Union (the United Kingdom, the United States) for the draft resolution before us and this statement of the way in which the Soviet Union (the United Kingdom, the United States) intends to act in accordance with the Charter of the United Nations are based upon the fact that the draft resolution is supported by other permanent members of the Security Council which are nuclear-weapon States and are also proposing to sign the treaty on the non-proliferation of nuclear weapons, and that these States have made similar statements as to the way in which they intend to act in accordance with the Charter."

Resolution 255 (1968) Adopted by the Security Council at its 1433rd Session, 19 June 1968

The Security Council,

Noting with appreciation the desire of a large number of States to subscribe to the Treaty on the Non-Proliferation of Nuclear Weapons, and thereby to undertake not to receive the transfer from any transferor whatsoever of nuclear weapons or other nuclear explosive devices or of control over such weapons or explosive devices directly or indirectly, not to manufacture or otherwise acquire nuclear weapons or other nuclear explosive devices, and not to seek or receive any assistance in the manufacture of nuclear weapons or other nuclear explosive devices,

Taking into consideration the concern of certain of these States that, in conjunction with their adherence to the Treaty on the Non-Proliferation of Nuclear Weapons, appropriate measures be undertaken to safeguard their security,

Bearing in mind that any aggression accompanied by the use of nuclear weapons would endanger the peace and security of all States,

1. *Recognises* that aggression with nuclear weapons or the threat of such aggression against a non-nuclear-weapon State would create a situation in which the Security Council, and above all its nuclear-weapon State permanent members, would have to act immediately in accordance with their obligations under the United Nations Charter;

2. *Welcomes* the intention expressed by certain States that they will provide or support immediate assistance, in accordance with the Charter, to any non-nuclear-weapon State Party to the Treaty on the Non-Proliferation of Nuclear Weapons that is a victim of an act or an object of a threat of aggression in which nuclear weapons are used;

3. *Reaffirms* in particular the inherent right, recognised under Article 51 of the Charter, of individual and collective self-defence if an armed attack occurs against a Member of the United Nations, until the Security Council has taken measures necessary to maintain international peace and security.

Treaty for the Prohibition of Nuclear Weapons in Latin America

Preamble

In the name of their peoples and faithfully interpreting their desires and aspirations, the Governments of the States which sign the Treaty for the Prohibition of Nuclear Weapons in Latin America,

Desiring to contribute, so far as lies in their power, towards ending the armaments race, especially in the field of nuclear weapons, and towards strengthening a world at peace, based on the sovereign equality of States, mutual respect and good neighbourliness,

Recalling that the United Nations General Assembly, in its Resolution 808 (IX), adopted unanimously as one of the three points of a co-ordinated programme of disarmament "the total prohibition of the use and manufacture of nuclear weapons and weapons of mass destruction of every type",

Recalling that militarily denuclearised zones are not an end in themselves but rather a means for achieving general and complete disarmament at a later stage,

Recalling United Nations General Assembly Resolution 1911 (XVIII), which established that the measures that should be agreed upon for the denuclearisation of Latin America should be taken "in the light of the principles of the Charter of the United Nations and of regional agreements",

Recalling United Nations General Assembly Resolution 2028 (XX), which established the principle of an acceptable balance of mutual responsibilities and duties for the nuclear and non-nuclear powers, and

Recalling that the Charter of the Organization of American States proclaims that it is an essential purpose of the Organization to strengthen the peace and security of the hemisphere,

Convinced:

That the incalculable destructive power of nuclear weapons has made it imperative that the legal prohibition of war should be strictly observed in practice if the survival of civilisation and of mankind itself is to be assured,

That nuclear weapons, whose terrible effects are suffered, indiscriminately and inexorably, by military forces and civilian population alike, constitute, through the persistence of the radioactivity they release, an attack on the integrity of the human species and ultimately may even render the whole earth uninhabitable,

That general and complete disarmament under effective international control is a vital matter which all the peoples of the world equally demand,

That the proliferation of nuclear weapons, which seems inevitable unless States, in the exercise of their sovereign rights, impose restrictions on themselves in order to prevent it, would make any agreement on disarmament enormously difficult and would increase the danger of the outbreak of a nuclear conflagration,

That the establishment of militarily denuclearised zones is closely linked with the maintenance of peace and security in the respective regions,

That the military denuclearisation of vast geographical zones, adopted by the sovereign decision of the States comprised therein, will exercise a beneficial influence on other regions where similar conditions exist,

That the privileged situation of the signatory States, whose territories are wholly free from nuclear weapons, imposes upon them the inescapable duty of preserving that situation both in their own interests and for the good of mankind,

That the existence of nuclear weapons in any country of Latin America would make it a target for possible nuclear attacks and would inevitably set off, throughout the region, a ruinous race in nuclear weapons which would involve the unjustifiable diversion, for warlike purposes, of the limited resources required for economic and social development,

That the foregoing reasons, together with the traditional peace-loving outlook of Latin America, give rise to an inescapable necessity that nuclear energy should be used in that region exclusively for peaceful purposes, and that the Latin American countries should use their right to the greatest and most equitable possible access to this new source of energy in order to expedite the economic and social development of their peoples,

Convinced finally:

That the military denuclearisation of Latin America – being understood to mean the undertaking entered into internationally in this Treaty to keep their territories forever free from nuclear weapons – will constitute a measure which will spare their peoples from the squandering of their limited resources on nuclear armaments and will protect them against possible nuclear attacks on their territories, and will also constitute a significant contribution towards preventing the proliferation of nuclear weapons and a powerful factor for general and complete disarmament, and

That Latin America, faithful to its tradition of universality, must not only endeavour to banish from its homelands the scourge of a nuclear war, but must also strive to promote the well-being and advancement of its peoples, at the same time co-operating in the fulfilment of the ideals of mankind, that is to say, in the consolidation of a permanent peace based on equal rights, economic fairness and social justice for all, in accordance with the principles and purposes set forth in the Charter of the United Nations and in the Charter of the Organization of American States,

Have agreed as follows:

Obligations

ARTICLE 1

1. The Contracting Parties hereby undertake to use exclusively for peaceful purposes the nuclear material and facilities which are under their jurisdiction, and to prohibit and prevent in their respective territories:

   (*a*) The testing, use, manufacture, production or acquisition by any means whatsoever of any nuclear weapons, by the Parties themselves, directly or indirectly, on behalf of anyone else or in any other way, and

   (*b*) The receipt, storage, installation, deployment and any form of possession of any nuclear weapons, directly or indirectly, by the Parties themselves, by anyone on their behalf or in any other way.

2. The Contracting Parties also undertake to refrain from engaging in, encouraging or authorising, directly or indirectly, or in any way participating in the testing, use, manufacture, production, possession or control of any nuclear weapon.

Definition of the Contracting Parties

ARTICLE 2

For the purposes of this Treaty, the Contracting Parties are those for whom the Treaty is in force.

Definition of territory

ARTICLE 3

For the purposes of this Treaty, the term "territory" shall include the territorial sea, air space and any other space over which the State exercises sovereignty in accordance with its own legislation.

Zone of application

ARTICLE 4

1. The zone of application of this Treaty is the whole of the territories for which the Treaty is in force.

2. Upon fulfilment of the requirements of Article 28, paragraph 1, the zone of application of this Treaty shall also be that which is situated in the western hemisphere within the following limits (except the continental part of the territory of the United States of America and its territorial waters): starting at

a point located at 35° north latitude, 75° west longitude; from this point directly southward to a point at 30° north latitude, 75° west longitude; from there, directly eastward to a point at 30° north latitude, 50° west longitude; from there, along a loxodromic line to a point at 5° north latitude, 20° west longitude; from there, directly southward to a point at 60° south latitude, 20° west longitude; from there, directly westward to a point at 60° south latitude, 115° west longitude; from there, directly northward to a point at 0° latitude, 115° west longitude; from there, along a loxodromic line to a point at 35° north latitude, 150° west longitude; from there, directly eastward to a point at 35° north latitude, 75° west longitude.

Definition of nuclear weapons

ARTICLE 5

For the purposes of this Treaty, a nuclear weapon is any device which is capable of releasing nuclear energy in an uncontrolled manner and which has a group of characteristics that are appropriate for use for warlike purposes. An instrument that may be used for the transport or propulsion of the device is not included in this definition if it is separable from the device and not an indivisible part thereof.

Meeting of signatories

ARTICLE 6

At the request of any of the signatory States or if the Agency established by Article 7 should so decide, a meeting of all the signatories may be convoked to consider in common questions which may affect the very essence of this instrument, including possible amendments to it. In either case, the meeting will be convoked by the General Secretary.

Organisation

ARTICLE 7

1. In order to ensure compliance with the obligations of this Treaty, the Contracting Parties hereby establish an international organisation to be known as the "Agency for the Prohibition of Nuclear Weapons in Latin America", hereinafter referred to as "the Agency". Only the Contracting Parties shall be affected by its decisions.

2. The Agency shall be responsible for the holding of periodic or extraordinary consultations among Member States on matters relating to the purposes, measures and procedures set forth in this Treaty and to the supervision of compliance with the obligations arising therefrom.

3. The Contracting Parties agree to extend to the Agency full and prompt co-operation in accordance with the provisions of this Treaty, of any agreements they may conclude with the Agency and of any agreements the Agency may conclude with any other international organisation or body.

4. The headquarters of the Agency shall be in Mexico City.

Organs

ARTICLE 8

1. There are hereby established as principal organs of the Agency a General Conference, a Council and a Secretariat.

2. Such subsidiary organs as are considered necessary by the General Conference may be established within the purview of this Treaty.

The General Conference

ARTICLE 9

1. The General Conference, the supreme organ of the Agency, shall be composed of all the Contracting Parties; it shall hold regular sessions every two years, and may also hold special sessions whenever this Treaty so provides or, in the opinion of the Council, the circumstances so require.

2. The General Conference:

(a) May consider and decide on any matters or questions covered by this Treaty, within the limits thereof, including those referring to powers and functions of any organ provided for in this Treaty.

(b) Shall establish procedures for the control system to ensure observance of this Treaty in accordance with its provisions.

(c) Shall elect the Members of the Council and the General Secretary.

(d) May remove the General Secretary from office if the proper functioning of the Agency so requires.

(e) Shall receive and consider the biennial and special reports submitted by the Council and the General Secretary.

(f) Shall initiate and consider studies designed to facilitate the optimum fulfilment of the aims of this Treaty, without prejudice to the power of the General Secretary independently to carry out similar studies for submission to and consideration by the Conference.

(g) Shall be the organ competent to authorise the conclusion of agreements with Governments and other international organisations and bodies.

3. The General Conference shall adopt the Agency's budget and fix the scale of financial contributions to be paid by Member States, taking into account the systems and criteria used for the same purpose by the United Nations.

4. The General Conference shall elect its officers for each session and may establish such subsidiary organs as it deems necessary for the performance of its functions.

5. Each Member of the Agency shall have one vote. The decisions of the General Conference shall be taken by a two-thirds majority of the Members present and voting in the case of matters relating to the control system and measures referred to in Article 20, the admission of new Members, the election or removal of the General Secretary, adoption of the budget and matters related thereto. Decisions on other matters, as well as procedural questions and also determination of which questions must be decided by a two-thirds majority, shall be taken by a simple majority of the Members present and voting.

6. The General Conference shall adopt its own rules of procedure.

The Council

ARTICLE 10

1. The Council shall be composed of five Members of the Agency elected by the General Conference from among the Contracting Parties, due account being taken of equitable geographic distribution.

2. The Members of the Council shall be elected for a term of four years. However, in the first election three will be elected for two years. Outgoing Members may not be re-elected for the following period unless the limited number of States for which the Treaty is in force so requires.

3. Each Member of the Council shall have one representative.

4. The Council shall be so organised as to be able to function continuously.

5. In addition to the functions conferred upon it by this Treaty and to those which may be assigned to it by the General Conference, the Council shall, through the General Secretary, ensure the proper operation of the control system in accordance with the provisions of this Treaty and with the decisions adopted by the General Conference.

6. The Council shall submit an annual report on its work to the General Conference as well as such special reports as it deems necessary or which the General Conference requests of it.

7. The Council shall elect its officers for each session.

8. The decisions of the Council shall be taken by a simple majority of its Members present and voting.

9. The Council shall adopt its own rules of procedure.

The Secretariat

ARTICLE 11

1. The Secretariat shall consist of a General Secretary, who shall be the chief administrative officer of the Agency, and of such staff as the Agency may require. The term of office of the General Secretary shall be four years and he may be re-elected for a single additional term. The General Secretary may not be a national of the country in which the Agency has its headquarters. In case the office of General Secretary becomes vacant, a new election shall be held to fill the office for the remainder of the term.

2. The staff of the Secretariat shall be appointed by the General Secretary, in accordance with rules laid down by the General Conference.

3. In addition to the functions conferred upon him by this Treaty and to those which may be assigned to him by the General Conference, the General Secretary shall ensure, as provided by Article 10, paragraph 5, the proper operation of the control system established by this Treaty, in accordance with the provisions of the Treaty and the decisions taken by the General Conference.

4. The General Secretary shall act in that capacity in all meetings of the General Conference and of the Council and shall make an annual report to both bodies on the work of the Agency and any special reports requested by the General Conference or the Council or which the General Secretary may deem desirable.

5. The General Secretary shall establish the procedures for distributing to all Contracting Parties information received by the Agency from governmental sources and such information from non-governmental sources as may be of interest to the Agency.

6. In the performance of their duties the General Secretary and the staff shall not seek or receive instructions from any Government or from any other authority external to the Agency and shall refrain from any action which might reflect on their position as international officials responsible only to the Agency; subject to their responsibility to the Agency, they shall not disclose any industrial secrets or other confidential information coming to their knowledge by reason of their official duties in the Agency.

7. Each of the Contracting Parties undertakes to respect the exclusively international character of the responsibilities of the General Secretary and the staff and not to seek to influence them in the discharge of their responsibilities.

Control system

ARTICLE 12

1. For the purpose of verifying compliance with the obligations entered into by the Contracting Parties in accordance with Article 1, a control system shall

be established which shall be put into effect in accordance with the provisions of Articles 13–18 of this Treaty.

2. The control system shall be used in particular for the purpose of verifying:

(a) That devices, services and facilities intended for peaceful uses of nuclear energy are not used in the testing or manufacture of nuclear weapons,

(b) That none of the activities prohibited in Article 1 of this Treaty are carried out in the territory of the Contracting Parties with nuclear materials or weapons introduced from abroad, and

(c) That explosions for peaceful purposes are compatible with Article 18 of this Treaty.

IAEA safeguards

ARTICLE 13

Each Contracting Party shall negotiate multilateral or bilateral agreements with the International Atomic Energy Agency for the application of its safeguards to its nuclear activities. Each Contracting Party shall initiate negotiations within a period of 180 days after the date of the deposit of its instrument of ratification of this Treaty. These agreements shall enter into force, for each Party, not later than eighteen months after the date of the initiation of such negotiations except in case of unforeseen circumstances or *force majeure*.

Reports of the Parties

ARTICLE 14

1. The Contracting Parties shall submit to the Agency and to the International Atomic Energy Agency, for their information, semi-annual reports stating that no activity prohibited under this Treaty has occurred in their respective territories.

2. The Contracting Parties shall simultaneously transmit to the Agency a copy of any report they may submit to the International Atomic Energy Agency which relates to matters that are the subject of this Treaty and to the application of safeguards.

3. The Contracting Parties shall also transmit to the Organization of American States, for its information, any reports that may be of interest to it, in accordance with the obligations established by the Inter-American System.

Special reports requested by the General Secretary

ARTICLE 15

1. With the authorisation of the Council, the General Secretary may request any of the Contracting Parties to provide the Agency with complementary or

supplementary information regarding any event or circumstance connected with compliance with this Treaty, explaining his reasons. The Contracting Parties undertake to co-operate promptly and fully with the General Secretary.

2. The General Secretary shall inform the Council and the Contracting Parties forthwith of such requests and of the respective replies.

Special inspections

ARTICLE 16

1. The International Atomic Energy Agency and the Council established by this Treaty have the power of carrying out special inspections in the following cases:

(a) In the case of the International Atomic Energy Agency, in accordance with the agreements referred to in Article 13 of this Treaty;

(b) In the case of the Council:

(i) When so requested, the reasons for the request being stated, by any Party which suspects that some activity prohibited by this Treaty has been carried out or is about to be carried out, either in the territory of any other Party or in any other place on such latter Party's behalf, the Council shall immediately arrange for such an inspection in accordance with Article 10, paragraph 5.

(ii) When requested by any Party which has been suspected of or charged with having violated this Treaty, the Council shall immediately arrange for the special inspection requested in accordance with Article 10, paragraph 5.

The above requests will be made to the Council through the General Secretary.

2. The costs and expenses of any special inspection carried out under paragraph 1, sub-paragraph (b), sections (i) and (ii) of this article shall be borne by the requesting Party or Parties, except where the Council concludes on the basis of the report on the special inspection that, in view of the circumstances existing in the case, such costs and expenses should be borne by the Agency.

3. The General Conference shall formulate the procedures for the organisation and execution of the special inspections carried out in accordance with paragraph 1, sub-paragraph (b), sections (i) and (ii) of this article.

4. The Contracting Parties undertake to grant the inspectors carrying out such special inspections full and free access to all places and all information which may be necessary for the performance of their duties and which are directly and intimately connected with the suspicion of violation of this Treaty. If so requested by the authorities of the Contracting Party in whose territory the inspection is carried out, the inspectors designated by the General Conference shall be accompanied by representatives of said authorities, provided that this does not in any way delay or hinder the work of the inspectors.

5. The Council shall immediately transmit to all the Parties, through the General Secretary, a copy of any report resulting from special inspections.

6. Similarly, the Council shall send through the General Secretary to the Secretary-General of the United Nations, for transmission to the United Nations Security Council and General Assembly, and to the Council of the Organization of American States, for its information, a copy of any report resulting from any special inspection carried out in accordance with paragraph 1, sub-paragraph (b), sections (i) and (ii) of this article.

7. The Council may decide, or any Contracting Party may request, the convening of a special session of the General Conference for the purpose of considering the reports resulting from any special inspection. In such a case, the General Secretary shall take immediate steps to convene the special session requested.

8. The General Conference, convened in special session under this article, may make recommendations to the Contracting Parties and submit reports to the Secretary-General of the United Nations to be transmitted to the United Nations Security Council and the General Assembly.

Use of nuclear energy for peaceful purposes

ARTICLE 17

Nothing in the provisions of this Treaty shall prejudice the rights of the Contracting Parties, in conformity with this Treaty, to use nuclear energy for peaceful purposes, in particular for their economic development and social progress.

Explosions for peaceful purposes

ARTICLE 18

1. The Contracting Parties may carry out explosions of nuclear devices for peaceful purposes – including explosions which involve devices similar to those used in nuclear weapons – or collaborate with third parties for the same purpose, provided that they do so in accordance with the provisions of this article and the other articles of the Treaty, particularly Articles 1 and 5.

2. Contracting Parties intending to carry out, or to co-operate in carrying out, such an explosion shall notify the Agency and the International Atomic Energy Agency, as far in advance as the circumstances require, of the date of the explosion and shall at the same time provide the following information:

  (a) The nature of the nuclear device and the source from which it was obtained,

  (b) The place and purpose of the planned explosion,

  (c) The procedures which will be followed in order to comply with paragraph 3 of this article, (*d*) The expected force of the device, and

(*e*) The fullest possible information on any possible radioactive fall-out that may result from the explosion or explosions, and measures which will be taken to avoid danger to the population, flora, fauna and territories of any other Party or Parties.

3. The General Secretary and the technical personnel designated by the Council and the International Atomic Energy Agency may observe all the preparations, including the explosion of the device, and shall have unrestricted access to any area in the vicinity of the site of the explosion in order to ascertain whether the device and the procedures followed during the explosion are in conformity with the information supplied under paragraph 2 of this article and the other provisions of this Treaty.

4. The Contracting Parties may accept the collaboration of third parties for the purpose set forth in paragraph 1 of the present article, in accordance with paragraphs 2 and 3 thereof.

Relations with other international organisations

ARTICLE 19

1. The Agency may conclude such agreements with the International Atomic Energy Agency as are authorised by the General Conference and as it considers likely to facilitate the efficient operation of the control system established by this Treaty.

2. The Agency may also enter into relations with any international organisation or body, especially any which may be established in the future to supervise disarmament or measures for the control of armaments in any part of the world.

3. The Contracting Parties may, if they see fit, request the advice of the Inter-American Nuclear Energy Commission on all technical matters connected with the application of this Treaty with which the Commission is competent to deal under its Statute.

Measures in the event of violation of the Treaty

ARTICLE 20

1. The General Conference shall take note of all cases in which, in its opinion, any Contracting Party is not complying fully with its obligations under this Treaty and shall draw the matter to the attention of the Party concerned, making such recommendations as it deems appropriate.

2. If, in its opinion, such non-compliance constitutes a violation of this Treaty which might endanger peace and security, the General Conference shall report thereon simultaneously to the United Nations Security Council and the General Assembly through the Secretary-General of the United Nations, and to the

Council of the Organization of American States. The General Conference shall likewise report to the International Atomic Energy Agency for such purposes as are relevant in accordance with its Statute.

United Nations and Organization of American States

ARTICLE 21

None of the provisions of this Treaty shall be construed as impairing the rights and obligations of the Parties under the Charter of the United Nations or, in the case of States Members of the Organization of American States, under existing regional treaties.

Privileges and immunities

ARTICLE 22

1. The Agency shall enjoy in the territory of each of the Contracting Parties such legal capacity and such privileges and immunities as may be necessary for the exercise of its functions and the fulfilment of its purposes.

2. Representatives of the Contracting Parties accredited to the Agency and officials of the Agency shall similarly enjoy such privileges and immunities as are necessary for the performance of their functions.

3. The Agency may conclude agreements with the Contracting Parties with a view to determining the details of the application of paragraphs 1 and 2 of this article.

Notification of other agreements

ARTICLE 23

Once this Treaty has entered into force, the Secretariat shall be notified immediately of any international agreement concluded by any of the Contracting Parties on matters with which this Treaty is concerned; the Secretariat shall register it and notify the other Contracting Parties.

Settlement of disputes

ARTICLE 24

Unless the Parties concerned agree on another mode of peaceful settlement, any question or dispute concerning the interpretation or application of this Treaty which is not settled shall be referred to the International Court of Justice with the prior consent of the Parties to the controversy.

Signature

ARTICLE 25

1. This Treaty shall be open indefinitely for signature by:
   (a) All the Latin American Republics, and
   (b) All other sovereign States situated in their entirety south of latitude
   35° north in the western hemisphere; and, except as provided in
   paragraph 2 of this article, all such States which become sovereign,
   when they have been admitted by the General Conference.

2. The General Conference shall not take any decision regarding the admission
of a political entity part or all of whose territory is the subject, prior to the date
when this Treaty is opened for signature, of a dispute or claim between an
extra-continental country and one or more Latin American States, so long as the
dispute has not been settled by peaceful means.

Ratification and deposit

ARTICLE 26

1. This Treaty shall be subject to ratification by signatory States in accordance
with their respective constitutional procedures.

2. This Treaty and the instruments of ratification shall be deposited with the
Government of the Mexican United States, which is hereby designated the
Depositary Government.

3. The Depositary Government shall send certified copies of this Treaty to
the Governments of signatory States and shall notify them of the deposit of each
instrument of ratification.

Reservations

ARTICLE 27

This Treaty shall not be subject to reservations.

Entry into force

ARTICLE 28

1. Subject to the provisions of paragraph 2 of this article, this Treaty shall
enter into force among the States that have ratified it as soon as the following
requirements have been met:
   (a) Deposit of the instruments of ratification of this Treaty with the
   Depositary Government by the Governments of the States mentioned
   in Article 25 which are in existence on the date when this Treaty is

opened for signature and which are not affected by the provisions of Article 25, paragraph 2;

(b) Signature and ratification of Additional Protocol I annexed to this Treaty by all extra-continental or continental States having *de jure* or *de facto* international responsibility for territories situated in the zone of application of the Treaty;

(c) Signature and ratification of the Additional Protocol II annexed to this Treaty by all powers possessing nuclear weapons;

(d) Conclusion of bilateral or multilateral agreements on the application of the Safeguards System of the International Atomic Energy Agency in accordance with Article 13 of this Treaty.

2. All signatory States shall have the imprescriptible right to waive, wholly or in part, the requirements laid down in the preceding paragraph. They may do so by means of a declaration which shall be annexed to their respective instrument of ratification and which may be formulated at the time of deposit of the instrument or subsequently. For those States which exercise this right, this Treaty shall enter into force upon deposit of the declaration, or as soon as those requirements have been met which have not been expressly waived.

3. As soon as this Treaty has entered into force in accordance with the provisions of paragraph 2 for eleven States, the Depositary Government shall convene a preliminary meeting of those States in order that the Agency may be set up and commence its work.

4. After the entry into force of this Treaty for all the countries of the zone, the rise of a new power possessing nuclear weapons shall have the effect of suspending the execution of this Treaty for those countries which have ratified it without waiving requirements of paragraph 1, sub-paragraph (c) of this article, and which request such suspension; the Treaty shall remain suspended until the new power, on its own initiative or upon request by the General Conference, ratifies the annexed Additional Protocol II.

Amendments

ARTICLE 29

1. Any Contracting Party may propose amendments to this Treaty and shall submit its proposals to the Council through the General Secretary, who shall transmit them to all the other Contracting Parties and, in addition, to all other signatories in accordance with Article 6. The Council, through the General Secretary, shall immediately following the meeting of signatories convene a special session of the General Conference to examine the proposals made, for the adoption of which a two-thirds majority of the Contracting Parties present and voting shall be required.

2. Amendments adopted shall enter into force as soon as the requirements set forth in Article 28 of this Treaty have been complied with.

Duration and denunciation

ARTICLE 30

1. This Treaty shall be of a permanent nature and shall remain in force indefinitely, but any Party may denounce it by notifying the General Secretary of the Agency if, in the opinion of the denouncing State, there have arisen or may arise circumstances connected with the content of this Treaty or of the annexed Additional Protocols I and II which affect its supreme interests or the peace and security of one or more Contracting Parties.

2. The denunciation shall take effect three months after the delivery to the General Secretary of the Agency of the notification by the Government of the signatory State concerned. The General Secretary shall immediately communicate such notification to the other Contracting Parties and to the Secretary-General of the United Nations for the information of the United Nations Security Council and the General Assembly. He shall also communicate it to the Secretary-General of the Organization of American States.

Authentic texts and registration

ARTICLE 31

This Treaty, of which the Spanish, Chinese, English, French, Portuguese and Russian texts are equally authentic, shall be registered by the Depositary Government in accordance with Article 102 of the United Nations Charter. The Depositary Government shall notify the Secretary-General of the United Nations of the signatures, ratifications and amendments relating to this Treaty and shall communicate them to the Secretary-General of the Organization of American States for its information.

TRANSITIONAL ARTICLE

Denunciation of the declaration referred to in Article 28, paragraph 2, shall be subject to the same procedures as the denunciation of this Treaty, except that it will take effect on the date of delivery of the respective notification.

In witness whereof the undersigned Plenipotentiaries, having deposited their full powers, found in good and due form, sign this Treaty on behalf of their respective Governments.

Done at Mexico, Distrito Federal, on the Fourteenth day of February, one thousand nine hundred and sixty-seven.

ADDITIONAL PROTOCOL I

The undersigned Plenipotentiaries, furnished with full powers by their respective Governments,

Convinced that the Treaty for the Prohibition of Nuclear Weapons in Latin America, negotiated and signed in accordance with the recommendations of the General Assembly of the United Nations in Resolution 1911 (XVIII) of 27 November 1963, represents an important step towards ensuring the non-proliferation of nuclear weapons,

Aware that the non-proliferation of nuclear weapons is not an end in itself but, rather, a means of achieving general and complete disarmament at a later stage, and

Desiring to contribute, so far as lies in their power, towards ending the armaments race, especially in the field of nuclear weapons, and towards strengthening a world at peace, based on mutual respect and sovereign equality of States,

Have agreed as follows:

Article 1. To undertake to apply the statute of denuclearisation in respect of warlike purposes as defined in Articles 1, 3, 5 and 13 of the Treaty for the Prohibition of Nuclear Weapons in Latin America in territories for which, *de jure* or *de facto*, they are internationally responsible and which lie within the limits of the geographical zone established in that Treaty.

Article 2. The duration of this Protocol shall be the same as that of the Treaty for the Prohibition of Nuclear Weapons in Latin America of which this Protocol is an annex, and the provisions regarding ratification and denunciation contained in the Treaty shall be applicable to it.

Article 3. This Protocol shall enter into force, for the States which have ratified it, on the date of the deposit of their respective instruments of ratification.

In witness whereof the undersigned Plenipotentiaries, having deposited their full powers, found in good and due form, sign this Protocol on behalf of their respective Governments.

ADDITIONAL PROTOCOL II

The undersigned Plenipotentiaries, furnished with full powers by their respective Governments,

Convinced that the Treaty for the Prohibition of Nuclear Weapons in Latin America, negotiated and signed in accordance with the recommendations of the General Assembly of the United Nations in Resolution 1911 (XVIII) of 27 November 1963, represents an important step towards ensuring the non-proliferation of nuclear weapons,

Aware that the non-proliferation of nuclear weapons is not an end in itself but, rather, a means of achieving general and complete disarmament at a later stage, and

Desiring to contribute, so far as lies in their power, towards ending the armaments race, especially in the field of nuclear weapons, and towards promoting and strengthening a world at peace, based on mutual respect and sovereign equality of States,

Have agreed as follows:

Article 1. The statute of denuclearisation of Latin America in respect of warlike purposes, as defined, delimited and set forth in the Treaty for the Prohibition of Nuclear Weapons in Latin America of which this instrument is an annex, shall be fully respected by the Parties to this Protocol in all its express aims and provisions.

Article 2. The Governments represented by the undersigned Plenipotentiaries undertake, therefore, not to contribute in any way to the performance of acts involving a violation of the obligations of Article 1 of the Treaty in the territories to which the Treaty applies in accordance with Article 4 thereof.

Article 3. The Governments represented by the undersigned Plenipotentiaries also undertake not to use or threaten to use nuclear weapons against the Contracting Parties of the Treaty for the Prohibition of Nuclear Weapons in Latin America.

Article 4. The duration of this Protocol shall be the same as that of the Treaty for the Prohibition of Nuclear Weapons in Latin America of which this Protocol is an annex, and the definitions of territory and nuclear weapons set forth in Articles 3 and 5 of the Treaty shall be applicable to this Protocol, as well as the provisions regarding ratification, reservations, denunciation, authentic texts and registration contained in Articles 26, 27, 30 and 31 of the Treaty.

Article 5. This Protocol shall enter into force, for the States which have ratified it, on the date of the deposit of their respective instruments of ratification.

In witness whereof the undersigned Plenipotentiaries, having deposited their full powers, found in good and due form, sign this Additional Protocol on behalf of their respective Governments.

INDEX